Financial Management

A PRIMER

Financial Management

A PRIMER

Stephen R. Foerster

W. W. NORTON & COMPANY
NEW YORK • LONDON

The text of this book is composed in Rotis.
Composition by Nan Sinauer
Manufacturing by Victor Graphics
Book design by Rubina Yeh

Library of Congress Cataloging-in-Publication Data
  Foerster, Stephen Robert.
    Financial management : a primer / Stephen R. Foerster.
        p. cm.
    Includes bibliographical references and index.
    ISBN 0-393-92420-3 (pbk.)
    1. Business enterprises--Finance. I. Title.
  HG4026.F664 2003
  658.15--dc21

                                   2002044369

W. W. Norton & Company, Inc., 500 Fifth Avenue, New York, N.Y. 10110
                      www.wwnorton.com
W. W. Norton & Company Ltd., Castle House, 75/76 Wells Street, London W1T 3QT

  3 4 5 6 7 8 9 0

To Linda,
Jennifer, Christopher, Thomas, and Melanie

Brief Contents

Contents

List of Figures

Preface

Welcome to the wonderful world of finance! What is the first thing that comes to mind if someone mentions corporate finance or financial management to you? For many students and nonfinancial managers, the initial response is "It sounds like something I don't need to know" or "It sounds like a complex subject" or "It deals with lots of numbers" or "It doesn't sound like the most exciting business subject I have studied." Yet my teaching experience involving commerce undergraduates, M.B.A.s, and executives has led me to conclude that almost everyone can overcome these initial perceptions and feelings through an educational process that

- shows how finance integrates with other areas of business
- shows the practical side of finance, rather than just the theoretical concepts
- shows that finance is a dynamic, interesting, and topical area of study

Understanding finance is critical to understanding business in general, since finance is a key driver of a firm's activities. Understanding finance also implies understanding what is behind many of the stories featured every day in the financial press.

This book aims to address these issues by

- integrating both nonfinancial and financial areas of business
- emphasizing practical examples and applications of concepts

- conveying much information visually (via charts, exhibits, and tables) and being generally easy to read
- maintaining a concise length (relative to most traditional finance texts)
- providing a comprehensive case study that summarizes the concepts addressed in the book

Financial Management: A Primer is aimed primarily at nonfinancial executives and managers, as well as current M.B.A. and undergraduate students (who are aspiring managers), who want to better understand the role of financial managers and to better communicate with financial managers, accountants, and controllers. It is meant to be a practical guide to financial management—a primer for those who have never had direct exposure to the field of finance. The emphasis is on the application of tools in order to better understand a firm's financial situation.

The three major objectives of the book are to provide nonfinancial managers with insights into the various activities of the firm that affect cash flows, to assist managers (and future managers) in developing analytical skills for evaluating business problems and opportunities from a financial perspective, and to assist in the understanding of the key concepts of some of the major decisions facing financial managers. An overview of each chapter and a road map are presented in chapter 1.

This book should prove valuable to interested individuals and nonfinancial executives as part of an executive course or a university course in applied corporate finance, as a case course in financial management, or as a supplement to financial theory courses. For those instructors interested in developing a case course or supplementing chapters with case studies, a list of cases related to relevant chapters is presented at the end of this book. All of the cases are available from Ivey Publishing and include teaching notes for instructors (sample copies and teaching notes are available free of charge to academics).

This book assumes no prior knowledge of finance but attempts to provide a tremendous amount of value added—I hope it will be one of the best investments you will ever make!

I am indebted to my colleagues who have used earlier drafts of the book with their students and to the many students who provided comments that helped with its clarity. I am also indebted to my accounting colleague, Claude Lanfranconi, who provided feedback on accounting-related material, and particularly my finance colleague, Larry Wynant, who helped improve the book through his detailed comments and was the first person to read my completed manuscript. Finally, I owe a great deal to W. W. Norton's Jack Repcheck, whose comments improved the book immensely, and special thanks to Andrew Lo for his encouragement and support.

Stephen Foerster
November 2002

Financial Management

A PRIMER

1. Overview of Finance

1.1 What Is Financial Management?

You may have heard the expression "Cash is king!" This expression high-lights the importance of a "noble" profession: the management of cash. Financial management involves the management of cash, the bloodline of any corporation.

Why is cash important to a business? A firm needs to invest in *real assets* in order to function as a business.[1] These assets may be tangible, such as plant and equipment, or intangible, such as research and the development of patents. In order to pay for these real assets, a firm must either have cash on hand or be able to obtain cash from some external sources. If a firm is able to obtain cash from an external source, it is able to do so by taking on a certain obligation. It does so by issuing or developing a piece of paper (albeit a carefully worded, important piece of paper) that represents a claim on its real assets. These pieces of paper are known as financial assets. For example, if a firm wishes to buy a new building, it may arrange a bank loan. The firm agrees to a schedule of interest payments and principal payments, like a home mortgage, with the terms set out in a piece of paper known as a contract. If the firm is unable to make the payments, then the bank is able to claim the building and sell it in order to recoup the money it lent to the firm. *Common shareholders* are special claimants known as residual claimants.

---

[1]Italicized terms are defined in the glossary in appendix A.

These shareholders receive pieces of paper known as stock certificates that allow them to share whatever *profits* are left in the business after other claimants, such as lenders, have been satisfied. Thus these shareholders collectively are the ultimate owners of the firm and entrust managers—including financial managers—to act in their best interest.

Financial management represents the bridge between the firm's real assets and its financial assets. Financial managers are concerned with four main functions: assessing the current business, assessing future financing needs, developing long-term financing strategies, and assessing future investments. To elaborate, financial managers are concerned with

- understanding the current business situation and measuring the current performance of the firm
- assessing the future financial needs of the firm in the short term (say, over the next year)
- determining the best way to raise money to pay for real assets, known simply as financing, and assessing other financing decisions, including determining how best to manage money generated by the operations of the business: whether it should be paid to the firm's shareholders as *dividends* or reinvested in the firm through *retained earnings*
- investing money in the various operations of the business, known simply as *investing* or *capital budgeting,* and determining the overall value of the firm and seeking ways to maximize its value

The relationships between real assets and financial assets are described in a simplified model in Figure 1.1. Arrows indicate the direction of the cash flows. Cash is invested through the capital budgeting process to purchase real assets (1). These real assets, in turn, generate cash for the business (2). If additional cash is required, say, to buy new equipment, the financial manager can obtain loans (3) or raise cash by issuing new common shares (4). Any cash generated by the business can either be paid as dividends to the shareholders (5) or be reinvested in the business (6).

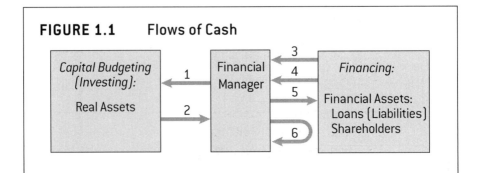

FIGURE 1.1   Flows of Cash

FIGURE 1.2   Financial Management Issues

- What amount of financing is required for the firm?
- How should the required financing be raised?
- What investments should the firm make?
- How can the financial decisions help to add value to the firm and its shareholders?

Financial managers are concerned with both short-term and long-term decisions. Short-term decisions focus on day-to-day cash flow and *working capital* management, the relationship between the firm's short-term *assets* and *liabilities*, while long-term decisions impact on the firm's overall *capital structure*, or mix of debt and equity. The ultimate task of the financial manager is to ensure that the firm is maximizing value for its shareholders. Figure 1.2 summarizes some of the key issues facing financial managers, and Figure 1.3 summarizes some of the key concepts that nonfinancial managers need to understand to better communicate with financial managers.

FIGURE 1.3   Key Concepts Related to Financial Management

- Assessment of the current business
    Business size-up
    Performance measurement (financial statement analysis)
    Day-to-day cash management

- Assessment of future financing requirements
    Financial statement projections

- Issues related to long-term financing decisions
    Understanding capital markets
    Determining the cost of capital
    Raising long-term capital

- Issues related to investments
    Understanding investment decisions
    Valuation: measuring and adding value

1.2   Relationship with Accounting

In order to make capital budgeting and financing decisions, the financial manager requires key financial information such as the cash inflows and outflows of the firm. The financial manager relies on the accountant to provide such information in a systematic and organized fashion. The role of accounting is to support the financial manager by identifying relevant data related to the activities of the firm and then presenting the relevant data in an agreed-on and standardized manner, known as "generally accepted accounting practices." The accountant communicates this relevant information not only internally to managers but also externally to stakeholders such as shareholders, lenders, analysts, and other interested parties.

Communication by accountants involves providing a "scorecard" that summarizes the relevant economic activity of the firm. Accountants utilize a number of key measurement tools. For example, the *balance sheet* provides a snapshot at a point in time indicating the amount of real assets of the firm as well as the financing of these real assets. The *income statement* provides a measure of the profitability of the firm over a particular time, such as a year. This information is also vital to the financial managers for use internally.

Accountants play an important role in creating budgets useful for financial planning. Accounting information is also useful in terms of problem solving, for example, evaluating decisions such as whether to acquire a new asset. The types of information provided by accountants are critically important to financial managers as well as nonfinancial managers.

1.3   Finance as Part of a Business

As Figure 1.1 indicates, the role of the financial manager is crucial to the running of the business. However, the finance role is only one of a number of critical functions within a business. It is important to explore the relationship that each function has with finance. For example, operations allows for the development of the product or service to be sold. Marketing plays a crucial role in generating revenues for the business. The human resources function manages the people who contribute to the success of the business. Information systems allows for efficient communications among employees and managers. Each of these functions, in some way, either is involved with the generation of cash or is a consumer of cash. Understanding and appreciating the implications of cash inflows and outflows helps nonfinancial managers better communicate with financial managers.

1.4   Road Map of Remaining Chapters

The book is divided into four parts. The next three chapters are related to an assessment of the current business: sizing-up the business from both a nonfinancial and financial perspective. This current business assessment is critical to the understanding of the financial health of the firm. Chapter 2 focuses on sizing-up a business and determining its key success factors by examining external factors such as the economy and industries, as well as focusing on a firm's strengths and weaknesses in such nonfinancial areas as marketing, operations, and human resources management. Chapter 3 focuses on sizing-up a business from a finance perspective by examining historical ratios or measures of performance in order to determine a firm's liquidity, efficiency, capacity to take on more debt, and overall profitability. Chapter 4 focuses on day-to-day cash flow management, including management of accounts receivable, inventory, and accounts payable.

Chapter 5 focuses on assessing the future financial needs of the firm and on projecting the firm's financial requirements through pro forma income statements, balance sheets, and cash budgets. The importance of spreadsheet analysis is also examined.

The next three chapters focus on long-term financing needs. Chapter 6 provides a bridge from short-term to long-term financing needs by providing an overview of capital markets as well as various debt and equity issues. Chapter 7 focuses on assessing a firm's cost of capital by estimating the cost of debt and the cost of equity. Chapter 8 focuses on issues related to the design of an optimal capital structure, including such trade-offs as cost, risk, and flexibility.

The next two chapters focus on other investment issues. Chapter 9 examines the investment decision process and summarizes time value of money concepts such as present value, which forms the basis for bond and equity valuation. Chapter 10 focuses on the measurement and creation of value. Traditional valuation techniques such as discounted cash flow analysis are presented here, as well as the concept of economic value added (EVA), which is part of value-based management. Finally, chapter 11 integrates all of the previous chapters by providing a comprehensive case study of Wal-Mart.

Figure 1.4 summarizes this chapter-by-chapter road map. A glossary of key terms is presented in appendix A. Each chapter contains self-study questions that summarize the key concepts covered in the chapter. Solutions are presented in appendix B. Present value and future value tables are given in appendix C.

FIGURE 1.4   Overview of Book

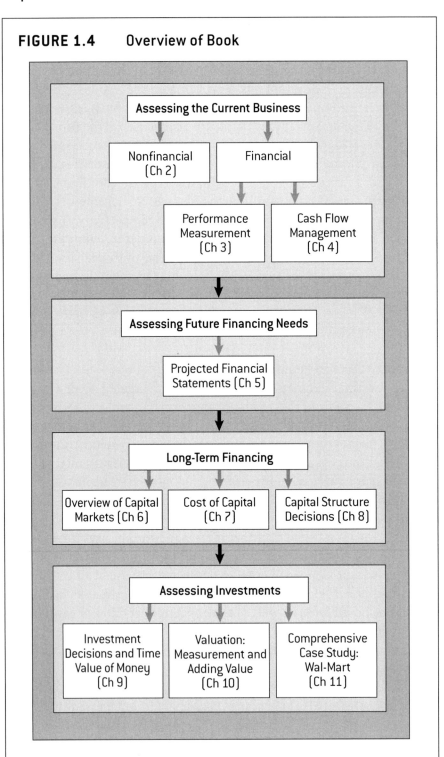

1.5   Additional Readings

There are a number of in-depth corporate finance books (each about a thousand pages in length):

Brealey, Richard, and Stewart Myers. *Principles of Corporate Finance.* 7th ed. Chicago, IL: Irwin/McGraw-Hill, 2003.

Ross, Stephen, Randolph Westerfield, and Jeffrey Jaffe. *Corporate Finance.* 5th ed. Chicago, IL: Irwin/McGraw-Hill, 1999.

There are shorter corporate finance texts aimed more at practitioner audiences:

Helfert, Erich. *Techniques of Financial Analysis: A Guide to Value Creation.* 10th ed. Chicago, IL: Irwin/McGraw-Hill, 2000.

Higgins, Robert. *Analysis for Financial Management.* 6th ed. Chicago, IL: Irwin/McGraw-Hill, 2001.

2. Business Size-up: A Nonfinancial Perspective

Often finance is associated strictly with number crunching and quantitative analysis. While it is true that financial management involves the management of cash, cash does not originate from or end up in the chief financial officer's (CFO's) desk drawer. It is the other parts of the business that are involved in the generation of and the need for cash. It is critical to understand what external factors impact the generation of cash and the need for the spending of cash and how, internally, various functional areas impact the cash flows of the firm. How should a firm in a particular industry be running its business in order to succeed? Does a particular firm have what it takes? We can't hope to understand a firm's current financial position or its anticipated financial needs if we don't take the time to understand the industry and the business.

This chapter is the first of three chapters that focus on assessing the current business of the firm. This chapter focuses on sizing-up a business and determining its key success factors by examining external factors such as the economy and industries, as well as a firm's strengths and weaknesses in such nonfinancial areas as marketing, operations, and human resources management. A size-up is a critical component to understanding the opportunities and risks and hence the impact on the cash flows of a business. A size-up helps managers understand the historical position the firm has evolved from and helps anticipate future financing needs. A size-up is an important tool both internally (used by current management) and externally (for example, used by potential lenders). A size-up analysis should be revisited on an annual basis. The key motivation for performing a size-up is to understand a firm's business in order to understand its financial position.

2.1   A Business Assessment Framework

There are two major components to sizing-up a business: external and internal. Two key external factors that can impact the cash flows of a business are the performance of the economy and the structure and nature of the industry. Understanding the overall relationship between the economy and the industry helps determine the impact of changing economic variables on the overall industry profitability. The industry key success factors can serve as a benchmark by which to assess the strengths and weaknesses of the firm within the particular industry.

There are a number of functional areas that combine to form a particular business. Outside of the finance area, some of the major areas involve operations, marketing, and human resources. Understanding each area and insights into the strengths and weaknesses of each area can help assess both the short-term and long-term financing needs of the firm. An overall framework is presented in Figure 2.1.

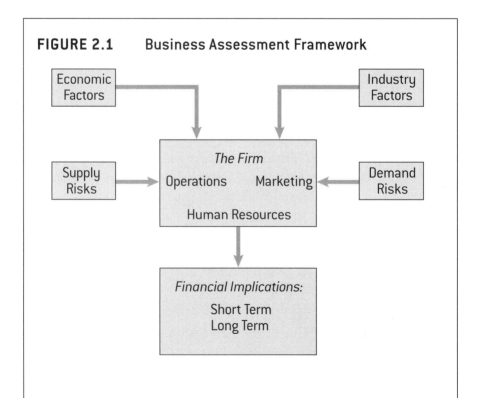

FIGURE 2.1   Business Assessment Framework

The external factors related to the economy and industry impact on the firm's financial situation. Supply and demand risks impact on the operations of the firm and the marketing of the firm, respectively. These areas, along with the overall human resources management of the firm, impact on the financial situation of the firm.

2.2   Economic Size-up

When asked where the economy is going, economists often talk as if they have more than two hands ("on the one hand…, on the other hand…, and on the other hand … "). In fairness to economists, predicting economic activity is a challenging task. Yet understanding the relationship between economic activity in general and the revenues and profit of a particular business can provide important insights into the anticipated financial needs of the firm.

The economic activity of a country is typically measured by the total amount of goods and services produced over a particular period, such as a year. This measure is known as *gross domestic product,* or GDP. An indication of economic activity is determined by focusing on real (inflation-adjusted) changes in GDP, either on a year-over-year or on a quarter-by-quarter basis. Over the long term, a country tends to have an increased capacity to expand economic activity, either by employing more labor or by building more plants and equipment. However, the actual output of goods and services may not, in the short term, increase at the same rate as the capacity. Consequently, a gap occurs between the capacity and the actual outcome. The changing size of this gap is also referred to as the *business cycle.* The typical relationship is presented in Figure 2.2. The peak of the business cycle tends to occur when the gap is smallest, while the trough tends to occur when the gap is largest. When real GDP changes are positive, the economy is said to be expanding, while two consecutive quarterly declines in real GDP are said to describe a *recession.* (An alternative definition: when a friend of yours loses his job, that's a recession; if you lose your job, that's a depression!) In North America over the past sixty years, the average expansion has been around five years and the average recession has been around one year. The performance of the overall economy will matter critically to an industry such as real estate that experiences a boom of new housing in good times and a dearth in bad times.

There are four components or segments that contribute to the overall measure of GDP. The largest component for any country is typically the consumer segment, which is driven by the consumption patterns of individual

FIGURE 2.2   **Business Cycle**

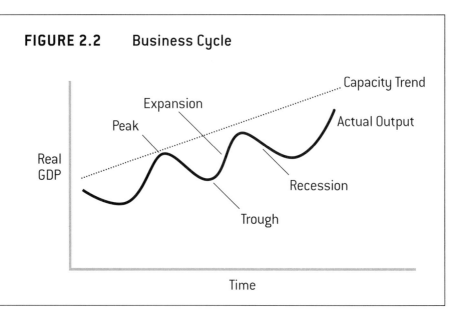

consumers. The second-largest component is the business investment component. This segment includes any business investments, such as plants and
equipment and research and development, and also investments by individuals in housing. The third-largest component is the government sector,
which includes any transfer payments to individuals. The final component
is the net export segment, which includes exports less imports by a country.

At various stages in a business cycle, some sectors may be growing or
shrinking at different rates. Business cycles can be caused by a decline in
demand for goods and services by any of these sectors. Alternatively, business
cycles can be related more directly to financial variables. Inflation, measured
as consumer price increases, tends to occur at a greater rate as the economy
expands. There is often a direct link between inflation and the money supply
in the economy. Too much money "chasing" too few goods often causes inflation. As inflation increases, so does the overall level of interest rates.

Interest rates represent the price of money. From the demand side, interest rates represent what an individual borrower would be willing to pay a
lender, given the opportunities the borrower is facing. From the supply side,
(nominal) interest rates can be decomposed into two components: real rates
and expected inflation. Real rates represent a "fair" return that a lender would
like to receive in the absence of any inflation. This real return includes a
return to supply money (which causes the lender to forgo consumption today)
as well as a default premium depending on the perceived riskiness of the borrower. Expected inflation is often a function of the current position in the

business cycle. During expansions, inflation—and hence the nominal interest rate level in general—tends to increase. This often happens when consumers increase their borrowing needs. Nominal rates tend to peak shortly after the peak in the overall economy, then decline during a recession.

Understanding changing economic factors and various business cycle stages is crucial for managers for a variety of reasons. Some businesses are critically tied to the overall economy. The profitability of many firms varies directly with the general economic performance, although for some businesses and industries, the relationship is more pronounced than for others. Thus changing economic activity will directly impact revenues. Also, costs tend to change throughout a business cycle. As well, depending on a business's reliance on borrowing, a changing economic environment will have a direct impact on its financial performance. There may be additional economic factors that affect a particular business. For example, if a firm is dependent on a particular commodity as a raw material input, such as aluminum, then changes in the price of aluminum can have important implications for the pricing of the product. Not only does economic performance help to explain past financial performance; anticipating future economic performance is invaluable in projecting future financial statements. Figure 2.3 includes a checklist of key questions to consider related to an assessment, or size-up, of general economic conditions.

FIGURE 2.3   Economic Size-up

- What is the current business cycle stage?

- What is the relationship between the business cycle and revenues?

- What is the relationship between the business cycle and costs?

- How important are changing interest rates to the financial position of firms within this industry?

- What is the current outlook for the overall economy (i.e., GDP forecast)?

- What is the current outlook for interest rates (i.e., next year)?

- Are there any key economic variables whose changes might impact on the financial performance of firms in this industry?

2.3   Industry Analysis

In order to understand the financial position facing the firm, it is critical to appreciate both the current and anticipated industry conditions. An industry analysis can provide insights into the current financial position of the firm as well as how its financial needs might change as industry conditions change. The analysis can also help to identify key risks and opportunities facing the firm.

2.3.1   Industry Life Cycles

The starting point for any industry analysis is the definition of a particular industry. An industry can be categorized by the type of product or service offered or by the particular market segment the product or service is directed toward. Industry categories can be very broad or very narrow. New industry categories are emerging all the time and replacing obsolete industry categories.

Industries, like individuals, go through a number of life-cycle stages. Various benchmarks, such as revenues or profit, exhibit different rates of growth at different stages. Figure 2.4 summarizes a comparison of revenue changes through time for five different life-cycle stages. Stage 1 represents the ini-

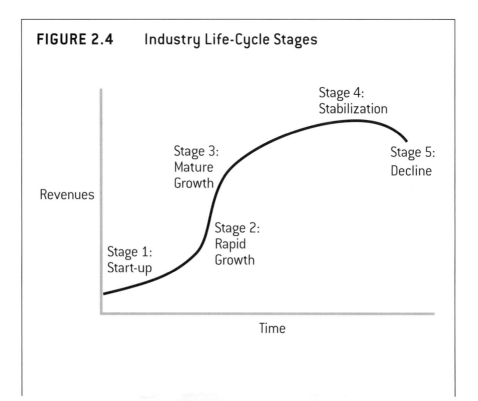

FIGURE 2.4   Industry Life-Cycle Stages

Stage 4:
Stabilization

Stage 3:
Mature
Growth

Stage 5:
Decline

Revenues

Stage 2:
Rapid
Growth

Stage 1:
Start-up

Time

tial, or start-up, stage of a business. At this point, firms in this industry tend to have very low revenues but high prospects for revenue growth. Profit is typically negative. In stage 2, revenues tend to grow rapidly and positive profit materializes. This is often the point at which private firms go public through an *initial public offering* process. This is often the point of consolidation of firms within the industry and a shakeout of many firms with poor prospects. In stage 3, competition intensifies, revenues continue to grow but at a slower rate, and firms tend to become more efficient as costs are controlled. Stage 4 is a phase of stabilization. Any growth in revenues tends to occur at about the same rate as the growth of the overall economy. Stage 5 represents a declining phase as substitute products cause overall revenue generation in the industry to decline.

It is critical to establish which life-cycle stage a particular firm is in. Such categorization is important when interpreting the current financial position of the firm as well as when determining the projected financial position of the firm.

2.3.2   Industry Competitive Environment

With the exception of firms that enjoy a monopoly position in regulated industries, firms face various intensities of competition within an industry. A number of factors have been identified that contribute to the intensity of competition: ease of entry, availability of substitute products, the power of suppliers and customers, the extent of rivalry among the current competitors, and factors unique to a particular industry.

The easier it is to enter a particular industry, the lower the profit margins and growth prospects within the industry. Conversely, if there are huge barriers to entry, then an industry is much more attractive to existing firms. Some barriers include the need for huge capital expenditures such as plants and equipment; the need to establish distribution channels, existing patents, and proprietary technology; and government regulation. Existing competitors might be expected to react strongly to any new potential entrants.

If an industry is offering a unique product or service that is very much in demand, then there are opportunities among firms in the industry to enjoy large profit margins. However, if prices are perceived to be too high, substitute products may become available, causing profit margins to be squeezed and resulting in a decline in revenues. Even in the absence of high prices, new innovations can occur to cause a product or service to become less appealing.

The relative strength of the bargaining power of suppliers and customers can have an impact on the profitability of an industry. Powerful suppliers are often those who are concentrated and offer a unique product or service. In addition, large customers who deal in large volumes and may be purchasing a relatively standardized product or service from a variety of sources can cause a squeeze on profit margins.

More intense existing rivalries can result in lower profit margins as well. Competition tends to be more intense when a particular product or service is like a commodity, with very few distinguishing features. As well, if the typical firm within an industry tends to have high fixed costs, competition tends to be more intense as firms attempt to utilize as much capacity as possible.

There are often a number of factors unique to a particular industry that can intensify competition. For example, the revenue generation in one industry is often dependent on the demand for goods and services in another industry. As an example, the sale of newsprint will depend, in part, on the communications industry and the demand for newspapers, which will, in turn, depend on the availability of electronic substitutes as well as economic conditions that affect advertising demand and revenues. All of these factors impact on the overall growth opportunities within the industry.

2.3.3   Industry Opportunities and Risks

By analyzing the so-called PEST factors—political, economic, social, and technological—insights can be gained into both opportunities and risks facing a particular industry. Political factors refer to legislative changes that might add to or eliminate regulation in a particular industry, thus posing an additional cost or providing a new opportunity. For example, favorable tax changes or incentives can result in lower price offerings and increased demand in an industry. Economic factors were discussed in section 2.2 "Economic Size-up." Some industries generate revenue growth that is closely tied to the performance of the overall economy. These industries are known as cyclical industries. Other industries, such as utilities, have more stable revenues regardless of the business cycle stage. Social trends can have a long-term impact on an industry. For example, if the consumption of a particular product is determined to have a detrimental health impact, sales may be negatively affected. Technological improvements can lead to major efficiency gains. Thus analysis of these PEST factors can help identify both opportunities and risks that can impact on the financial performance and requirements of a firm.

2.3.4   Key Industry Success Factors

The ultimate outcome of the industry analysis is the identification of key success factors that articulate what resources or skills are necessary to successfully compete in the industry. Key success factors are a checklist by which the internal strengths and weaknesses of a firm can be judged. They provide a crucial benchmark that will be utilized as part of the internal firm size-up, since the firm's capabilities in various areas such as operations, marketing, and human resources are compared with them. The crux of the analysis should focus on customer needs. Ultimately, consumers are searching for either the lowest price or a product or service offering particular features. For a firm to succeed in a business in the long term, either it must be a low-cost producer in the industry or it must find a niche by offering a product or service that is unique. Thus in a particular industry, the key to success might be in operations, by being more efficient through technology investment and offering a product or service at the lowest price; or the key might be in marketing, by packaging the product in an appealing manner or by utilizing the best distribution channel. Alternatively, the ability to manage labor relations in a heavily unionized industry might be the key to success. In general, every key success factor will have important financial implications.

A summary of key industry size-up questions that need to be addressed is presented in Figure 2.5.

FIGURE 2.5   Industry Size-up

- What industry segment and life-cycle stage is this business in?
- How profitable is the industry currently?
- What is the competitive environment? How intense is the competition? Are there significant barriers to entry? Do suppliers or customers have bargaining power? Is there a threat of the emergence of substitute products?
- What are the overall prospects for growth in the industry?
- What are the key opportunities or risks associated with this industry related to the political, economic, social, and technological environments?
- Overall, what are the key success factors for the industry?

2.4 Firm Operations Management and Supply Risks

After examining the current and anticipated economic conditions and completing an industry analysis and determining key success factors, the size-up analysis moves from an external perspective to an internal one, with the focus on the firm's capabilities in various areas. The analysis begins by examining the operations of the firm. The key question to address is: Assuming customer demand is strong, to what extent is the firm able to fulfill that demand by providing the service or making the product available to the customer? The analysis focuses on identifying what are known as supply risks or on the ability of the firm to supply the product or service.

There are a number of areas that can be assessed. Figure 2.6 describes the key areas of operations assessment: quality, process, facilities, inventory,

---

FIGURE 2.6   Firm Operations and Supply Risk Assessment

- Quality
  How important is quality to the customer?
  How does the firm attempt to control quality?

- Process
  What process does the firm currently employ?
  How critical are technological innovations and investments?

- Facilities
  What is the current capacity of facilities?
  How close is the firm to full capacity?

- Inventory
  What type of inventory does the firm have?
  What inventory management system is currently in use?

- Labor
  What skills are required?
  How skilled is the workforce relative to the skills required?
  What is the current labor environment?

and labor. Quality management is concerned with the extent to which the firm is able to provide a reasonable amount of product or service quality subject to constraints such as costs. While the firm is often concerned with meeting production specifications, quality to consumers is often related to the value or quality relative to the price paid. Poor quality can result in substantial costs for the firm in terms of repairs, higher warranty costs, or damage to reputation and future business. From an assessment perspective, the importance of quality must be determined and the firm's operations must be evaluated.

Process management involves determining the appropriate process to provide the product or service. In a manufacturing setting, the process choices involve job shops or a variety of workstations, line flow or a series of sequential operations, and projects or the production of a single item. In a service setting, these processes also apply, but they apply to the customer. It is important for the firm to ensure that the choice of process, which has cost and time implications, is meeting the needs of the customer. Another dimension of process is the choice of technology investment. The goal is to maximize the investment in technology, trading off potential efficiency gains with the costs of the new technology.

Facilities management involves ensuring sufficient capacity or maximum output is available. Facility refers to the physical plant and equipment available to produce the goods or offer the service. There is a trade-off between being able to meet demand and the costs of having facilities and equipment available but idle. Thus planning and anticipating demand is a crucial part of facilities management. On a day-to-day basis, this long-term planning translates into scheduling or determining how the available capacity will be best utilized.

Inventory management applies primarily to a manufacturing business and ensures a proper mix of different types of inventory: raw materials, work in process, and finished goods. Raw materials are inputs for the finished goods. Work in process represents inventory that has not been completed. As with other operations components, managing inventory involves tradeoffs. From a supply perspective, having huge amounts of inventory ensures that any demand for the product can be readily met. On the other hand, there are huge costs to holding large amounts of inventory in terms of the costs of the raw materials, storage space, and administration. Thus there is a tradeoff between the risks of stock-outs versus the opportunity to meet unexpectedly large demand.

Finally, labor management involves ensuring the hiring and maintenance of a sufficiently skilled workforce. Management must match workers with their job, provide adequate training, clearly define responsibilities, communicate effectively, provide adequate supervision, and set standards and performance rewards. Management must ensure that the firm is paying an appropriate amount for the skill level of employees. Management should work toward a positive labor environment and must always be cognizant of labor's union status.

After each of these components of operations management is examined and compared with the overall industry key success factors, a final assessment of the supply risks can be made. Inevitably, this assessment will be somewhat subjective, yet extremely useful as part of the subsequent financial analysis. For example, a final assessment can be made on a 1-to-10 scale, with 1 indicating low supply risk and 10 indicating high supply risk. If the firm is currently producing a high-quality product at a reasonable cost, is employing the latest technology, is not currently at capacity, has an effective inventory management system in place, and has a skilled labor force and a positive labor environment, then the supply risk will be judged to be very low. However, if the current product or service is judged to be poor quality, yet quality is determined to be a key industry success factor, then the firm would be expected either to invest in order to improve quality, or to suffer a decline in future revenues. A supply risk assessment will also be useful to highlight critical inputs to projected financial statements. For example, if there is a high supply risk attributable to a possible work stoppage, projected financial needs should incorporate such a possibility through sensitivity analysis (described in chapter 5).

2.5 Firm Marketing Management and Demand Risk

Having completed an assessment of the firm's operations and supply risk, the internal size-up continues with an examination of its marketing management and demand risk. The key question to address is: Assuming the firm is able to readily supply the product or service, to what extent is customer demand available? The analysis focuses on identifying demand risks, or the possibility of the fluctuation of demand for the product or service related to the complete marketing mix.

Analysis of a firm's marketing capabilities relates to the soundness and appropriateness of a firm's marketing mix, also known as the "4 P's" of mar-

---

FIGURE 2.7   Firm Marketing and Demand
Risk Assessment

- Target Market
  What is the particular target market?
  How important are the who, what, where, when, and how of
  the purchase decision?

- Product
  What are the critical physical and intangible attributes?

- Price
  Is the price level appropriate relative to the competition?

- Place
  Is the distribution channel appropriate?

- Promotion
  Is the promotional campaign having a positive impact on
  the buyer?

---

keting: product, price, place, and promotion. Each of these P's is examined
below. However, before a marketing strategy can be established, a firm must
select the appropriate target market. Figure 2.7 lists the key areas of a market
assessment.

Markets can be segmented by the groups that have distinctive needs or
characteristics or by geographical location. The firm needs to establish the
current size, potential for growth, and profitability of a particular segment.
Ideally, a target market would be selected if the customer base were large,
there were little competition, and the firm's capabilities matched the needs
of the customers.

Understanding the buying choice/rejection process of consumers is critical. A firm must understand the critical aspects of the process: who, what,
where, when, and how. There can be a distinction between who buys the
product and who actually consumes the product. Key marketing efforts can
be directed at the group that is most influential to the purchase decision.
Consumers may be buying a physical item or such intangibles as service,
convenience of purchase, sales advice, or delivery. Location is often an important part of the process. Timing of purchases can vary by time of day or by

month of the year. Finally, the "how" encompasses the prepurchase process as well as the purchase decision. A firm's market research can help to better articulate this buying process.

Once a target market is established, the firm can develop a marketing program based on the 4 P's. The product decision involves the determination of the actual physical product, quality, special features, packaging, warranties, and services. The price decision involves determining not only an absolute price but also a price relative to the competition. The promotion decision involves the method of persuading the consumer or decision maker to buy the product or service, either through advertising, point-of-purchase display, or other forms of promotion. Finally, the place decision involves determining the most appropriate distribution channel to reach the target market. Location is often critical to the purchase decision.

After each of these components of marketing management are examined and compared with the industry key success factors, a final assessment of the demand risks can be determined. As with the supply risk assessment, a final assessment can be made based on a 1-to-10 scale, where 1 indicates low demand risk and 10 indicates high demand risk. If the firm is targeting an attractive market and has in place an appropriate marketing mix with a product very much in demand offered at an appropriate price and with an effective promotional campaign and appropriate distribution channel, then the demand risk will be judged to be very low. The demand risk assessment will also be useful to highlight critical inputs to projected financial statements. For example, if there is a high demand risk attributable to a faddish product offering or a weak sales force, projected financial needs should incorporate such a possibility through sensitivity analysis. This sensitivity analysis might include a reassessment of financial needs assuming a 10 percent decline in sales.

2.6 Firm Human Resources Management and Strategy

The focus of human resources management is on the capabilities and character of the management team, including the chief executive officer (CEO), the president, senior management, and all other managers. It is often a challenge to examine a firm's management from inside; it is sometimes easier to look at the management team from an external perspective: How would prospective lenders or investors view management? Does the current management team offer opportunities or risks to the firm? Given the previous discussions of the operations and marketing areas, it is the management and implementation of strategies that ultimately determine success or failure for the firm.

There are a number of key management capabilities that are required to improve the chances of business success. Managers in functional areas such as operations, marketing, information systems, and finance must be capable. As well, general managers must be able to supply leadership skills.

The size of the firm as well as the growth stage of the firm must be considered as part of the analysis since there are different challenges during different life-cycle stages. For example, there are many challenges associated with the start-up of a business. Many new businesses fail due to lack of management depth. There are often problems when a successful entrepreneur fails to plan for succession, which can lead to the downfall of a promising business. There are also challenges facing businesses that expand too rapidly, particularly into new areas beyond their original core capabilities.

In all types of businesses, but particularly in smaller organizations, the experience and skills of the key senior managers are an overwhelming determinant of the firm's success. Previous experience running other businesses and technical training can be evaluated. Commitment to the firm can also be demonstrated by a manager's financial stake in the business. Ultimately, shareholders want to ensure that managers are acting in their best interest, to maximize the value of their shares.

For the management team in general, technical knowledge and experience in a functional area are important. In addition, establishing relationships among customers, suppliers, distributors, lenders, and shareholders will be critical to the success of the firm. Clearly one person will not have the skills to establish all of these relationships, so the extent to which the members of the management team work together is crucial. In addition, attracting new managers will be critical to success.

Leadership skills are another key success factor. Managers must be able to motivate other employees and must be able to effectively delegate authority. Managers must be able to create enthusiasm and stimulate loyalty. Success often is impacted by the overall structure of the organization, the performance measurement system, the reward system, and the overall level of communication between managers and employees and among managers. Managers, as leaders, must be able to clearly articulate a strategy and focus for the firm.

FIGURE 2.8   Human Resources Management

- What life-cycle stage is the firm in?
- What management challenges is the firm currently facing?
- Are the current management challenges being addressed?
- What is the overall strategy and focus of the firm?
- Who are the key principals in the firm?
- What technical skills do they possess?
- What business experience do they have (previously and in the firm)?
- What leadership skills do they possess?
- What ownership position do they have?
- What is the character of the key managers?
- How much management depth does the firm have?
- What are the overall management team's strengths and weaknesses?

At an individual level, each manager can be judged by his or her character. For example, honesty, integrity, fairness in dealing with others, willingness to admit mistakes rather than to lay blame, and overall management style can all be judged. Figure 2.8 summarizes some of the key human resources factors that should be considered.

2.7   Importance for Financial Analysis

It is important to undertake a thorough business size-up before attempting to analyze a firm's current financial position or future financial needs. Each component of the size-up should provide important implications for the financial analysis. For example, the economic size-up should establish the relationship between the overall economic performance and the industry performance (in terms of revenues and profit) and should provide a sense of the outlook for interest rates. The industry size-up should generate a list of key success factors based on opportunities and risks related to the particular industry life-cycle stage, the growth prospects for the industry, the intensity and nature of the competition, and any other unique characteristics of the industry. This industry analysis provides a benchmark with which to measure the capabilities of the firm, assessing the strengths and weaknesses of the firm as compared to the industry key success factors.

The internal analysis of the operations, marketing, and human resources management will help to highlight key supply and demand risks and internal capabilities, all of which have financial implications. For example, if the firm relies more heavily on variable-rate loans and interest rates are expected to rise, then higher borrowing costs should be incorporated in financial projections. If a key industry success factor is providing a product with technical specifications that can only be produced with the latest technology, then the firm must anticipate major technology investments. On the basis of the internal assessment, any shortfalls related to what is required to succeed will have important financial implications. As well, simply understanding economic and industry characteristics can assist in an understanding of the recent and anticipated performance of the firm. For example, if the last few years have shown little or no economic growth, this might have had a negative impact on the revenues of all firms within the industry, and might also have been the cause of slower payments by customers. Without this knowledge, it would be impossible to interpret the firm's financial performance in a meaningful manner.

2.8   Size-up Example

The following example illustrates the business size-up process, implications, and conclusions. Finco is a financial institution with a focus on retail banking.

The external analysis begins with an assessment of the economy. While GDP growth was negative over the past year, many economists are currently divided: Some are calling for a continued slump while others are projecting an increase in GDP growth of up to 3 percent this year. The economy is estimated to be just past the trough in the business cycle. The industry's overall economic activity is closely tied to the overall activity of the general economy. An implication is that interest rates, which have fallen during the recession, are projected to continue to decline over the next 6 to 12 months and then gradually to rise as the economy strengthens. Lower interest rates not only will help by lowering the cost of financing for firms in this industry but will also have a positive impact on demand as consumers are more likely to borrow when rates are lower.

The overall industry growth prospects are fairly good. Demographic trends suggest baby boomers, the largest population segment, will become more concerned with investments and wealth management. However, the industry is in a mature stage, so growth in profits will probably not be far off from the overall growth in the economy. Existing competition is fairly intense, although consolidation is expected to continue. The primary industry characteristic is regulation. There is a potential for a relaxation of the rules that will allow for better opportunities. However, current regulation provides some power for consumers. Key success factors include the ability to offer attractive savings rates and reasonably attractive loan rates, commensurate with risks; good customer service; and efficiency of operations.

An internal assessment of Finco begins with operations management. The firm has recently invested heavily in order to upgrade its information systems. As a consequence, the firm is able to offer its customers a quicker turnaround response on loan applications. In addition, Finco has invested heavily in remodeling many of its branches to make them more appealing to customers. However, a weakness is that Finco's employee turnover is higher than the industry norm. This suggests that Finco may need to reassess its wage structure since it is ending up investing much more in training and development than if it had lower turnover.

An assessment of Finco's marketing management identifies a strategy of focusing on high-net-worth clients. While this is an attractive segment, it is also an intensely competitive segment. This segment has been determined to be fairly price sensitive. Recently, Finco has earned a reputation of leading other banks in terms of loan-rate reductions. While there appear to be short-term benefits in terms of revenues, most other banks are quick to react. Thus Finco has also been trying to emphasize the quality dimension in its banking services by offering a pleasant and convenient environment.

An assessment of Finco's human resources identifies a clear, focused strategy, but some problems with management retention as well. The higher-than-normal turnover is having a negative impact on morale.

Relative to industry key success factors, Finco appears to be providing good prices and service but is facing challenges in terms of management and employee turnover. Financial implications are that if the economy does improve, as many anticipate, then the overall revenues of Finco will grow as well. However, it would be appropriate, when projecting financial statements, to do a sensitivity analysis on revenues. For example, projections can be repeated assuming revenues are 10 percent lower than the current year, reflecting an ongoing recession. In order to reflect the turnover problem, operating costs should include wage increases as attempts are made to rectify the problem. Overall, without looking at the numbers, Finco appears to be in strong shape. The next step is the understanding of the financial statements and the development of projected financial statements.

2.9   Summary

1. A qualitative business size-up is a critical precursor to any financial analysis. The analysis includes both an external assessment of the economy and industry as well as an internal assessment of the firm's capabilities and strengths and weaknesses in the areas of operations, marketing, and human resources management.
2. An economic size-up focuses on identifying the current business cycle stage, the relationship between overall economic activity and the industry's performance, and the anticipation of interest rate changes.
3. An industry size-up identifies the industry life-cycle stage and prospects for growth, the intensity and nature of the competition, the overall risks and opportunities, and the key success factors.
4. An operations size-up identifies the firm's strengths and weaknesses related to the operations management of quality, process, facilities, inventory, and labor and provides for an assessment of the supply risk facing the firm.
5. A marketing size-up identifies the firm's strengths and weaknesses related to the marketing management areas of the identification of a target market, and the development of an appropriate marketing mix consisting of product, price, place, and promotion and provides for an assessment of the demand risk facing the firm.
6. A human resources size-up identifies the firm's strengths and weaknesses related to the human resources management areas of strategy, capabilities, and character.
7. The business size-up is utilized to better understand the current financial position of the firm, through financial performance measures, and to assist in developing projected financial statements.

2.10   Additional Readings

The classic work on competitiveness is
Porter, Michael. *Competitive Advantage: Creating and Sustaining Superior Performance.* New York: Free Press, 1985.

A good examination of business size-up, in the context of commercial lending, can be found in
Hatch, Jim, and Larry Wynant. *Canadian Commercial Lending.* Toronto: Carswell, 1995.

2.11   Self-Study Problems

1. What information would need to be gathered to assess the economy's current position within the business cycle?
2. Compare the typical profitability of a stage 2 firm versus that of a stage 4 firm.
3. Develop a list of key success factors in the automotive manufacturing industry.
4. Develop a list of factors that would result in a firm's having high supply risk and high demand risk.

3. Financial Size-up: Ratio Analysis and Performance Measures

A colleague in accounting introduces a class on finance for nonfinancial executives by telling them that it is probably too late: They have missed an exciting opportunity to become accountants! At this point, they will have to simply settle for being able to communicate with accountants. Similarly, the focus of this chapter is not to turn you into an accountant but rather to aid in financial assessments and decisions.

This chapter is the second of three chapters that focus on assessing the current business of the firm. It focuses on sizing-up a business from a financial perspective by examining historical ratios or measures of performance in order to attempt to measure a firm's liquidity and efficiency, capacity to take on more debt, and overall profitability. The initial focus is on the fundamental accounting communication tools: financial statements known as balance sheets, income statements, and cash flow statements. Financial statements are the key scorecards of a firm. They allow for both internal (by managers) and external (by analysts and investors) assessments of the financial health of the firm as well as an understanding of the flow of the firm's cash over time.

3.1 Balance Sheets

Most corporations prepare three financial statements (in some cases there are statutory requirements). The first statement, the balance sheet, represents a snapshot of the financial position of the firm at any point in time. A balance sheet is made up of two parts. The first part (originally referred to as the left-hand side) represents all of the firm's assets. The second part (originally referred to as the right-hand side) represents all of the claims on those assets. For example, the second part is usually made up of liabilities such as bank loans, and common equity (or shareholder equity). A not-so-subtle observation of all balance sheets is that they balance: The first part must always equal the second part. Simply put,

$$\text{Total assets} = \text{total liabilities} + \text{equity}$$

Rearranging this simple equation,

$$\text{Equity} = \text{total assets} - \text{total liabilities}$$

This rearrangement highlights the concept that equityholders represent residual claimants as they have a claim on any assets once debtholders have been satisfied. Consequently, equityholders are the true owners of the firm. As an analogy, the true worth of a homeowner is the difference between the value of the house and any mortgage owing.

Assets represent what the firm owns, controls, or derives some future benefit from. By convention, all assets are listed at their cost at the time of purchase. This is known as the *book value* of the assets. Assets are categorized as short term—usually lasting less than one year—and long term, or fixed. Some assets which do not fit cleanly into either category are known as "other assets."

Short-term assets are referred to as *current assets*. These assets include cash or *marketable securities* such as government Treasury bills, *accounts receivable*, *inventory*, and *prepaid expenses*. Cash is what is needed to run the day-to-day operations of the business. Any excess cash is often invested in very short-term, liquid, risk-free government certificates. If a business offers credit terms, then accounts receivable represent sales that have been generated but not yet paid for by customers. Inventory represents the amount of goods that a business has available but has not yet sold. Inventory may consist of finished goods ready for sale, work in progress, or raw materials. Prepaid expenses represent intangible assets that will be used in the near future, such as an annual insurance policy that is paid midyear and is only half used-up by year-end. These current assets are represented in the following equation:

$$\text{Current assets} = \text{cash} + \text{marketable securities} + \text{accounts receivable} + \text{inventory} + \text{prepaid expenses}$$

Fixed assets, sometimes referred to as capital assets, typically include any land or property that a firm owns, buildings or plants, and equipment. In most cases, land is assumed to remain useful indefinitely. However, this is not the case for buildings and equipment, which tend to wear out or become obsolete over time and need to be replaced. A reflection of the reduction in the value of these assets over time is known as *depreciation*. Depreciation is actually an allocation over a particular period (such as a year) to match costs against revenues. Accumulated depreciation represents the accumulated allocation from the time of purchase to the current time. The net value of property, plant, and equipment at any point in time is calculated as the original costs less any accumulated depreciation. In order to estimate the annual depreciation costs, a useful life for the asset must be estimated. There are certain conventions for estimating depreciation. The simplest method, known as straight-line depreciation, simply takes the estimate of the useful life of the asset and divides it into the original cost. For example, if a piece of equipment costs $50,000 and its useful life is estimated at ten years, then the annual depreciation would be $5,000. After three years, the accumulated depreciation would be $15,000, with the residual, or net, value at $35,000.

There is one final class of assets, known collectively as "other assets." This category includes such intangible assets as patents or *goodwill*, which arises from a situation whereby the firm acquires another asset (or company) and pays more than the asset's book value. In summary, total assets are represented by

$$\text{Total assets} = \text{current assets} + \text{fixed assets} + \text{other assets}$$

Liabilities and equity are represented on the right-hand side of the balance sheet. Liabilities are categorized as current, long-term, and "other."

Current liabilities include any debt-related commitments due over the next year. These current liabilities include *accounts payable, notes payable,* the current portion of any long-term debt, and any other short-term obligations. Accounts payable represent money owed by the firm to its suppliers for supplies received but not yet paid for. Notes payable represent short-term obligations such as a written promise to repay short-term bank loans. The current portion of long-term debt represents any principal repayments due within the next year. Other current liabilities represent obligations that have been accrued but not paid, such as income taxes owing. These current liabilities are represented in the following equation:

$$\text{Current liabilities} = \text{accounts payable} + \text{notes payable} + \text{current portion} \\ \text{of long-term debt} + \text{other current liabilities}$$

Long-term debt represents money borrowed that needs to be repaid in more than one year (which excludes the current portion), such as a long-term loan from a bank or a *bond* issued by the firm that represents a contractual obligation to repay a number of lenders.

Another category of liabilities (often stated separately) is *deferred income taxes*, or deferred tax liability. This item often arises because firms are allowed to keep two sets of books, or financial statements: one for its shareholders and one for the tax department. (Firms don't report cash taxes paid in the financial statements in order to more fairly reflect reported income.) The tax department often allows for depreciation expenses to be written off in early years at a rate greater than the straight-line method. Returning to the previous depreciation example, although the straight-line method calculates the year 1 depreciation as $5,000, the tax department may allow for a year 1 depreciation of $15,000. The impact for the firm is that in year 1, expenses are $10,000 greater; this implies that taxable income will be $10,000 less, since depreciation expenses are subtracted from operating profit before taxes are calculated. If the firm has a tax rate of 40 percent, it will pay a tax of $4,000 less than if the tax was calculated on its accounting income. This difference between actual income taxes paid and reported income tax must be recognized in order to make the balance sheet balance, and the result is the item of deferred income taxes. In summary, liabilities are represented by the following equation:

$$\text{Total liabilities} = \text{current liabilities} + \text{long-term liabilities} + \text{other liabilities}$$

The final category on the right-hand side of the balance sheet is the *equity* section, also known as the shareholders' equity or net worth section. From a practical perspective, there are only two important categories in this section (although more categories often appear on the accounting statements): *preferred shares* (or preferred equity) and all other categories that collectively represent *common equity*.

Although preferred shares often appear under the equity section of the financial statements, preferred shares are actually a hybrid between debt and equity, sharing features of each. Instead of interest payments as with debt, preferred shareholders receive regular dividends. However, from the firm's perspective, the dividend payments are paid after income taxes are paid and are thus not expensed like interest payments. Another distinction from debt is that preferred shareholders do not receive any principal repayment. The term *preferred* relates to the fact that these shares have preference over common shares in terms of dividend payments—no common share dividends can be paid until preferred dividends are paid—and in the event of *bankruptcy* by the firm, in which case preferred shareholders would stand in line before common shareholders.

As noted earlier, the common shareholders are the actual owners of the firm, since they share any remaining profits once other stakeholders—debtholders and preferred shareholders—have been taken care of. There are often a number of subcategories in the common equity section, but the distinctions are not really of any practical importance (except to accountants). Some categories include common stock or paid-in capital (representing the initial nominal value of the equity), treasury stock (representing stock that a corporation has bought back from shareholders), and retained earnings (the accumulated amount of profits not paid out in dividends). It is best to simply lump these together and refer to them as common equity or to separate the retained earnings portion. For the remainder of this book, unless otherwise noted, *equity* or *shareholders' equity* is meant to refer to common equity. It is important to note that equity does not represent cash: it simply represents a claim on assets. In summary, for simplicity common equity is represented by the following relationship:

$$\text{Common equity} = \text{common stock} + \text{retained earnings}$$

As an example of the terms discussed above, Figure 3.1 presents the actual balance sheets for Coca-Cola as of December 31, 2000 and 2001. Note that the rather large line item "other assets" includes a number of equity investments by Coca-Cola in other companies, principally bottling companies.

3.2   Income Statements

The second statement that all corporations are required to prepare is the income statement. This statement is useful to measure the overall profitability of the firm. The income statement records the *revenues* (or sales), costs and expenses, and profit (or income) of the firm over a particular period, such as a year. The most basic relationship is

$$\text{Revenues} - \text{costs and expenses} = \text{profit}$$

Revenues come mainly from the operations of the business in the form of sales of the product or service. In some cases, revenues can come from other noncore business sources, for example, from interest earned on marketable securities.

FIGURE 3.1   Balance Sheets for Coca-Cola

AS OF DECEMBER 31 (IN $ MILLIONS)	2001	2000
Assets		
Current assets		
Cash	1,866	1,819
Marketable securities	68	73
Accounts receivable	1,882	1,757
Inventories	1,055	1,066
Prepaid expenses	2,300	1,905
Total current assets	7,171	6,620
Fixed assets		
Land (property)	217	225
Plant and equipment (PE)	6,888	6,389
Less accumulated depreciation	2,652	2,446
Total plant and equipment	4,236	3,943
Total fixed assets (PPE)	4,453	4,168
Goodwill and intangible assets	2,579	1,917
Other assets	8,214	8,129
Total assets	22,417	20,834
Liabilities and Equity		
Current liabilities		
Accounts payable	3,679	3,905
Loans and notes payable	3,743	4,795
Current maturities of long-term debt	156	21
Accrued income tax	851	600
Total current liabilities	8,429	9,321
Long-term debt	1,219	835
Other liabilities	961	1,004
Deferred income taxes	442	358
Shareholders' equity	11,366	9,316
Total liabilities and equity	22,417	20,834

SOURCE: Adapted from 2001 *Coca-Cola Annual Report*.

Costs and expenses are reported separately. Costs refer to the direct costs of generating goods that are sold or of providing the services rendered. In the case of a wholesale firm, *costs of goods sold* (or costs of sales) can be determined by examining all of the material purchases as well as any changes in inventory. The inventory on hand at the start of the period, known as beginning inventory, plus any purchases of materials during the year, results in the costs of goods that are available for sale. In order to calculate the costs of goods actually sold during the year, ending inventory must be subtracted. The resulting relationship is

Costs of goods sold = beginning inventory + purchases − ending inventory

The difference between revenues and cost of goods sold is known as the *gross profit* (or gross margin) of the firm:

Revenues − costs of goods sold = gross profit

After the gross profit has been calculated, expenses are subtracted in order to determine the amount of income or profit before taxes are deducted. Expenses are other costs associated with doing business. Operating expenses typically include any general, selling, and administrative (GS&A) expenses associated with running the business and selling the product or offering the service, as well as any interest expenses associated with any debt the firm may have. The resulting relationship is

Gross profit − expenses = income before taxes

The next item is the provision for income taxes and is usually calculated in North America to be around 35 percent of pretax income (although if a firm has experienced losses in the previous year, the taxes paid in subsequent years may be lower since tax losses in one year can be carried forward and applied to earnings in a subsequent year). The result, after accounting for income taxes, is the *net income* (or loss) of the firm for that particular period. Net income is also referred to as "net profit" or "net income after taxes" or "net profit after taxes." The relationship is

Income before taxes − income taxes = net income

While this completes the income statement, there is one more important step that allows for a connection between the income statement and the balance sheet. If a firm has any preferred shares, then the preferred dividends would be paid out of the net income, leaving income that is available to common shareholders:

Net income − preferred dividends = net income available to
common shareholders

If a firm does not have preferred shares, then "net income" and "net income available to common shareholders" are the same thing. This amount represents what the common shareholders earned in that particular year. However, it does not necessarily represent the cash that the common shareholders would receive. From this amount, some might be paid to common shareholders in the form of common dividends, while the remainder would be retained in the firm. The common dividends would be a cash payment, while the remainder would be reflected on the balance sheet as an increase in retained earnings. Typically, a firm would have a dividend policy or guideline, for example, targeting approximately 30 percent of net income available to common shareholders to be paid as common dividends. It is important to note that the firm is under no obligation to pay common dividends. In fact, some newer firms in a growth stage have a policy not to pay any common dividends. The hope, for common shareholders, is that by reinvesting any profit, the business can grow even more in the future. The relationship is captured in Figure 3.2 for a firm that does not have any preferred shares but

FIGURE 3.2 **The Relationship between Net Income and Retained Earnings**

Balance Sheet, December 31, Year 0		Balance Sheet, December 31, Year 1	
Assets	$24,000	Assets	$30,000
Liabilities	10,000	Liabilities	12,000
Equity		Equity	
Common shares	8,000	Common shares	8,000
Retained earnings	6,000	Retained earnings	10,000
Total liabilities and equity	$24,000	Total liabilities and equity	$30,000

Income Statement, Year-End December 31, Year 1	
Revenue	$80,000
Less costs of goods sold	50,000
Gross profit	30,000
Less expenses	15,000
Income before taxes	15,000
Less income taxes	6,000
Net income	9,000
Less common dividend	5,000
Increase in retained earnings	$4,000

FIGURE 3.3   Income Statements for Coca-Cola

FOR YR. ENDED DEC. 31 (IN $ MILLIONS)	2001	2000
Revenues		
Net operating revenues	20,092	19,889
Other income (losses)	282	(190)
Total revenues	20,374	19,699
Costs of goods sold	6,044	6,204
Gross profit	14,330	13,495
Expenses		
Selling, general, and administrative expenses	8,696	9,994
Net interest expenses (income)	(36)	102
Total expenses	8,660	10,096
Earnings (income) before taxes	5,670	3,399
Income tax	1,691	1,222
Earnings after taxes (net income)	3,979	2,177
Average number of shares outstanding (millions)	2,487	2,477
Net income per share	$1.60	$0.88

SOURCE: Adapted from 2001 *Coca-Cola Annual Report*.

pays common dividends. The year 0 retained earnings are $6,000. Net income available to common shareholders in year 1 is $9,000. After the $5,000 common share dividend payment, retained earnings increase by $4,000 to $10,000.

As an actual example of the terms in Figure 3.2, Figure 3.3 presents the income statements for Coca-Cola for the years ended December 31, 2000 and 2001. One additional representation, often reported on financial statements, is the net income divided by the number of common shares outstanding. The result is a measure known as net income per (common) share, or more commonly *earnings per share*, or EPS.

3.3 Cash Flow Statements

The third financial statement that most firms prepare is known as the cash flow statement. The cash flow statement focuses, not surprisingly, on the flow of cash or the change in the cash position between the beginning of the period (for example, one year ago) and the end of the period. While the income statement also examines flows during a period, that statement uses the *accrual* method of accounting. The accrual method attempts to match costs and revenues rather than report cash inflows and outflows. Recall that if a business offers credit terms, then it may generate revenues during one period but not receive payment until the next period. Similarly, it may incur expenses in one period but not make payments until the next period. In contrast, the cash flow statement reports the straightforward inflow and outflow of cash.

There are three main categories of cash inflows and outflows. The first category includes any cash flows related to the operating activities of the firm. This refers to any day-to-day activities that bring in cash from customers or pay cash out to suppliers. A usual starting point is the net income as reported on the income statement. However, since that number is based on the accrual method, adjustments must be made to convert it to a cash basis. One adjustment is to add back any depreciation or amortization, since these items are noncash items. Recall that these items were subtracted from revenues in order to reflect wear and tear on equipment but do not represent actual cash flows. Similarly, another adjustment is to add (or subtract) any increase (decrease) in deferred taxes. The final major item includes any changes in operating assets and liabilities. For example, an increase (decrease) in accounts receivable represents a cash outflow (inflow), an increase (decrease) in inventory represents a cash outflow (inflow), and an increase (decrease) in accounts payable represents a cash inflow (outflow).

The second major category represents cash flows from investing activities. Any investments in new business, acquisitions, or purchases of new equipment represent cash outflows, while divestitures, or asset sales, represent cash inflows.

The third major category represents cash flows from financing activities. If any new debt or equity is issued, this represents a cash inflow to the business, while the retirement of any debt or the buyback of any stock represents a cash outflow. As well, the payment of any preferred or common dividends represents a cash outflow.

One other category may appear on the cash flow statements of firms with nondomestic activities: cash flows attributable to exchange rate movements.

This item can arise, for example, if a firm agrees to pay a foreign supplier a set amount of foreign currency but ends up paying more (or less) depending on the prevailing exchange rates.

As a real-world example of the categories discussed above, Figure 3.4 presents the actual cash flow statements for Coca-Cola for the years ended Decem-

FIGURE 3.4   Cash Flow Statements for Coca-Cola

FOR YR. ENDED DEC. 31 (IN $ MILLIONS)	2001	2000
Operating Activities		
Net income	3,969	2,177
Depreciation and amortization	803	773
Deferred taxes	56	3
Net change in operating assets and liabilities	(462)	(852)
Other (net)	(256)	1,484
Net cash provided by operating activities	4,110	3,585
Investing Activities		
Purchases of investments and acquisitions	(1,107)	(905)
Proceeds from disposals of investments	455	290
Purchases of property, plant, and equipment (PPE)	(769)	(733)
Proceeds from disposal of PPE	91	45
Other investing activities	142	138
Net cash used in investing activities	(1,188)	(1,165)
Financing Activities		
Issuances of debt	3,011	3,671
Payments of debt	(3,937)	(4,256)
Issuance of stock	164	331
Purchases of stock for treasury	(277)	(133)
Dividends	(1,791)	(1,685)
Net cash used in financing activities	(2,830)	(2,072)
Effect of exchange rate changes	(45)	(140)
Cash		
Net increase during year	47	208
Balance at beginning of year	1,819	1,611
Balance at end of year	1,866	1,819

SOURCE: Adapted from 2001 *Coca-Cola Annual Report*.

ber 31, 2000 and 2001. A cash flow statement is particularly useful in determining the future needs of a firm. For example, a growing business will usually have increased needs for cash related to accounts receivable and inventories. A cash flow statement is also important to a firm that is facing financial difficulty and needs to manage its cash inflows and outflows very carefully.

3.4　Performance Measures

Once the financial statements have been reported, the next step is to interpret how the statements reflect performance. There are a number of diverse stakeholders who are concerned with the firm's financial performance: the management team, the shareholders, and the lenders. Each has a particular focus; some place more emphasis on a particular measure than others. While the performance measures reflect past performance, often these measures can be used to assist in generating forecasted financial statements. Thus these measures provide an important bridge from the past to the future. Since most of these measures represent calculations based on two items from the financial statements—a numerator and a denominator—these measures are often collectively known as financial ratios or *ratio analyses*.

These measures allow for both an internal and external assessment. Internally, ratios can be compared through time. Externally, ratios can be compared with other firms within the industry or with overall industry benchmarks. These measures can help to raise some red flags in terms of anticipated future financial performance.

It is important to keep in mind that all accounting numbers have limitations. They are simply estimates and as such are often incomplete. You must always be asking where these numbers are coming from because if the measures are poor, then any ratios based on them will be poor as well.

3.4.1　Return on Equity

There are virtually countless ratios that could be generated from the balance sheet and income statement. The focus below is on some of the major ratios that are particularly useful. An interesting starting point is the *return on equity* (ROE) measure. This is one of the most important financial benchmarks. ROE is calculated as

$$\text{Return on equity} = \frac{\text{net income (available for common shareholders)}}{\text{common shareholders' equity}}$$

This important benchmark indicates a measure of the overall profits of the firm for a particular period relative to the shareholders' investment in the firm. Recall the goal of the firm is to maximize the value to shareholders. This measure is an indication of the success of the firm in meeting this goal. It should be noted that there are some limitations to this measure. For example, there can be differences between the book value of the equity and the *market value* of the equity. Nonetheless, this measure is an important one. There are a variety of ways of calculating ROE. For example, equity can be calculated as the beginning equity (as in the examples below) or as the average between the beginning and ending equity amounts. There is no right or wrong method, but consistency is important. In the formulation above, ROE refers to the return on common equity. This implies that if a firm has preferred equity as well, any preferred dividends must be subtracted from net income in order to arrive at the amount available for common shareholders (this is implicit in the description of net income in the measures below).

Additional intuition can be gained by decomposing the ROE measure, as follows:

$$\text{ROE} = \frac{\text{net income}}{\text{revenues}} \times \frac{\text{revenues}}{\text{assets}} \times \frac{\text{assets}}{\text{equity}}$$

Note that, from basic algebra, this decomposition simplifies to "net income divided by equity" as above:

$$\text{ROE} = \frac{\text{net income}}{\text{revenues}} \times \frac{\text{revenues}}{\text{assets}} \times \frac{\text{assets}}{\text{equity}} = \frac{\text{net income}}{\text{equity}}$$

This decomposition of ROE creates three components: the *profit margin, asset turnover,* and *financial leverage* measures. The profit margin indicates the contribution to ROE through the generation of profits from the business. The asset turnover indicates the contribution through effective resource management. The financial leverage indicates the contribution through the effective use of borrowing.

3.4.2   Profitability Measures

Profitability measures typically focus on the income statement and examine how the firm is able to generate profits from a particular level of revenue generation. The goal of the firm should be to increase profits per unit of revenues, all else equal. It is a straightforward exercise to perform a *vertical analysis* by creating ratios of each item on the income statement as a percentage of revenues. In practice, there are a few particularly relevant ratios.

The first focuses on the gross profit relative to sales or revenues from operations:

$$\text{Gross margin percentage} = \frac{\text{gross profit}}{\text{revenues}}$$

The *gross margin percentage* focuses on the operating profit. By examining these ratios over time or in comparison to industry averages, important insights can be gained into the cost structure of the firm. For example, due to a recession or to the entry of new competitors, margins may have become squeezed over time. This example highlights the importance of understanding the industry and the firm in order to better interpret the ratios and trends.

Another ratio focuses on expenses:

$$\text{Expense ratio} = \frac{\text{expenses}}{\text{revenues}}$$

The expense ratio highlights the impact of expenses on profitability. A further examination might reveal the impact of fixed versus variable costs as a firm with high fixed costs experiences a downturn in demand. Alternatively, lower borrowing costs might decrease the interest portion of expenses.

3.4.3   Resource Management Measures

Recall that the asset turnover measure compares the revenues the firm is able to generate relative to the asset base. This overall performance measure highlights the importance of managing the resources available to the firm. Ideally, the firm would like to have as high an asset turnover ratio as possible. This measure captures the capital intensity of the business: the more capital intense, the lower the asset turnover. Not surprisingly, firms with higher profit margins tend to have lower asset turnover ratios.

There are a number of methods available to measure the ability of management to efficiently manage the resources of the firm. Two methods focus on the management of the short-term assets of inventory and accounts receivable, while a related method focuses on the management of accounts payable. These measures combine information from both the income statement and the balance sheet.

The first measure focuses on inventory:

$$\text{Age of inventory (days)} = \frac{\text{inventory}}{\text{average daily costs of sales}}$$

The age of the inventory measures the average time between the purchase of materials (to create the goods) and the sale of the goods. Firms often have a variety of raw materials, works in progress, and finished goods. The numerator of this ratio is typically measured by examining a snapshot at a particular point in time, say, December 31, on the basis of the outstanding inventory on that day.

An alternative measure of average inventory throughout the year is sometimes used and may be more appropriate in a seasonal business. The denominator is calculated by taking the total costs of goods sold (or costs of sales) for the year divided by 365 (alternatively 360 days may be used throughout):

$$\text{Average daily costs of sales} = \frac{\text{annual costs of sales}}{365}$$

The average days of inventory represent how long the firm's assets are tied up in inventory before sales are made. The interpretation of this ratio— whether large amounts are typical or whether just-in-time inventory practices are more prevalent—depends very much on the type of industry.

An alternative representation of the age of inventory, known as the *inventory turnover* measure, simply divides the costs of goods sold by the ending inventory. This representation indicates how many times in a year, on average, the inventory "turns," or needs to be replaced. Equivalently, taking 365 and dividing by the age of inventory can calculate this number.

The second measure focuses on accounts receivable:

$$\text{Age of accounts receivable (days)} = \frac{\text{accounts receivable}}{\text{average daily (credit) sales}}$$

The age of accounts receivable, also known as the *collection period,* measures the average time between credit sales and the collection of sales. Firms typically offer customers terms of up to 30 days within which to pay for goods or services received. As with the previous ratio, the numerator of this ratio either provides a snapshot at a particular point in time, say, December 31, based on outstanding accounts receivable on that day, or is based on an average. If a business offers credit to all of its customers, the denominator is calculated by taking the total revenues for the year divided by 365:

$$\text{Average daily (credit) sales} = \frac{\text{annual (credit) sales}}{365}$$

Some businesses deal in a mix of both cash and credit. However, financial statements do not usually provide a mix of the cash and credit breakdown. In such a case, it is typical to simply use the overall revenue number. From an interpretation perspective, unless the mix changes over time or unless the mix is very different from the industry average, the ratio, however measured, can provide important insights. If the business is all credit, then a benchmark of comparison is the stated credit term. For example, if the firm requests payment in 30 days, yet the age of accounts receivable is 50 days, this suggests a lax enforcement of these terms and a further investigation into the reason for this situation is warranted.

The third measure, age of accounts payable, focuses on the liability side and is a mirror image of the accounts receivable measure:

$$\text{Age of accounts payable (days)} = \frac{\text{accounts payable}}{\text{average daily purchases}}$$

The age of accounts payable, also known as the *payable period,* measures the average time between the firm's purchase of materials and its payment to suppliers. Suppliers typically offer customers terms of up to 30 days within which to pay for materials and often offer discounts of, say, 2 percent if payment is made within 10 days. As with the previous ratios, the numerator of this ratio either provides a snapshot at a particular point in time, say, December 31, based on outstanding accounts payable on that day, or is based on an average. The denominator is calculated by taking the total purchases for the year divided by 365:

$$\text{Average daily purchases} = \frac{\text{annual purchases}}{365}$$

In some cases, financial statements do not provide sufficient details concerning the amount of material purchases made by the firm in a particular year. In such cases, it is often common to simply use the costs of goods sold as a proxy for purchases. What is important is to be consistent with the measure, in which case important insights can be gained from examining trends and comparing with industry averages. A benchmark of comparison is the stated payment term. For example, if suppliers request payment in 30 days, yet the age of accounts payable is 45 days, this suggests the firm may have stretched the payment to its suppliers as much as possible and the firm may need to be prepared to reduce the age of payables.

In terms of overall resource management, all else equal, the firm would like to have as little money tied up in inventory as possible, would like to receive payment from customers as quickly as possible, and would like to take as long as possible to pay suppliers. Overall, the firm would like to be able to generate as high revenues as possible for a given asset base.

3.4.4   Liquidity and Leverage Measures

Liquidity focuses on a firm's abilities to meet both short-term and long-term obligations; leverage measures focus on the firm's overall optimal use of debt. Utilizing debt can be good for a firm and can assist in generating higher return for shareholders, but it also involves more risks. Most of the capacity and leverage ratios focus on balance sheet items.

Short-term measures of liquidity include the *current ratio* and the *acid test*. The current ratio simply compares current assets and current liabilities:

$$\text{Current ratio} = \frac{\text{current assets}}{\text{current liabilities}}$$

The current ratio measures the extent to which the firm is able to cover its short-term obligations, due within the next year, with its short-term assets. In general, this ratio should be far greater than one-to-one. The rationale is that if the firm were able to liquidate all of its short-term assets such as turning accounts receivable into cash and selling its inventory, then it would be able to use this cash to meet its short-term obligations.

The acid test ratio is calculated as follows:

$$\text{Acid test} = \frac{\text{cash + accounts receivable}}{\text{current liabilities}}$$

where cash includes any marketable securities as well. The acid test is similar to the current ratio but is a tougher test of liquidity. In the case of a forced liquidation, the firm would have a more difficult time turning inventory, and prepaid expenses in particular, into cash. By excluding these items, a more realistic picture of the firm's ability to meet short-term obligations with short-term assets emerges. As with the current ratio, it is desirable for this ratio to be greater than one-to-one.

Long-term measures of leverage and the firm's overall capacity for debt include the *debt-to-equity* ratio and the long-term-debt–to–total-capital ratio. The debt-to-equity ratio is calculated in a straightforward manner:

$$\text{Debt-to-equity ratio} = \frac{\text{total debt}}{\text{equity}}$$

We usually incorporate both common equity and preferred equity in this ratio. However, it should be noted that this ratio is sometimes calculated using long-term debt only in the numerator. The lower this ratio, the more room a firm has to issue new debt or take on other liabilities in the future. There is no general benchmark for this ratio; it depends on the type of industry. More stable industries and those with higher fixed costs, such as utilities, tend to have higher debt-to-equity ratios.

The long-term-debt–to–capital ratio is

$$\text{Long-term-debt–to–capital ratio} = \frac{\text{long-term debt}}{\text{long-term debt + equity}}$$

This ratio provides a better picture of what is known as the capital structure of the firm, since it focuses on "permanent" or long-term capital. This ratio presents a picture of the percentage of the firm's capital that is made up of debt.

One final leverage ratio is the *interest coverage ratio,* calculated as follows:

$$\text{Interest coverage} = \frac{\text{earnings before interest and taxes}}{\text{interest expenses}}$$

This measure is of particular interest to any lenders. The ratio is calculated by taking the earnings before tax number and adding back the interest expenses number to get earnings before interest and taxes. This is the amount of operating earnings available to pay interest expenses. If this amount is less than the amount of interest owing during the year—in other words, if the interest coverage ratio is less than one-to-one—then the firm is in danger of defaulting on its loan obligations, which would have serious consequences for the future of the firm.

The performance ratios are summarized in Figure 3.5.

FIGURE 3.5   Summary of Performance Ratios

PERFORMANCE MEASURE	NUMERATOR	DENOMINATOR
Return on equity	Net income	Equity
Profitability		
Gross margin percentage	Gross profit	Revenues
Expense ratio	Expenses	Revenues
Resource Management		
Age of inventory	Inventory	Avg. daily cost of goods
Age of receivables	Accounts receivable	Average daily sales
Age of payables	Accounts payable	Avg. daily purchases
Liquidity and Leverage		
Current ratio	Current assets	Current liabilities
Acid test	Cash + acc. receivable	Current liabilities
Debt to equity	Total debt	Equity
Long-term debt to capital	Long-term debt (LTD)	LTD + equity
Interest coverage	EBIT	Interest expenses

FIGURE 3.6   Coca-Cola Performance Ratios

PERFORMANCE MEASURE	2001	2000
Return on equity	35.0%	23.4%
Profitability		
Gross margin*	71.3%	67.9%
Expense ratio*	43.1%	50.8%
Resource Management		
Age of inventory	63.7 days	62.7 days
Age of receivables*	34.2 days	32.2 days
Age of payables[†]	222.2 days	229.7 days
Liquidity and Leverage		
Current ratio	0.9×	0.7×
Acid test	0.5×	0.4×
Debt to equity[‡]	0.9×	1.2×
Long-term debt to capital	0.1×	0.1×
Interest coverage	n.m.[§]	34.3×

*Based on operating revenues.
[†]Based on costs of goods sold.
[‡]Current, long-term, and other liabilities.
[§]"n.m." not meaningful.

3.4.5   Application: Coca-Cola

The performance measures are applied to Coca-Cola for both 2000 and 2001 year-ends. The performance ratios are summarized in Figure 3.6.

3.5   Summary

1. Balance sheets provide a snapshot at a particular time of the assets of a firm compared with its liabilities and equity. Balance sheets always balance.
2. Income statements examine the revenues, costs, expenses, and profit of a firm over a particular period of time.

3. Balance sheets and income statements connect through the retained earnings account.
4. Cash flow statements reconcile any changes in cash balances between two periods and examine cash inflows and outflows generated by operating activities, investing activities, and financing activities.
5. Performance measures focus on the profitability, resource management, and liquidity and leverage position of a firm. An important overall measure of performance is the return on equity, which examines the net income generated relative to the equity of the firm.
6. Profitability measures focus on the ability of a firm to earn a sufficient operating profit with reasonable expenses.
7. Resource management measures focus on the ability of a firm to manage its inventory, accounts receivable, and accounts payable.
8. Liquidity and leverage measures focus on the ability of a firm to meet its short-term and long-term debt obligations.

3.6   Additional Readings

Reviews of basic accounting can also be found in

Anthony, Robert. *A Review of Essentials of Accounting.* 6th ed. Reading, MA: Addison-Wesley, 1997.

Merrill Lynch. *How to Read a Financial Report.* 7th ed. New York: Merrill Lynch, Pierce, Fenner & Smith, 1993.

3.7   Self-Study Problems

1. Bigco's balance sheet one year ago indicated retained earnings of $450 million. This year, Bigco's net income was $35 million. It paid its preferred shareholders a dividend of $5 million and its common shareholders a regular dividend of $6 million and a special one-time dividend of $10 million. What should be the retained earnings amount on this year's balance sheet?
2. Recalculate Coca-Cola's return on equity for both 2000 and 2001 as the product of the gross margin, asset turnover, and financial leverage ratios. On the basis of this analysis discuss why Coca-Cola's return on equity increased between 2000 and 2001.
3. Recalculate all of the ratios for Coca-Cola as presented in Figure 3.6. Comment on the strength or weakness and the trend of each ratio.

4. Day-to-Day Cash Flow Management

This chapter is the third of three chapters that focus on assessing a firm. This chapter focuses on day-to-day cash management. As discussed in chapter 3, cash inflows and outflows can arise from the operating, investing, or financing activities of the firm. A key factor in the success of a firm is its ability to manage these cash inflows and outflows.

While investing and financing activities are usually long term and do not typically occur on a daily basis, the management of cash flows related to operating activities is often a primary focus of the firm and is the focus of this chapter. Also, as will be shown, day-to-day cash flow management has important implications for the long-term financial requirements of the firm.

This chapter describes the typical cash flow cycle a business faces as it tries to balance cash inflows and cash outflows. Cash flows related to operations—inventory management, accounts receivable management, and accounts payable management—are then specifically examined. Finally, the implication of growth in revenues for financing requirements is examined.

4.1   Cash Flow Cycles

Consider the following example of a simple business in the start-up phase; carefully follow the flow of cash as the example builds. The example highlights the connection among the various activities of the firm related to its

---

FIGURE 4.1   **Start-up Example 1**

Assets		Liabilities and Equity	
Cash	$1,000	Liabilities	$0
Inventory	$0	Initial equity	$1,000
Total assets	$1,000	Total liabilities and equity	$1,000

---

operations, financing decisions, and investing (or capital budgeting) decisions. Anne Treprenoor invests $1,000 cash, her own money, in the business. She plans to buy prepackaged coffee for use in office coffee machines. She then plans to sell the coffee to offices within walking distance of her downtown home. Initially, Anne plans to run her business on an all-cash basis, and there are no other associated costs. Anne has made a *financing* decision by putting her own equity in the business. Her opening balance sheet is shown in Figure 4.1.

She then makes an *investment* decision by purchasing $1,000 in coffee packages as her initial inventory (although most investment decisions, such as the purchase of fixed assets, are long term). She hopes to be able to sell each package for twice as much as she paid for it. After her initial investment in inventory, her balance sheet is shown in Figure 4.2. Note that at this point her asset amount remains the same but the cash item has decreased by $1,000 while the inventory item has increased by $1,000. The line indicates the movement of the cash item to the inventory item.

Anne spends the morning telephoning various offices. She is very successful and ends up with more orders than she can fill with her initial inventory. She then calls her supplier and asks for an additional $500 in inventory, for which she promises to pay the next day with the proceeds from her sales.

FIGURE 4.2   **Start-up Example 2**

Assets

Liabilities and Equity

Cash $1,000 – $1,000 = $0 ⟵ $1,000 ⟶ Inventory $1,000

		Liabilities	$0
Cash $1,000 – $1,000 = $0		Liabilities	$0
Inventory	$1,000	Initial equity	$1,000
Total assets	$1,000	Total liabilities and equity	$1,000

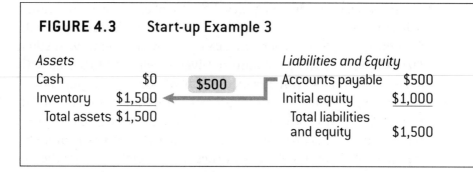

FIGURE 4.3   Start-up Example 3

Assets   *Liabilities and Equity*
Cash $0 $500   Accounts payable $500
Inventory $1,500   Initial equity $1,000
Total assets $1,500   Total liabilities
                                                            and equity $1,500

The supplier agrees. Her new balance sheet is shown in Figure 4.3. Note that both her assets and liabilities have increased by $500. On the asset side, her inventory has increased by $500 to $1,500, while her accounts payable is now $500. The arrow indicates the association between the increase in accounts payable and the corresponding increase in inventory.

Anne is able to convert $1,200 of the $1,500 in inventory into $2,400 in sales, on the basis of the *operations* of her business (recall she is able to sell the coffee for twice as much as she paid for it). The sales include $400 in cash and the remaining $2,000 as a promise to repay within the next week. Her inventory decreases by $1,200 from $1,500 to $300. Cash increases from zero to $400. Accounts receivable increase from zero to $2,000. Profits of $1,200 (ignoring any taxes in this simple example) result in an increase in retained earnings of $1,200. At the end of the day, her balance sheet and income statements are as shown in Figure 4.4.

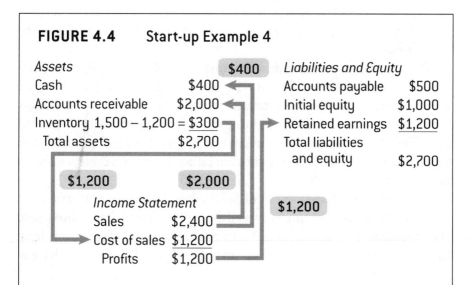

FIGURE 4.4   Start-up Example 4

Assets $400   *Liabilities and Equity*
Cash $400   Accounts payable $500
Accounts receivable $2,000   Initial equity $1,000
Inventory 1,500 – 1,200 = $300   Retained earnings $1,200
Total assets $2,700   Total liabilities
                                                            and equity $2,700

$1,200 $2,000

                Income Statement $1,200
                Sales $2,400
                Cost of sales $1,200
                Profits $1,200

This simple example demonstrates the cycle of cash flows. To summarize each item, cash initially increased to $1,000 on the basis of Anne's equity contribution, then to $0 with her purchase of the initial inventory, and then to $400 with the cash sales. Accounts receivable increased to $2,000 with the credit sales. Inventory initially increased to $1,000 with the purchase of the initial inventory, then increased to $1,500 with the addition of $500 in inventory, and then decreased by $1,200 to $300 after the first day of sales. Accounts payable increased to $500 with the materials purchased on credit. The day's sales of $2,400, less the cost of sales of $1,200, left profit for the day of $1,200. The profit increased equity by $1,200, from the initial amount of $1,000 to $2,200 by the end of the day.

The assets on the left-hand side represent any investments Anne has made. In this example, the current assets, accounts receivable, and inventory directly relate to the *operations* of her business. In the future, if Anne decides to buy a car or equipment related to the storage of the materials, then she will *invest* in fixed assets. This decision should be made on the basis of the return she anticipates to get. For example, the purchase of a car may result in greater sales, as Anne is able to cover a larger territory in less time.

The liabilities and equity on the right-hand side represent Anne's *financing*. However, part of the financing, through accounts payable, was directly related to the *operations* of her business. Most financing decisions relate to the desired mix of long-term debt and equity. If Anne does decide to make some major fixed asset purchases, she may need to approach a bank and get the bank to act as a lender. In such a case, Anne would incur a long-term debt obligation rather than the short-term obligation to her supplier. The income statement, which appears in the middle of Figure 4.4, represents the results of the *operating* activities of the business. Note that this income statement is connected to both the left-hand and right-hand sides of the balance sheet.

The sources and uses of cash are summarized in Figure 4.5, another financial statement known as the *statement of change in financial position* or the *sources and uses statement.* This statement focuses on balance sheet changes over time and is useful in highlighting the cash impact of each. Unlike the cash flow statement described in chapter 3, this statement groups items together not on the basis of activities but rather directly on their positive or negative impact on cash.

In this example, Anne's source of cash (or her ability to invest) came from credit terms through suppliers as well as profitability of the business (and corresponding increase in retained earnings). Anne's uses of cash came from the credit terms she offered to her customers, as well as her purchase of

FIGURE 4.5   Start-up Example 5

Sources of Cash

Increase in accounts payable	$500
Increase in retained earnings	$1,200
	$1,700

Uses of Cash

Increase in accounts receivable	$2,000
Increase in inventory	$300
	$2,300

Increase (decrease) in cash	($600)
Beginning cash	$1,000
Ending cash	$400

inventory. Since her uses exceeded her sources by $600, her cash balance decreased from $1,000 to $400.

In general, the potential sources are mirror images of the potential uses of cash. These items are summarized in Figure 4.6.

4.2   Cash Flows Related to Operating Activities

Cash flows related to operating activities impact primarily on current assets, such as accounts receivable and inventory, and current liabilities, such as accounts payable. Additional insights can be gained by simplifying the analysis to focus on these three items.

Consider, as an example, a manufacturer of personal computers. In order to build the computers, various materials need to be purchased, such as processing chips and hardware parts. The computer-manufacturing firm orders and takes delivery of the materials and agrees to certain credit terms, such as repayment within 30 days. The materials become part of its inventory and are assembled over the next few weeks. After assembly, the finished goods may remain in the warehouse for several more weeks or months until sales are made to retail stores. The firm offers the retail stores credit terms, such as repayment within 30 days.

FIGURE 4.6   Summary of Sources and Uses of Cash

Sources of Cash

- Decreases in current assets such as accounts receivable and inventory
- Increases in current liabilities such as accounts payable (slower payments)
- Decreases in fixed assets and other investments (sell-offs)
- Increases in long-term debt (new issues)
- Increases in retained earnings (profit)
- Increases in equity (new issues)

Uses of Cash

- Increases in current assets such as accounts receivable and inventory
- Decreases in current liabilities such as accounts payable (faster payments)
- Increases in fixed assets and other investments (new purchases and acquisitions)
- Decreases in long-term debt (principal repayment)
- Decreases in retained earnings (losses)
- Decreases in new equity (share repurchases)

Suppose the manufacturer is quite large and has the opportunity to choose among a number of different suppliers. It chooses suppliers, in part, on the available credit terms. While stated terms indicate 30-day repayment, in practice, the manufacturer averages 45 days to repay. In addition, the firm has an efficient operations process and inventory management system and attempts to assemble the computers in a few days and minimizes finished goods inventory through a just-in-time inventory system. On average, inventory is only carried for 15 days. Finally, given the importance in the industry of this manufacturer and the demand for this product, the customers (retail stores) attempt to maintain good relations with the manufacturer by paying for the computers, on average, within the agreed-on 30 days.

On the basis of this information, we can approximate the cash flow cycle by focusing on three key ratios described in chapter 3. Age of inventory, 15 days in this example, indicates the time between the order of materials and the sale of finished goods. Age of receivables, or the collection period, 30 days in this example, indicates the time between the credit sales and the receipt of cash from the customers. Thus a total of 45 days has elapsed between the order for materials and the receipt of cash from the sales. This represents the cash inflow part of the cycle. On the cash outflow part of the cycle, once the materials have been ordered, the manufacturer takes approximately 45 days to repay its suppliers, as measured by the age of accounts payable. In this example, illustrated in Figure 4.7, cash inflows and outflows from operating activities just happen to be in balance. The implication is that the firm is generally able to manage its day-to-day operations efficiently by matching its primary current liability with its primary current assets.

Now consider a different situation. Suppose the manufacturer is much smaller and does not have the opportunity to choose among a number of different suppliers. It chooses the only available supplier and must stay strictly within the terms of 30-day repayment or risk losing the supplier. In addition, the firm has a less efficient operations process and a primitive inventory management system. On average, inventory is carried for 45 days. Finally, given the relatively small size in the industry and this manufacturer's lack of reputation, the customers (retail stores) can stretch their payments to 40 days instead of the stipulated 30 days.

On the cash outflow part of the cycle, once the materials have been ordered, the manufacturer takes approximately 30 days to repay its suppli-

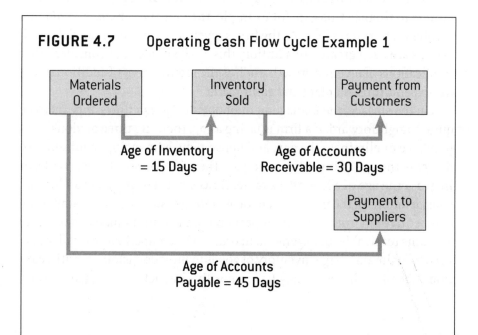

FIGURE 4.7   Operating Cash Flow Cycle Example 1

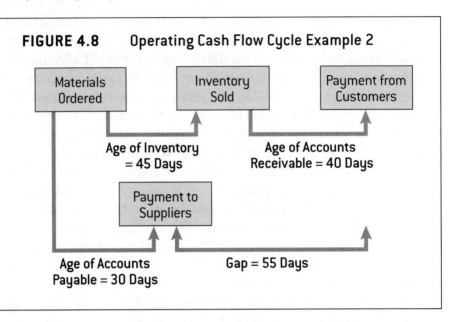

FIGURE 4.8   Operating Cash Flow Cycle Example 2

ers, as measured by the age of accounts payable. However, cash inflows require a much longer time period, estimated as the sum of the age of inventory, 45 days, and the age of receivables, 40 days, for a total inflow cycle of 85 days. This example is illustrated in Figure 4.8.

In this example, there is now a gap between the time payment to suppliers is required and the time payment from customers is received. The firm must be able to bridge this gap of 55 days (on average). The firm must be able to finance this gap, for example, through a bank *line of credit* or a revolving short-term loan. As the firm's revenues grow, the financial implications are even greater. In addition, this analysis does not consider other implications of revenue growth, such as the requirement of additional capital expenditures on plant and equipment.

On the surface, the management of operating cash flows appears to be quite straightforward. If a firm is facing a gap, there are three obvious ways to reduce or eliminate the gap, and hence reduce financing requirements: decrease the age of inventory, decrease the age of accounts receivable, or increase the age of accounts payable. However, there are some additional considerations in the management of operating cash flows. For example, the competitive environment can impact on both inventory management and accounts receivable management. In order to be competitive, a retailer may need to maintain a large inventory of goods to provide customers with selection. Liberal credit terms may have a positive impact on sales, particularly during weak economic conditions or during times of higher interest rates. Depending on the power of the suppliers, a firm may need to be prompt in payment of accounts payable. As well, suppliers often offer discounts for quick payment—for example, a 2 percent discount for payment within ten days instead of the regular 30-day terms—that may make it attractive to the firm. All of these considerations relate back to the discussion of the business size-up, which should indicate the viability of such alternative strategies.

4.3   Sustainable Growth

Day-to-day cash flow management has implications for long-term funding. A firm's requirements for funding often depend on the life-cycle stage it is in, as indicated previously in Figure 2.5. In particular, firms in a growth phase will face funding challenges. The necessity for additional financing depends on the firm's growth in revenues relative to its *sustainable growth rate:* the maximum rate at which revenues can grow without the firm's having to issue new equity, to change its payout of dividends (relative to earnings), or to change its debt policy (i.e., mix of debt relative to equity). If a firm grows at this rate, then the only new equity required will be satisfied through retained earnings, and the only new debt required, combined with the increase in retained earnings, will result in a similar debt-to-equity ratio. The sustainable growth rate is estimated as

Sustainable growth rate = return on equity × retention ratio

Recall that ROE is measured as the net income after tax available to common shareholders divided by the amount of beginning common equity. The *retention ratio* is the fraction of net income after tax available to common shareholders that is *not* paid out in common dividends but is reinvested, or retained, in the firm. The retention ratio is the inverse of the *dividend payout ratio*, which indicates the fraction of net income after tax available to common shareholders that is paid out as common dividends. For example, if the ROE is 12 percent and the retention ratio is 0.6, then the sustainable growth rate is 12 percent × 0.6 = 7.2 percent. If sales grow at this rate, then no new equity issues, change in debt to equity, or change in dividend payout are required. Note that if a firm does not pay common dividends but rather reinvests all of its retained earnings, then the retention ratio is 1.0 and the sustainable growth rate simply equals the return on equity.

4.4   Summary

1. The statement of change in financial position reconciles all of the cash inflows versus outflows and highlights the sources and uses of cash during the year.
2. Decreases in assets and increases in liabilities and equity represent sources of cash while increases in assets and decreases in liabilities and equities represent uses of cash.
3. The operating cash flow cycle compares the combined age of inventory and receivables with the age of payables in order to identify a funding gap.
4. Sustainable growth represents the maximum growth in revenue of the firm while maintaining a fixed debt policy and a dividend payout policy.
5. Sustainable growth is estimated as the product of the return on equity measure and the retention rate.

4.5   Additional Readings

A more in-depth discussion of accounting issues can also be found in
Anthony, Robert. *Essentials of Accounting.* 6th ed. Reading, MA: Addison-Wesley, 1997.

A good example of sustainable growth can be found in the article
Taggart, Robert. Spreadsheets Exercises for Linking Financial Statements, Valuation, and Capital Budgeting. *Financial Practice and Education* 9, No. 1 (1999): 102–10.

4.6   Self-Study Problems

1. Identify some of the major sources and uses of cash for Coca-Cola during 2001 on the basis of the information provided in the financial statements in Figures 3.1 and 3.3.
2. Discuss the implications of attempting to reduce the funding gap by (a) reducing the age of inventory, (b) reducing the age of accounts receivable, and (c) increasing the age of accounts payable.
3. What is the sustainable growth rate of a firm with a profit margin (net income to sales) of 5 percent, an asset turnover ratio (sales to assets) of 3.1, a financial leverage ratio (assets to equity) of 1.5, and a dividend payout ratio of 0.4?

5. Projecting Financial Requirements: Pro Forma Financial Statements

The previous chapters of the book have focused on assessing the current business from both nonfinancial and financial perspectives. This chapter makes the transition to a focus on the future: What is the anticipated *amount* of financing for the firm? The next three chapters examine additional aspects related to the *type* of long-term financing for the firm.

The chapter begins with an example, introduced in chapter 4, related to the sustainable growth rate of a firm. If the firm grows at this rate, then it can maintain its debt policy (or debt-to-equity ratio) and its dividend policy. While additional lending will be required, these requirements are balanced by internally generated funds reinvested in the firm through retained earnings. More general pro forma (projected) income statements and balance sheets are then developed, followed by pro forma cash budgets. The importance of sensitivity analysis is examined and the use of spreadsheet analysis is highlighted.

5.1   Sustainable Growth Example

Recall from chapter 4, the sustainable growth rate is the maximum rate of growth of sales that a firm can sustain while maintaining its debt policy (debt-to-equity mix) and dividend policy (payout as a fixed percentage of earnings). This example develops projected financial statements, assuming the firm grows at the sustainable growth rate. All of the financial ratios remain constant. Note that the sustainable growth rate provides a simplified summary of the pro forma statement relationships.

In order to develop this example, it is useful to recall two key relationships and the implications of each. First, the equation for sustainable growth can be rewritten as

$$\text{Sustainable growth rate} = \text{return on equity} \times b$$

where b represents the retention ratio, or the proportion of earnings after tax available to common shareholders not paid out in common dividends. Note that the dividend payout ratio is simply $(1 - b)$. For example, if the retention ratio is 0.6, then the payout ratio is 0.4.

The second key relationship, developed earlier as the decomposition of ROE, can be rewritten as

$$\text{ROE} = \frac{\text{revenues}}{\text{assets}} \times \frac{\text{assets}}{\text{equity}} \times \frac{\text{net income}}{\text{revenues}}$$

or simply as

$$\text{ROE} = \text{asset turnover} \times \text{financial leverage} \times \text{profit margin}$$

The two key implications of sustainable growth—the dividend policy, as captured by the constant b, and the debt policy, as captured by the financial leverage measure—remain constant. Implicitly, the asset turnover, or efficiency, measure and the profit margin remain constant as well.

Once we understand these key relationships, we can build the financial statements in three stages. First, we can establish income statement relationships. Second, we can estimate the sustainable growth rate and connect the income statement with the balance sheet. Third, we can establish balance sheet relationships.[1]

In this example, we wish to establish a process for developing a relatively robust set of financial statements that will serve as a template for most situations you will encounter. In order to build these general statements, we need to make a number of key assumptions and also establish a number of

---

[1] Note that a number of examples in this chapter are also presented in an Excel workbook called *Financial Forecasting Spreadsheet*, available on the Web site: www.wwnorton.com/college/econ/finman. Footnotes throughout this chapter will indicate the specific spreadsheets that are part of the workbook. The sustainable growth example appears in the spreadsheet called "Sustainable Growth."

relationships among the variables. For example, we need to assume a particular retention ratio. Combined with a ROE estimate, we need to establish the relationship of ROE × b in order to estimate the sustainable growth rate. Each assumption or relationship is referred to below as an item. Each item is presented in a logical manner, starting with income statement relationships, then moving to sustainable growth, and finally balance sheet relationships. In this example, we will need 25 items to establish relatively robust financial statements. While this may seem like a lot of assumptions and relationships, if we understand each item and take it one step at a time, the process is not as intimidating as it may first appear.

We begin by establishing income statement relationships. We assume the firm starts with an asset base of $100. We also assume the asset turnover ratio (sales to assets) is constant at a rate of 3.0. This implies that projected sales in year 1 will be $300 ($100 × 3.0). Once we establish this key number, the asset turnover ratio, which we will refer to as item 1, virtually all of the remaining assumptions and relationships can be tied to the projected sales figure.

The second key assumption, item 2, is the financial leverage ratio, which we assume to be 2.5. This implies the ratio of assets to equity is 2.5. Recall that assets are equal to liabilities (or debt) plus equity. If the *assets-to-equity* ratio is 2.5, then by inverting this ratio, we know that the *equity-to-assets* ratio is 1/2.5, or 0.4. In other words, initial equity is 40 percent of our asset base of $100. This implies our initial equity is $40 and total liabilities will therefore be $100 – $40, or $60.

We now have established two of the three components of ROE: the asset turnover and the financial leverage. It turns out that the last component, the profit margin, requires a lot of interim calculations as part of our development of the income statement. Before we examine those interim calculations, let's "cut to the chase" and note that the profit margin, item 17, turns out to be 0.016, or 1.6 percent of the sales. With that established, we can move directly to the second key relationship, sustainable growth, and estimate ROE as the product of the asset turnover, financial leverage, and profit margins: 3.0 × 2.5 × 1.6 percent = 12 percent, item 18. If we assume a retention ratio b, item 19, of 0.60, then the sustainable growth rate, item 20, is ROE × b = 12 percent × 0.60 = 7.2 percent. These relationships are summarized in Figure 5.1.

This implies that, assuming sales grow at exactly 7.2 percent per year and dividend and debt policy remain constant, then the growth can be funded internally (through retained earnings) and externally to the extent that such other performance measures (asset turnover and gross margin) remain constant.

FIGURE 5.1   Sustainable Growth Estimation

ITEM	DESCRIPTION	VALUE
1	Asset turnover (AT)	3.0
2	Financial leverage (FL)	2.5
.		
.		
.		
17	Profit margin (PM)	1.6%
18	ROE $= AT \times FL \times PM$	$3.0 \times 2.5 \times 1.6\% = 12\%$
19	Retention ratio (b)	0.60
20	Sustainable growth rate $=$ ROE $\times b$	$12\% \times 0.60 = 7.2\%$

Now that we have established the big picture, we can return to the profit margin calculation—earnings after tax relative to sales—and develop interim relationships that will help establish various income statement items. These will be established in items 3 through 16. But first, a simple income statement is outlined in Figure 5.2.

This income statement outline is similar to the Coca-Cola income statement presented in Figure 3.3, with one minor exception: interest expenses are shown separately from other operating expenses such as selling expenses and depreciation. This allows us to calculate the earnings before interest and taxes, commonly known as EBIT.

In order to establish earnings after tax as a percentage of sales, we must also establish the following relationships relative to sales: gross profit; selling, general, and administrative (SG&A) expenses; depreciation expenses; interest expenses; and taxes (as a percent of earnings before tax).

The gross margin, item 3, is assumed to be a fixed percentage of sales: 21 percent. Implicitly, this assumes that the costs of goods sold represent 79 percent of sales. The next three items represent expenses as a percentage of sales. Item 4, SG&A, is assumed to be 15 percent of sales. Note that this assumes all of these expenses are *variable costs*, as opposed to *fixed costs*. Variable costs vary directly with sales. Examples of variable costs are packaging and shipping expenses. Certainly, it makes sense that many selling-related costs vary directly with the amount of sales. For other general and administrative expenses, the relationship is less straightforward as items such as head office and computing facilities may be fixed and not directly linked to sales (at least in the short term) but more loosely tied to sales. Nonetheless, for simplicity, we will proceed by assuming all SG&A expenses are variable. Item 9, depreciation, and item 13, interest, require additional interim assumptions.

Recall depreciation represents a charge reflecting the decreasing value of fixed assets, such as plant and equipment, through regular wear and tear. Depreciation as a percentage of fixed assets, item 5, is assumed to be 20 percent. In other words, assuming straight-line depreciation, the typical fixed asset is assumed to have a useful life of five years (and hence each year's depreciation is 1/5, or 20 percent). The relationship between fixed assets and total assets, item 6, is assumed to be 30 percent. This assumption implies current (short-term) assets represent 70 percent of assets. Combining items 5 and 6, item 7 indicates depreciation as a percentage of total assets is the product of depreciation to fixed assets and fixed assets to total assets: $0.20 \times 0.30 = 0.06$, or 6 percent. Item 8, the assets-to-sales ratio is simply the inverse of the sales-to-assets ratio of 3.0, or 1/3 (0.333). Finally, we can now calculate depreciation as a percentage of sales, item 9, as the product of depreciation as a percentage of total assets, item 7, and assets to sales, item 8: $0.06 \times 0.333 = 0.02$, or 2 percent.

In order to calculate interest expenses as a percentage of sales, the first step is to estimate the relationship between interest and long-term debt, item 10. This item, assumed to be 0.10, or 10 percent, represents the firm's borrow-

---

FIGURE 5.2   Income Statement Outline

INCOME STATEMENT

Sales
Less costs of goods sold
    Gross profit

Operating expenses
    Selling, general, and administrative
    Depreciation
       Total operating expenses

Earnings (profit) before interest and taxes (EBIT)
Less interest expenses
    Earnings (profit) before taxes (EBT)

Less taxes
    Earnings (profit) after taxes (EAT)

ing costs. This cost will depend on the overall level of interest rates, as well as the perceived riskiness of the firm. Item 11 indicates the relationship between long-term debt and total assets, assumed to be 0.40, or 40 percent. Item 12 again indicates the assets-to-sales ratio of 0.333. Finally, interest as a percentage of sales, item 13, is estimated as the product of interest to long-term debt, item 10; long-term debt to total assets, item 11; and assets to sales, item 12: $0.10 \times 0.40 \times 0.333 = 0.013$, or 1.3 percent.

Total expenses as a percentage of sales, item 14, can now be estimated as the sum of SG&A as a percentage of sales, item 4; depreciation expenses as a percentage of sales, item 9; and interest as a percentage of sales, item 13: $0.15 + 0.02 + 0.013 = 0.183$, or 18.3 percent.

The profit before tax margin, item 15, is estimated as the gross margin (gross profit as a percentage of sales), item 3, less total expenses as a percentage of sales, item 14: $0.21 - 0.183 = 0.027$, or 2.7 percent. Finally, with an assumed tax rate of 40 percent, item 16, we can estimate the profit margin, item 17, as the profit margin before tax, item 15, times 1 minus the tax rate, item 16: $0.027 \times (1 - 0.4) = 0.027 \times 0.6 = 0.016$, or 1.6 percent. Note that with a tax rate of 40 percent, each before-tax dollar turns into 0.60 after-tax dollars.

Figure 5.3 summarizes the profit margin calculations.

We are now in a position to establish the pro forma income statements. Recall our key starting point is the year 1 sales projection of $300, that is, the projected asset base of $100 times the asset turnover ratio (sales to assets) of 3.0. Most of the remaining assumptions are based on percentages of the sales item (except taxes, which are a percentage of before-tax earnings, or profits). We can also project year 2 sales on the basis of the calculated sustainable growth rate of 7.2 percent. Results are presented in Figure 5.4.

We can now proceed from the income statement to the balance sheet. A simplified balance sheet outline is presented in Figure 5.5 (no distinction has been made between current and fixed asset categories, and current and long-term liabilities categories). Recall the basic relationship: total assets (the left-hand side of the balance sheet) must equal total liabilities and equity (the right-hand side of the balance sheet).

In this sustainable growth example, we need to make some basic assumptions, as indicated in Figure 5.6. We start with initial total assets of $100, item 21—all other items are percentages (or fractions) of total assets. Current assets include cash, item 22, 10 percent of total assets; accounts receivable, item 23, 25 percent of total assets; and inventory, item 24, 35 percent of total assets. The remaining asset category, fixed assets, was described above in item 6 as 30 percent of total assets. Note that all of these asset categories must add up to 100 percent.

Switching to the right-hand side of the balance sheet, accounts payable, item 25 (and the only indicated current liability), is 20 percent of total assets. Long-term debt was previously described in item 11 as 40 percent of total assets (we are implicitly including any current portion of the long-term debt, due within one year). Finally, equity was previously described in item 4 as 40

FIGURE 5.3   Profit Margin Estimation

ITEM	RELATIONSHIP	VALUE
3	Gross margin (gross profit/sales or *GM*)	0.21
4	SG&A % of sales	0.15
5	Depreciation % of fixed assets (depreciation/FA)	0.207
6	Fixed assets/total assets (*FA/TA*)	0.30
7	Depreciation/TA = depreciation/FA $\times$ FA/TA	$0.20 \times 0.30 = 0.06$
8	Assets/sales (*TA/sales*)	0.333
9	Depreciation/sales = depreciation/TA $\times$ TA/sales	$0.60 \times 0.333 = 0.02$
10	Interest % of LT debt (int/LTD)	0.10
11	LT debt/total assets (LTD/TA)	0.40
12	Assets/sales (*TA/sales*)	0.333
13	Interest/sales = interest/LTD $\times$ LTD/TA $\times$ TA/sales	$0.10 \times 0.40 \times 0.333 = 0.013$
14	Expenses/sales = SG&A % + depreciation/sales + interest/sales	$0.15 + 0.02 + 0.013 = 0.183$
15	Pretax margin (PTM) = GM − expenses/sales	$0.210 - 0.183 = 0.027$
16	Tax rate (*t*)	0.40
17	Profit margin (PM) = PTM $\times (1-t)$	$0.027 \times (1-0.40) = 0.016$, or 1.6%

FIGURE 5.4   Sustainable Growth Pro Forma Income Statements

INCOME STATEMENT	Fraction of Sales*	YEAR 1	YEAR 2
		($ Amount)	
Sales		300.0	321.6
Less costs of goods sold		237.0	254.1
Gross profit	0.210	63.0	67.5
Operating expenses			
Selling, general, and administrative	0.150	45.0	48.2
Depreciation	0.020	6.0	6.4
Total operating expenses		51.0	54.7
Earnings before interest and taxes (EBIT)		12.0	12.9
Less interest expenses	0.013	4.0	4.3
Earnings (profit) before tax (EBT)		8.0	8.6
Less taxes	0.40 of EBT	3.2	3.4
Earnings (profit) after tax (EAT)		4.8	5.1
Dividends	0.40 of EAT	1.9	2.1
Change in retained earnings		2.9	3.1

*Unless otherwise noted.

percent of total assets. Note that all liability and equity categories must add up to 100 percent.

We are now in a position to estimate the pro forma balance sheets. Results are presented in Figure 5.7. Year 0 represents the initial balance sheet. Year 1 and year 2 assets increase at the sustainable growth rate of 7.2 percent.

On the basis of these pro forma income statements and balance sheets, we can estimate financial ratios. Profitability, resource management, and liquidity ratios are presented in Figure 5.8. As predicted, all of the ratios

FIGURE 5.5   Balance Sheet Outline

BALANCE SHEET

Assets
    Cash
    Accounts receivable
    Inventory
    Fixed assets
        Total assets

Liabilities
    Accounts payable
    Long-term debt
        Total liabilities

Equity
    Total liabilities and equity

FIGURE 5.6   Balance Sheet Estimation

ITEM	DESCRIPTION	VALUE
21	Initial total assets (TA)	$100
22	Cash % of TA	0.10
23	Accounts receivable % of TA	0.25
24	Inventory % of TA	0.35
6 (previous)	Fixed assets % of TA	0.30
25	Accounts payable % of TA	0.20
11 (previous)	Long-term debt % of TA	0.40
4 (previous)	Equity % of TA	0.40

FIGURE 5.7   Sustainable Growth Pro Forma Balance Sheets

BALANCE SHEET	Fraction of Assets	YEAR 0	YEAR 1	YEAR 2
			($ Amount)	
Assets				
Cash	0.10	10.0	10.7	11.5
Accounts receivable	0.25	25.0	26.8	28.7
Inventory	0.35	35.0	37.5	40.2
Fixed assets	0.30	30.0	32.2	34.5
Total assets		100.0	107.2	114.9
Liabilities				
Accounts payable	0.20	20.0	21.4	23.0
Long-term debt	0.40	40.0	42.9	46.0
Total liabilities		60.0	64.3	69.0
Equity	0.40	40.0	42.9	46.0
Total liabilities and equity		100.0	107.2	114.9

remain constant over time, provided the sustainable growth rate of sales and assets remains constant.

The preceding example is meant to illustrate important concepts and connections between income statements and balance sheets. Of course, it is very unlikely that a firm is able to maintain a growth rate exactly equal to the sustainable growth rate in every year. If it appears that the difference in the growth rate from the sustainable rate is not temporary, then the firm will need to take action.

Now suppose a firm's revenue growth is above the sustainable growth rate. The firm has three possible courses of action. First, it can cut its dividend in order to increase its retention ratio (the b in the sustainable growth equation; recall the sustainable growth rate equals ROE $\times b$). This alternative assumes the firm is facing attractive projects in which to invest. However, while this alternative appears to meet the requirements of increasing the sustainable rate, a firm's dividend policy often acts as a signal to equity

FIGURE 5.8   Pro Forma Sustainable Growth Financial Ratios

PRO FORMA PERFORMANCE RATIOS	YEAR 0	YEAR 1	YEAR 2
Return on equity		12%	12%
Profitability			
Gross margin		21% of sales	21% of sales
Operating expense ratio		17% of sales	17% of sales
Resource Management			
Age of inventory		57.78 days	57.78 days
Age of receivables		32.61 days	32.61 days
Age of payables		33.02 days	33.02 days
Liquidity and Leverage			
Current ratio	3.50×	3.50×	3.50×
Acid test	1.75×	1.75×	1.75×
Debt to equity	1.50×	1.50×	1.50×
Long-term debt to capital	0.50×	0.50×	0.50×
Interest coverage		3.00×	3.00×

investors. Firms are often very reluctant to reduce dividends in case investors interpret the cut as a desperate measure by the firm to preserve cash.

A second alternative is issuing debt in order to increase the financial leverage ratio, and hence increase the ROE, and hence increase the sustainable growth rate. A firm will often consider this alternative if it deems it has available debt capacity. Of course, there are limits to the firm's ability to issue additional debt, depending on the perceived riskiness of the firm.

A third alternative for the firm is to issue more equity. In other words, if the firm cannot rely on internal equity to finance its growth (through retained earnings), it may have to rely on external equity. Issuing equity may be difficult depending on prevailing market conditions.

A different situation occurs if the firm's revenue growth is permanently below the sustainable growth rate. In this case, the firm also faces three alternatives. First, the firm can do nothing, in which case it will generate excess cash. The problem with this alternative is that it signals the underutilization of assets that often has a negative impact on a firm's stock price or may even attract potential acquirers. Second, the firm can increase its dividend, thereby decreasing its retention ratio. However, since individual investors face taxes on dividends, such a policy is often discouraging. Finally, the firm can use the excess cash to acquire other businesses. Such a strategy only makes sense if the acquisitions can occur at a reasonable price and the acquired business provides a good fit with the existing business.

5.2   Pro Forma Income Statement

The preceding section was developed on the premise that the firm was growing at the sustainable growth rate. However, as noted above, this is often not the case, particularly in the short term. While the examples above are useful to the understanding of the relationships among various growth-related variables, it is a more common approach to developing pro forma statements *not* to assume sustainable growth as an *input.* A more common approach to developing pro forma income statements is described in this section.[2]

    This approach shares many of the elements described above, with the exception of the sustainable growth assumption. The most common variation of this approach starts with an estimate of projected sales, then makes assumptions about projected income statement relationships that are often related to past relationships. It is important to note that while this common approach is presented here, there are numerous variations and assumptions that can be made as well. The assumptions and refinements depend on the availability of data, the importance of particular assumptions, and the potential use of the financial statements.

    In this section and the next, we will take the position of a growing firm that is considering approaching its bank with a request for additional bank loan funding. We start with the pro forma income statement in this section, and then proceed to the pro forma balance sheet in the next section. We need to begin by estimating the projected profitability of the firm to determine the impact of retained earnings on the balance sheet. Rather than make assumptions about the loan required, we will allow the other variables to

---

[2]See the "Pro Formas (1)" spreadsheet.

determine the level of the required loan in order to make the balance sheet balance.

Projected sales (or revenues) for the next one or two years are usually developed by management. We are making the assumption that the firm is an ongoing business rather than a start-up. In this case, sales estimates are based on volume changes as well as unit price changes. Economic factors and industry-wide factors, such as competition, are incorporated into this forecast, consistent with the business size-up analysis described above. For simplicity, sales are often assumed to grow at a particular rate for the next one or two years (again note that this short-term growth rate is not necessarily equal to the sustainable growth rate).

The next assumption is often based on estimating the projected gross margin as a percentage of sales. Implicitly, this assumption also provides us with an estimate of the costs of goods sold as a percentage of sales.

The costs of goods sold are often decomposed on the income statement to provide more details than presented in the previous section. Recall the relationship established in chapter 3, which relates to a typical wholesale firm:

$$\text{Costs of goods sold} = \text{beginning inventory} + \text{purchases} - \text{ending inventory}$$

(Note that for a manufacturing firm, other items such as labor costs, manufacturing overhead, and depreciation of manufacturing equipment would also be included.) Each of these items is presented. Beginning inventory is readily available from existing financial statements: the pro forma beginning inventory for the upcoming year is simply last year's ending inventory. Ending inventory can be estimated from an assumption of inventory turnover or the age of inventory. Recall the following relationship:

$$\text{Age of inventory (days)} = \frac{\text{ending inventory}}{\text{average daily costs of sales}}$$

Since we now know the pro forma annual costs of sales, the pro forma average daily cost of sales is simply

$$\text{Pro forma average daily costs of sales} = \frac{\text{pro forma annual costs of sales}}{365}$$

If we are willing to assume a projected age of inventory, we can then solve for the pro forma ending inventory by rearranging the equation above:

$$\text{Pro forma ending inventory} = \text{pro forma age of inventory} \times \text{pro forma average daily costs of sales}$$

We can then solve for the estimated purchases during the year by rearranging this equation.

$$\text{Pro forma purchases} = \text{costs of goods sold} - \text{beginning inventory} + \text{ending inventory}$$

After the pro forma costs of goods sold and the gross margin have been established, we can estimate expenses. As described in chapter 4, SG&A expenses can be estimated either as a percentage of sales, assuming these expenses are all variable, or separately as fixed or variable.

Any depreciation expenses (not included in the costs of goods sold section) are estimated on the basis of the amount of fixed assets and the estimated depreciation schedule. For example, if the average useful life of assets is estimated as ten years and if the pro forma gross fixed assets are estimated to be $100,000, the depreciation expense would be estimated as $10,000 for the upcoming year.

The most challenging expense to estimate is the interest expense. Recall that the interest expense is not directly related to sales but rather to the amount of interest-bearing debt outstanding, as well as the anticipated interest rate. If a current loan has been established at a fixed rate, then the projected interest rate estimate is straightforward. If the loan has a variable rate, then an estimate of expected interest rates must be established. However, there is another challenge. In order to determine the pro forma interest expenses, we must determine the pro forma bank loan. But we have now stumbled across a chicken and egg problem since we cannot determine the pro forma loan amount until we estimate all other items, including the pro forma change in retained earnings. However, we cannot establish the pro forma change in retained earnings until we establish the pro forma profits, which in turn depend on an estimate of pro forma interest rates.

Fortunately, there are a number of potential solutions to this problem. We will deal with this problem here in the simplest manner. As a first-pass estimate, we will base the interest expenses on our best guess of what the loan will be. Management usually has a rough idea, for example, of what increase in the outstanding loan will be required to meet growing sales. In our first example below, we assume the best guess of next year's loan amount is simply this year's loan amount. This approach highlights an important point related to pro forma statements in general: it is not critical to get every number exactly correct but rather it is more important to understand the big picture that emerges from all of the assumptions.

After expenses have been determined, earnings before taxes are estimated in the usual way by subtracting expenses from the gross profit. Taxes are then estimated as a percentage of the pro forma earnings before tax, taking into account any proposed tax law changes. Pro forma earnings after tax are estimated by subtracting taxes from pro forma earnings before tax. Finally, any projected dividends must be accounted for in order to establish the projected change in retained earnings. An example is presented in Figure 5.9.

FIGURE 5.9   Pro Forma Income Statement

	ASSUMPTION		
Sales	Management estimate		$300.0
Costs of goods sold			
Beginning inventory	Last year's ending inventory	35.0	
+ Purchases	C.G.S. + ending inventory		
	– beginning inventory	239.5	
Costs of goods avail.		274.5	
– Ending inventory	57.8 days of costs of sales	37.5	
Costs of goods sold			237.0
Gross profit	0.210 fraction of sales		63.0
Operating expenses			
Selling, general, and administration	0.15 fraction of sales		45.0
Depreciation	0.20 fraction of beginning fixed assets		6.0
Total operating expenses			51.0
Earnings before interest and taxes			12.0
Interest expenses	0.10 fraction of *current* loan		4.0
Earnings before taxes (EBT)			8.0
Taxes	0.40 fraction of EBT		3.2
Earnings after taxes (EAT)			4.8
Dividends	Same as last year		1.9
Change in retained earnings			2.9

5.3   Pro Forma Balance Sheet

The pro forma balance sheet typically starts with assets, then proceeds to liabilities and equity, with the bank loan (or long-term debt) as the balancing amount.

An initial assumption is often made regarding the minimum cash balance sufficient to meet day-to-day requirements. Alternatively, if a business runs on a revolving line-of-credit basis (whereby money is borrowed from the bank only when needed), then the cash balance may be assumed to be zero.

Accounts receivable are estimated next. Accounts receivable can be estimated from an assumption related to the age of receivables. Reasonable assumptions can be derived on the basis of the analysis as part of the business size-up. Recall the following relationship:

$$\text{Age of accounts receivable (days)} = \frac{\text{accounts receivable}}{\text{average daily sales}}$$

Since we know the pro forma annual sales (estimated in the previous section), the pro forma average daily sales is simply

$$\text{Pro forma average daily sales} = \frac{\text{pro forma annual sales}}{365}$$

If we are willing to assume a projected age of accounts receivable, we can solve for the pro forma accounts receivable by rearranging the equation above:

$$\text{Pro forma accounts receivable} = \text{pro forma age of receivables} \times \text{pro forma average daily sales}$$

Ending inventory was estimated as part of the costs of goods sold on the income statement.

Fixed assets are estimated separately. If there are no new purchases of fixed assets, then the ending net fixed assets will equal the beginning net fixed assets less any depreciation projected for the year.

All of the current and fixed assets can be added to determine the projected total assets. We can then use this number from the left-hand side of the balance sheet as the final number on the right-hand side of the balance sheet: total liabilities and equity. In this manner, we ensure that the pro forma balance sheet will actually balance!

Next, we can move up the right-hand side of the balance sheet to the equity item. Recall the ending equity equals the beginning equity plus any change in retained earnings. Last year's ending equity is this year's beginning equity. We then simply add the pro forma change in retained earnings based on the projected profitability of the firm.

By subtracting the pro forma equity amount from the pro forma total liabilities and equity, we are left with the pro forma total liability amount.

We can then proceed to the current liabilities. The main current liability is the accounts payable item. As with inventory and accounts receivable, accounts payable can be estimated from an assumption related to the age of payables. Recall the following relationship:

$$\text{Age of accounts payable (days)} = \frac{\text{accounts payable}}{\text{average daily purchases}}$$

Since we know the pro forma annual purchases (estimated as part of the cost of goods sold component on the income statement), the pro forma average daily purchases is simply

$$\text{Pro forma average daily purchases} = \frac{\text{pro forma annual purchases}}{365}$$

If we are willing to assume a projected age of accounts payable, we can solve for the pro forma accounts payable by rearranging the equation above:

$$\text{Pro forma accounts payable} = \text{pro forma age of payables} \\ \times \text{pro forma average daily purchases}$$

The final item is the bank loan, or long-term debt. Recall we referred to this item as the balancing amount. Since we know the pro forma total liabilities, by subtracting the pro forma current liabilities, we are left with the pro forma bank loan. Note that it is possible, at this point, that the total liabilities are actually less than the current liabilities. If this occurs, then this negative loan balance implies that no loan is required and the negative balance can be interpreted as excess cash.

An example of the pro forma balance sheet process is indicated in Figure 5.10.[3] The number directly beside each balance sheet item represents the order in which the item is estimated, as described above.

---

[3]See the "Pro Formas (1)" spreadsheet.

FIGURE 5.10   Pro Forma Balance Sheet

	ASSUMPTION	YEAR 0	YEAR 1 PRO FORMA
Assets			
Cash ①	Assumed minimum	$10.0	$10.7
Accounts receivable ②	32.6 days of accounts receivable	25.0	26.8
Inventory ③	57.8 days of costs of sales	35.0	37.5
Fixed assets ④	8.2 new assets (before depreciation)	30.0	32.2
Total assets ⑤		100.0	107.2
Liabilities			
Accounts payable ⑨	33.0 days of payables	20.0	21.7
Long-term debt ⑩	Balancing amount	40.0	*42.7*
Total liabilities ⑧	Total liability and equity – equity	60.0	64.3
Equity ⑦	Beg. equity + change in retained earnings	40.0	42.9
Total liabilities and equity ⑥	Same as total assets	100.0	107.2

5.4   Pro Forma Cash Budgets

An alternative, and equivalent, method of projecting financial needs is through a more direct cash flow forecast, or *cash budget*. The cash budget forecasts the timing and amount of cash inflows and outflows, often on a monthly basis. The cash budget is particularly useful for firms facing seasonal financing needs. Thus the cash budget often is useful as more of a short-term than of a long-term financial forecasting vehicle.

The first step in the process is to forecast the amount and timing of any cash inflows. The primary source of such inflows is related to forecast sales.

If the firm's sales are on a cash-only basis, then the sales forecast and the cash inflow forecast will be identical. If the firm's sales are on credit, then the cash flows will depend on the credit terms. For example, if the credit terms require payment within 30 days, then any sales made in a particular month should translate into cash inflows in the following month.

The next step in the process is to forecast the amount and timing of any cash outflows. Some cash outflows result from the operations of the business, such as purchases of supplies or materials. As a preliminary step, these purchases can be forecast on a monthly basis and then the payment terms can be incorporated to forecast the timing of the outflows. For example, if the purchase terms require payments within 60 days, then any purchases made in a particular month should translate into cash outflows two months hence.

There are a number of other cash outflow categories. Selling, general, and administrative expenses are either fixed (i.e., stable from month to month) or variable (related to the sales in a particular month). Any capital expenditures—for example, purchases of new equipment—need to be forecast. Any outstanding loans require an estimate of interest payments (although this item can be difficult to forecast precisely since the loan interest may depend on the ability to secure new financing). Forecasted taxes depend on forecasted sales and profitability. Finally, any dividend payments must be forecast.

Once the monthly cash inflows and outflows have been estimated, the net monthly cash flow is calculated simply as the difference between the inflows and outflows. The net cash flow in any month is added to (in the case of an outflow) or subtracted from (in the case of an inflow) the beginning loan amount in order to calculate the ending loan amount. (In some cases, the loan amount is estimated in excess of any cash on hand.) This process is continued on a month-by-month basis.

An example of a cash budget is presented in Figure 5.11.[4] In this example, a business generates monthly sales on a credit-only basis, with receivables due within 30 days. Any purchases of supplies are due within 30 days as well. Note that the corresponding accounts receivable and accounts payable items for the month of January reflect sales and purchases that occurred the previous month. The forecasted cash inflows and outflows are meant to be consistent with the previous example's assumptions and forecasted financial statements. Note that the beginning bank loan of $30 is consistent with the beginning loan (long-term debt) in excess of the cash balance as pre-

---

[4]See the "Cash Budget" spreadsheet.

FIGURE 5.11   Cash Budget

	JAN	FEB	MAR	APR	MAY	JUN	JUL	AUG	SEP	OCT	NOV	DEC	TOTAL
Sales (all on credit)	$25.0	25.0	25.0	25.0	23.2	23.2	23.2	23.2	26.8	26.8	26.8	26.8	300.0
CASH INFLOWS													
(AR = 30 days)	25.0	25.0	25.0	25.0	25.0	23.2	23.2	23.2	23.2	26.8	26.8	26.8	298.2
OPERATIONS													
Purchases	20.0	20.0	20.0	20.0	18.0	18.0	18.0	19.0	21.5	21.6	21.7	21.7	239.5
CASH OUTFLOWS													
Payables (AP = 30 days)	**20.0**	20.0	20.0	20.0	20.0	18.0	18.0	18.0	19.0	21.5	21.6	21.7	238.1
SG&A	4.0	4.0	4.0	3.5	3.0	3.0	3.0	3.0	4.0	4.5	4.5	4.5	45.0
New equipment	0.0	0.0	0.0	0.0	0.0	0.0	0.0	0.0	0.0	0.0	0.0	8.2	8.2
Interest	0.3	0.3	0.3	0.3	0.3	0.3	0.3	0.3	0.3	0.3	0.3	0.3	4.0
Taxes	0.0	0.0	0.8	0.0	0.0	0.8	0.0	0.0	0.8	0.0	0.0	0.8	3.2
Dividends	0.0	0.0	0.5	0.0	0.0	0.5	0.0	0.0	0.5	0.0	0.0	0.5	1.9
Total cash outflows	24.3	24.3	25.6	23.8	23.3	22.6	21.3	21.3	24.6	26.3	26.4	36.0	300.4
Net monthly cash flows	0.7	0.7	−0.6	1.2	1.7	0.6	1.9	1.9	−1.4	0.5	0.4	−9.2	−1.9
Beg. of month loan	30.0	29.3	28.7	29.3	28.1	26.4	25.8	23.9	22.1	23.5	23.0	22.9	30.0
End of month loan	$29.3	28.7	29.3	28.1	26.4	25.8	23.9	22.1	23.5	23.0	22.7	31.9	31.9

sented on the current balance sheet in Figure 5.10 (i.e., 40 – 10), while the ending loan of $32 is consistent with the previous example's ending loan in excess of the cash balance as presented on the pro forma balance sheet (i.e., 42.7 – 10.7). Thus the cash budget and pro forma financial statements are equivalent methods of forecasting financing needs but each with a different emphasis.

5.5 Sensitivity Analysis and Spreadsheet Applications

Up to this point, the focus of energy has been directed toward the development of pro forma financial statements with a particular focus on determining the required long-term debt financing. After this considerable investment of time, it turns out that the fun is only beginning! We are now in a position to step back and thoroughly understand the relationships among the variables that make up the financial statements. While the analysis above represents our best guess of the relationships, each assumption required judgment and was made with a particular degree of confidence. One thing we know for certain about all financial forecasts: they are (almost always) wrong! However, this does not mean our efforts have been for naught. While the projected statements may be wrong down to the last dollar, if our best guesses have been reasonably accurate, then the statements provide a useful picture of what to expect in the future and assist in making good business decisions. For example, if the current bank loan is $250,000 and the forecast for next year is a bank loan of $400,000, the firm will take action now to secure an increase in the bank loan. It may turn out that only $350,000 is actually required in one year. While the financial forecast was not 100 percent accurate, it did help to make a good decision today.

5.5.1 Sensitivity Analysis

The pro forma statements allow us to examine whether the business can be reasonably financed. The debt-to-equity ratio and the interest coverage ratio provide a good summary that addresses this question. Besides providing the best guess of the projected financial position of the firm, pro forma statements are powerful tools to address the critical "what if" questions. These questions are related to the key assumptions made as part of the building of the pro forma statements. They usually focus on determining what will happen to the projected loan requirement if one or more key variables change. In particular, this analysis attempts to quantify how sensitive the projected loan amount (and hence the two key ratios: the debt-to-equity ratio and the interest coverage ratio) is to changing assumptions. For example, a large change in one variable may have less of an impact than a small change in another variable. We examine some of the key variables.

Often the most critical assumption is the projected sales assumption. Recall many of the items on the income statement, such as the gross margin and many of the expense items, were estimated as a percentage of forecasted sales. If an unexpected slowdown in the economy occurs, depending on the industry and the particular firm, sales may be severely impacted. While profits may decline, the loan amount will also change.

Another key assumption is the projected interest rate. If a firm has locked in to a fixed loan rate for a number of years, then this may not be a concern. However, many firms have floating or variable rate loans tied to the *prime rate* of interest or some other floating interest rate such as *LIBOR*. The prime rate is the rate at which the bank lends money to its most creditworthy customers. Depending on the credit rating of the firm, the bank might charge prime plus ½ percent or prime plus 2 percent (or more). The bank can change the prime rate at any time depending on overall market conditions and the general level of interest rates. Thus if inflation is expected to increase substantially, the prime rate may be much higher than anticipated. If the firm has a high debt ratio, then an increase in the loan interest rate may have a substantial negative impact on projected profits and a corresponding increase in the required loan.

A key set of balance sheet assumptions relates to the working capital items: accounts receivable, inventory, and accounts payable. Recall these three variables combine to determine the financing gap. The actual collection period may depend on a number of factors, including the overall economic conditions as well as the competitive position. An extended age of accounts receivable, all else equal, will lead to an increased loan requirement. In-stock inventory will depend, in part, on the ability of management to anticipate customer needs. An extended age of inventory, all else equal, will lead to an increased loan requirement. The age of accounts payable depends on the relationship between the firm and its suppliers, as well as its competitive position. An extended age of accounts payable, all else equal, will lead to a decreased loan requirement.

It is important to tie this sensitivity analysis back to the business size-up discussion in chapter 2. The main purpose of understanding the economy, the industry, and the business is to understand what is behind the numbers that form the projected statements. A proper and thorough size-up provides guidance in determining not only which assumptions to make as part of the pro forma statement development but also which variables to focus on as part of the sensitivity analysis.

5.5.2   Spreadsheet Applications

It is often reasonably straightforward to change one assumption—for example, the age of accounts payable—and determine the impact on the loan requirement. However, a more accurate and versatile approach is to develop pro forma statements from commonly available software spreadsheet packages (such as Microsoft Excel). In addition, spreadsheet analysis is particularly useful if more than one variable is being changed at the same time. This section describes some basic spreadsheet approaches.

Before proceeding with sensitivity analysis, we need to develop some simple spreadsheets. The creation of spreadsheets is often an extremely useful way to consolidate understanding of the financial statement relationships. The process is relatively straightforward. If you have never had the opportunity to create your own spreadsheet before, now is your chance!

The process involves inputting *formulas*, or equations, into spreadsheet cells, in addition to inputting *text* (i.e., actual words) as well as *numbers*. The formulas represent simple income statement and balance sheet relationships. An example is presented in Figure 5.12.[5] This example incorporates the pro forma income statement developed in Figure 5.9 and the pro forma balance sheet developed in Figure 5.10. The actual spreadsheets can also be copied from the Web site.

The first step is to input as *text*, in column A of your blank spreadsheet, the various financial statement items as in Figure 5.12. For example, in cell A2 (where A represents the column and 2 represents the row), type "Sales" (without the quotation marks). For clarity, you may also wish to input, also as text, the explanations of various assumptions in column C. Note that spreadsheet applications allow you to change the width of each column and also to change other style-related items such as the number of decimal places that are presented. (Don't worry if your spreadsheet looks a bit different but do make sure you are using *exactly* the same columns and rows as indicated below; otherwise, the formulas won't work.) The next step is to input the actual *numbers* in column B (which will be used in the formulas described

---

[5]See the "Spreadsheet" spreadsheet.

FIGURE 5.12   Spreadsheet Development

	A	B	C	D	E	F
1	**Income Statement**					
2	Sales		*Assumption*	*Col. F formulas*		300.0
3	Cost of goods sold					
4	Beginning inventory		Last year's end. inv.	=E25	⟶	35.0
5	+ Purchases		CGS + end. inv. − beg. inv.	=F6−F4		239.5
6	Cost of goods avail.			=F8+F7		274.5
7	− Ending inventory	57.8	Days of cost of sales	=B7*(F8/365)		37.5
8	Cost of goods sold			=F2*(1−B9)		237.0
9	Gross profit	0.21	Fraction of sales	=F2*B9		63.0
10	Operating Expenses					
11	SG&A	0.15	Fraction of sales	=B11*F2		45.0
12	Depreciation	0.2	Frac. of beg. fixed assets	=B12*E26		6.0
13	Total op. expenses			=SUM(F11:F12)		51.0
14	Earn. Bef. Int. & Taxes			=F9−F13		12.0
15	Interest expenses	0.1	Frac. of *current* loan	=B15*E30		4.0
16	Earn. Before Tax (EBT)			=F14−F15		8.0
17	Taxes	0.4	Fraction of EBT	=B17*F16		3.2
18	Earn. After Tax (EAT)			=F16−F17		4.8
19	Dividends	0.4	Fraction of EAT	=B19*F18		1.9
20	Change in ret. earn.			=F18−F19	⟶	2.9
21	**Balance Sheet**				Year 0	Year 1
22	Assets					
23	Cash		Assumed minimum	=10.7	10.0	10.7
24	Accounts receivable	32.6	Days of acc. rec.	=B24*F2/365	25.0	26.8
25	Inventory	57.8	Days of cost of sales	=F7	35.0	37.5
26	Fixed assets	8.2	New assets (before dep.)	=E26+B26−F12	30.0	32.2
27	Total assets			=SUM(F23:F26)	100.0	107.2
28	Liabilities				⟶	
29	Accounts payable	33	Days of payables	=B29*F5/365	20.0	21.7
30	Long-term debt		Balancing amount	=F31−F29	40.0	42.7
31	Total liabilities		Total liab. & eq. − equity	=F33−F32	60.0	64.4
32	Equity		Beg. + change in R.E.	=E32+F20	40.0	42.9
33	Total liab. and equity		Same as total assets	=F27	100.0	107.2

below) and in column D (under the "year 0" text heading, or current balance sheet).

Next, proceed directly to column F. In cell F2 (where F represents the column and 2 represents the row), the projected sales number 300 is inputted. You are now ready to input the *formulas* related to the pro forma statements. Note that 0.21 previously inputted in cell B9 represents the gross margin, or the gross profit as a fraction of sales. The next step is to enter a formula to represent the gross profit, as a dollar amount. In most spreadsheets, a formula is recognized as one that starts with =. The formula =F2*B9 is entered in cell F9, indicating the gross profit is equal to sales multiplied by (represented by *) the gross margin. *Important note: The formulas described in this section appear in column D in Figure 5.12. This is only to show you what formulas to enter in column F. These formulas are* not *to be entered in column D but rather are to be entered two cells to the right, in column F. Nothing should appear in your spreadsheet in column D.*

Other formulas simply represent the relationships described previously in this book. For example, ending inventory is estimated as the age of inventory times the average daily costs of goods sold. The projected age of inventory in days is 57.8, as indicated in cell B7. Average daily costs of goods sold equal the projected annual costs of goods sold in cell F8, divided by 365. The resulting formula in F7 is =B7*(F8/365). Note that spreadsheets such as Excel have built-in functions. For example, total operating expenses are calculated using the SUM function that indicates the range of numbers to add.

Earlier, we discussed the first-pass calculation of the interest expense using the *current* loan as the best guess of the pro forma loan. Using a spreadsheet, we can now refine this calculation using the iteration method. The spreadsheet allows us to estimate pro forma interest directly on the basis of the pro forma loan! To get around the chicken and egg problem described earlier, we use a spreadsheet option that effectively starts with the first-pass estimate described above, checks whether the first-pass pro forma loan is greater or less than the best guess, then does a second-pass calculation and continues to iterate until it has estimated precisely the actual loan. (The process appears seamless and the iteration routine is virtually instantaneous.) In order to ensure that Excel performs this iterative calculation (without giving a "circular reference" error message), we need to do the following when developing a new spreadsheet. Select "Tools" from the menu, then click on "Options" and go to the "Calculations" menu. Click on the "Iteration" box so that a check mark appears; then press the "OK" button. Finally, we modify the interest expense calculation, referring to the *pro forma* loan in cell F30 rather than the *current* loan in E30. The modified line is high-

FIGURE 5.13   Interest Expense: Iteration Method

	A	B	C	D	E	F
1	**Income Statement**					
14						
15	Interest expenses	0.1	Fraction of **pro forma** loan	=B15*F30	→	4.3
16						

lighted in Figure 5.13.[6] Note that there is a slight increase in the interest expense amount. It turns out that the pro forma loan based on the iteration method is $42.8 (only slightly higher than our $42.7 best guess). Since the loan is $2.8 higher than our best guess of $40, this implies that the interest expense will be higher by 10 percent (the loan interest rate) of this $2.8 amount, or $0.28. Thus the resulting pro forma interest expense is $4.3 instead of $4.0.

We are now in a position to demonstrate the power of spreadsheet sensitivity analysis by asking a series of "what if" questions and letting the computer do all the work. We begin with a focus on sales (we will perform our sensitivity analysis by the iterated method of interest expenses). What if sales are actually 10 percent greater than forecast?[7] We would then replace the pro forma sales number of 300 with 330. Consequently, the loan requirement would increase from $42.8 to $46.2—an increase of $3.4. Thus a 10 percent increase in sales results in a 7.9 percent increase in the required loan, assuming all other variables remain the same.

We can also consider changes in the working capital ratios. For example, what if customers are much slower paying back credit sales and take 45 days instead of 32.6 days?[8] The impact is an increase in the loan requirement from $42.8 to $53.3. If sales are 10 percent greater than expected *and* customers take longer to pay, then the loan requirement increases to $57.8.

5.6   Summary

1. If sales grow at a rate exactly equal to the sustainable rate (and the dividend policy remains stable), then pro forma financial ratios should remain constant as well.

---

[6]See the "Pro Forma (2)" spreadsheet.
[7]See the "Sensitivity (1)" spreadsheet.
[8]See the "Sensitivity (2)" spreadsheet.

2. Pro forma income statements are primarily based on forecasted sales and assumed relationships with sales.
3. Pro forma balance sheets are derived from the projected change in retained earnings, projected working capital relationships (i.e., age of receivables, age of inventory, and age of payables), and projected fixed asset changes. The required bank loan, or long-term debt, is often used as the balancing amount to make the pro forma balance sheet balance.
4. Pro forma (monthly) cash budgets are useful to highlight seasonal financing needs.
5. The pro forma loan requirement calculated from the cash budget should be consistent with the pro forma balance sheet loan requirement.
6. Sensitivity analysis highlights the impact of one (or more) change(s) on the pro forma financial statements on another key variable such as the loan requirement. Spreadsheets provide a powerful tool for performing sensitivity analysis.

5.7   Additional Readings

A useful book describing financial applications using spreadsheets is Benninga, Simon. *Financial Modeling.* Boston: MIT Press, 1997.

5.8   Self-Study Problems

1. Create a pro forma income statement based on the following assumptions: revenues of $150,000, costs of goods sold of 76 percent of revenues, total expenses of 14 percent of revenues, tax rate of 35 percent, beginning equity of $50,000, beginning inventory of $12,000, and ending inventory of 60 days. Also, calculate the projected purchases.
2. Create a pro forma balance sheet based on your results in question 1 as well as the following assumptions: minimum cash balance of $10,000, accounts receivable of 30 days, fixed assets of $60,000, and accounts payable of 35 days. Consider long-term debt as the balancing amount.
3. In question 2, what would be the impact on the pro forma long-term debt if sales were to change to $200,000 and the age of payables were to change to 45 days?
4. In questions 1 and 2, assume sales in the subsequent years increase by 15 percent. If all the other relationships remain the same, what will be the pro forma loan requirement in two years?

6. Overview of Capital Markets: Long-Term Financing Decisions

Up to this point, we have focused on understanding the current business as well as the short-term financial requirements of a firm. This chapter is the first of three chapters to examine various aspects related to the long-term financing needs of the firm, that is, needs for more than one year. As mentioned earlier, if a firm is not able to meet its financial requirements through internally generated funds and some short-term borrowing, then it will need to seek external financing through *capital markets*. Determining the appropriate type of financing is one of the most important decisions the firm faces. Recall, the firm can issue pieces of paper, which represent claims on the firm. These claims are known as the financial assets (to the buyers) or the *financial instruments* (to the firm). This chapter examines the distinctive features of three important types of financial instruments: bonds, preferred shares, and common shares. A general overview of capital markets (the markets in which these securities trade) is also presented, with a focus on the two major markets: the bond (or debt) market and the stock market. Finally, a discussion of the efficiency of capital markets is presented.

6.1 Bonds

From the firm's perspective, bonds are simply a form of borrowing. At a most basic level, bonds are loan contracts or promises made by the firm indicating a scheduled repayment of the *principal* amount along with interest payments. The bonds are said to be issued by the firm. Since the bonds represent a major form of long-term financing or a vehicle for raising funds, they are known as a type of financial instrument. Bond investors are the lenders, or *bondholders*. These investors are commonly large institutional investors such as pension funds and insurance companies. However, once the firm has issued a bond, the lender can choose to sell or trade that bond to another party, in exchange for money. There is usually an active market whereby corporate bonds, as well as bonds issued by governments, can be traded, known generically as a *securities market* (or capital market) or specifically as the bond market.

6.1.1 Bond Features

Bonds are typically issued at *par value*—also known as *face value*—indicating the principal amount to be repaid to the lender. Bonds are usually issued with a $1,000 par value (however, for pricing purposes, bond values are often quoted in $100s). The date on which repayment is due is known as the *maturity date*. Generally, maturity dates range from one year to twenty or more years. Interest payments are determined by the *coupon rate* attached to the bond. The coupon rate is expressed as a percentage of the par value of the bond. For example, if a bond has a coupon rate of 8 percent, this implies annual interest payments of $80. The typical corporate bond pays semi-annual interest, so the lender, or bond investor, would receive $40 every six months. If the bond issued today had a maturity date five years hence, the investor would receive ten equal coupon payments (the first one in six months and the last one in five years), and a principal repayment in five years as well.

Bonds often differ by the types of features they have. For example, some bonds include a *sinking fund* feature, which essentially requires the firm to repurchase a portion of its bonds on a regular basis throughout the life of the bond. The main purpose of this feature is to reassure bond investors that the firm will not be faced with the daunting task of meeting the whole of its principal repayment obligation at maturity. In some cases, the firm may simply repurchase a portion of its bonds in the bond market, or it can buy back bonds directly from the bondholders by paying the par value.

While most bond contracts specify a fixed coupon rate, other contracts indicate a *variable rate*. For example, the contract might specify repayment at the rate of prime (or LIBOR) plus a certain percentage (often in the ½ to 3 percent range).

Some bonds have *call provisions* as a feature. This provision is of particular benefit to the firm, allowing it to retire, or repay, the loan at specified times before maturity. This provision adds flexibility to the financial strategy of the firm and gives it the potential to refinance its debt obligations at a lower rate if interest rates decline.

Since bondholders do not have a direct say in how the business is run, bondholders' interests are protected to a degree through any bond *covenants*. These covenants place some restrictions on the firm in such a way as to enhance the prospect of repayment. For example, covenants might specify a maximum allowable debt-to-equity ratio for the firm, limit capital expenditures, or limit dividend payments.

6.1.2   Bond Ratings

When a firm is planning to issue a bond, potential investors want a method to assess the perceived riskiness of the bond investment. In other words, they would like to assess the possibility of *default* by the firm, or a failure to meet its interest and principal repayment obligations. Bond rating agencies provide an assessment of the creditworthiness of the firm.

Major rating agencies include Moody's and Standard & Poor's (S&P). These agencies assess the financial health of the firm. The process these agencies complete is similar to the business size-up process described in chapter 2. For long-term bonds (maturity of more than one year), the ratings are based on the likelihood of payment, the capacity and willingness of the firm to meet its financial commitments, the nature of the financial obligation (for example, the maturity and any special features of the bond), and any protection afforded by the firm in the event of bankruptcy or reorganization.

Typical ratings range from AAA, the highest rating, to AA, A, BBB, BB, B, and below. A summary of the description of various ratings, as provided by Standard & Poor's, is presented in Figure 6.1. Bonds with ratings of BBB and higher are known as investment grade bonds. Most institutional investors are restricted to investments in investment grade bonds. Investments rated below BBB are known as high-yield or junk bonds. Prior to 1980, most bonds in this category were known as fallen angels—bonds that initially received an investment grade but had since become riskier. Since that time, led by the initiative of well-known (and infamous) financier Michael Milken, a huge market developed for firms to initially issue risky bonds.

FIGURE 6.1   Standard & Poor's Long-Term
                    Credit Rating Definitions

AAA

An obligation rated AAA has the highest rating assigned by Standard & Poor's. The obligor's capacity to meet its financial commitment on the obligation is very strong.

AA

An obligation rated AA differs from the highest-rated obligations only in small degree. The obligor's capacity to meet its financial commitment on the obligation is extremely strong.

A

An obligation rated A is somewhat more susceptible to the adverse effects of changes in circumstances and economic conditions than obligations in higher-rated categories. However, the obligor's capacity to meet its financial commitment on the obligation is still strong.

BBB

An obligation rated BBB exhibits adequate protection parameters. However, adverse economic conditions or changing circumstances are more likely to lead to a weakened capacity of the obligor to meet its financial commitment on the obligation than of higher-rated obligors.

BB, B, CCC, CC, C

Obligations rated BB, B, CCC, CC, and C are regarded as having significant speculative characteristics. The rating BB indicates the least degree of speculation, and C the highest. While such obligations will likely have some quality and protective characteristics, these may be outweighed by large uncertainties or major exposures to adverse conditions.

D

An obligation rated D is in payment default.

SOURCE: www.standardandpoors.com.

6.2   Common Shares

The issuance of common shares represents a very different form of financing. Common shareholders (or common equityholders) are the ultimate owners of the firm. Common shareholders are often referred to as residual claimants since they have a claim on any of the income earned by the firm after other stakeholders, such as bondholders, have been taken care of (for example, after they have received their interest payments). Like bonds, an active market has developed for the trading of common shares.

Common shareholders benefit either directly or indirectly through the earnings of the firm. If the firm has earnings available to common shareholders, it has two choices related to what to do with these earnings. It can either pay dividends to the common shareholders or retain the earnings to finance future projects and investments. Typically, established firms have *dividend payout* policies whereby a certain percentage of earnings, such as 30 percent, is paid in dividends, on average, over a long period. Typically, dividends are paid on a regular quarterly schedule. In some cases, growing firms with frequent needs for additional investments elect not to pay any dividends. Note that, unlike the treatment of bondholders, firms are not bound by any contractual obligation to common shareholders whereby common dividends must be paid on a regular basis.

As ultimate owners of the firm, common shareholders have rights. One of the major rights is the voting power that highlights the ultimate control the shareholders collectively have. Voting power allows shareholders to appoint a board of directors to act in their best interests. The mandate of the board of directors is to ensure that management is making decisions that are consistent with maximizing the value of the common shares. Thus any actions taken by the firm's management team, including the chief executive officer, must ultimately be justified to the board. It should be noted that different countries have different regulations governing the rights of common shareholders.

6.3   Preferred Shares

The issuance of preferred shares offers another long-term form of financing to firms. Preferred shares are often described as hybrid securities. They have some similarities with bonds but some major differences. While technically categorized as equity financing (since from the debtholders' perspective, preferred equity provides a cushion in the event of bankruptcy), preferred shares are very different from common shares as well.

Like bonds, preferred shares are issued with a par value. Unlike bonds, for most preferred shares (known as perpetual preferreds), there is no intention on the part of the firm to repay the initial investment. Instead, preferred shareholders receive a steady stream of dividends. The dividend is specified as a predetermined rate, a percentage of the par value. For example, if the preferred share is issued at a par value of $40 and the dividend is specified as 6 percent of the par value, preferred shareholders can expect to receive $2.40 per share in dividends each year. As with common shares, preferred shares are typically paid quarterly.

Preferred shareholders differ from common shareholders. A firm must make dividend payments to preferred shareholders before common shareholders receive any dividends. An important feature with typical preferred shares is that if a firm does not make any regularly scheduled preferred dividend payments, the dividends owed cumulate to the preferred shareholder and must be paid before any further dividends can be paid to common shareholders. As well, in the event of bankruptcy and liquidation by the firm, preferred shareholders receive any claims before common shareholders.

From a firm's perspective, preferred shares are not as desirable as bonds since the firm is not able to deduct preferred dividend payments for tax purposes, whereas bond interest expenses are tax deductible. Preferred shares are generally the least common form of financing relative to bonds and common equity.

6.4   Capital Markets Overview

Up to this point, we have examined the major financial instruments or securities: bonds, common shares, and preferred shares. We now step back and examine the overall markets in which these securities are issued and traded.

6.4.1   Private versus Public

Capital markets can be segmented in a number of ways. One segmentation scheme is based on the method by which securities are issued. In many cases, the easiest and quickest method by which firms raise capital is through the *private placement* process. A private placement involves the purchase of a large block of securities by a large institutional investor such as a pension fund or an insurance company. The process is very common with the issuance of debt securities but not of equities. Since these types of investors are deemed to be more sophisticated, there are different regulations involved in the security issuance process. While the private placement process is much quicker and less expensive (in terms of administrative and selling costs), it does place restrictions on the ability of the institutional investors to resell the securities they have purchased (unless they are reselling to other large institutional investors). Consequently, the investors often demand a higher interest rate on bonds.

The alternative method for raising funds is through a *public offering*. In this process, securities are offered to both large institutional investors and smaller "retail" investors. This is the most common process by which equities are issued. This process often takes six months or more and is more expensive than private placement. However, the result is typically a wider range of either bondholders or stockholders. In the case of stockholders, this is often important for who ultimately controls the firm.

6.4.2   Initial Offerings versus Seasoned Issues

Capital markets can also be segmented by the timing of the issue. For example, if a firm is currently private and decides that, on the basis of its need for equity capital, it is going to issue equity available to the public (or it is going public), it undertakes a process known as an *initial public offering*, or IPO. This is a major step in the life a firm since the initial owners of the firm are now effectively sharing the ownership with a much larger group of shareholders. The firm faces more rigorous disclosure of its financial situation to the public and is more accountable to a larger group of stakeholders. However, there is an upside as well. The initial owners now have a much more liquid market in which to sell some or all of their stake in the firm, usually at a per-share price much higher than if the company were still private.

If a firm is already public and decides to issue additional common shares, the process is known as a *seasoned equity offering*, or SEO. Unlike the IPO, a seasoned offering is a much less dramatic step for the firm. However, depending on the size of the SEO relative to the amount of existing shares, the SEO can have an impact on the existing common share price. Note that after the SEO, there will be more common shares outstanding. If the firm is not able to utilize the new funds in such a way as to create additional profits and sufficient value for the common shareholders, then existing shareholders will find that their claim on the firm's profits has been diluted and the share price will decline. Thus the firm must clearly articulate the reason for issuing additional shares and must indicate how the issuance will add value in the long term.

6.4.3 Organized Exchanges versus Over-the-Counter Markets

Traditionally, organized exchanges have played a dominant role in the trading of securities. Organized equity exchanges are much more prevalent than organized bond exchanges since bond trading tends to take place primarily among large institutional investors. The largest organized equity exchange in the world is the New York Stock Exchange (NYSE). The major investment dealers, such as Merrill Lynch, are members of the exchange and arrange to have any client buy or sell orders routed through the NYSE. Firms must first apply to have their stock listed on a particular organized exchange. There are strict listing requirements based on the size and financial performance track record of the firm. Once listed, each stock is handled by a specialist whose job it is to bring buyers and sellers together at a fair price and, by buying and selling from their own accounts, ensure that an orderly market transpires. Automation has had a dramatic impact on the way exchanges are run. While the NYSE still maintains an actual floor where securities are traded, many exchanges worldwide have eliminated a floor and simply match buy and sell orders by way of an automated computer system.

The other major mechanism for trading securities is the *over-the-counter* (OTC) market. Instead of having one specialist in a particular location setting the price for a stock, an OTC market allows for greater participation among a larger number of brokers who are prepared to make a market for a stock. Most bond markets are OTC. The National Association of Security Dealers Automated Quotation (NASDAQ) system is the largest OTC equity market in the world and has grown to challenge the traditional dominance of the NYSE. Historically, a NYSE listing was associated with prestige, and most firms strove to meet the qualifications for such a listing. More recently, some of the best-known firms in the world, particularly in the technology area, have decided to remain listed exclusively on NASDAQ.

6.4.4 Role of Intermediaries

Traditionally, *financial intermediaries* have played an important role related to the issuance and trading of securities. Financial intermediaries include the exchanges discussed above, as well as investment banks or investment dealers. These intermediaries attempt to facilitate the buying and selling process, first between corporations and investors and second among investors. For example, investment bankers have traditionally played a critical role in the IPO process. They provide advice related to the appropriateness and timing of an IPO; then they determine an appropriate price to be offered. They then facilitate the issuing or *underwriting* process whereby the securities are sold to the public, often assuming the risk in the offer by buying the securities from the firm at a preset price and reselling them to the public at a (hopefully) higher price.

The role of intermediaries is rapidly changing as the Internet provides more direct access to capital markets. Some initial public offerings over the Internet are becoming more common. Trading by individuals is rapidly changing the role of intermediaries who must constantly assess how they can add value for their clients.

6.5   Understanding Financial Information

We can now examine bonds and stocks from the perspective of the investor rather than the firm. While the firm is concerned with raising a particular amount of capital at one particular time, an investor is concerned with the day-to-day value of the investment. Information is available from a variety of sources indicating the value of securities.

6.5.1   Bond Tables

Given the predominance of large institutional bond investors (versus smaller retail investors), much less financial information is readily available related to corporate bonds compared to stocks. Nonetheless, an example of corporate bond information is present in Figure 6.2. In this example, the issuer represents the corporation, Coca-Cola, which has issued this particular bond. The

FIGURE 6.2   Coca-Cola Bond Listing

November 5, 2002

ISSUER	COUPON	MATURITY	PRICE	YIELD	PRICE $ CHG
Coca-Cola	5.75	Mar 15/11	107.41	4.67	−0.13

bond matures on March 15, 2011. Based on a par value or face value of $100, annual coupon payments are $5.75, or $2.875 every six months. The current price of this bond is $107.41. We can surmise that when the bond was initially issued (we do not know when the issue date was), interest rates were at a higher level than they are currently. Note that the bond represents a promise of fixed payments. Since interest rates have fallen, this bond with fixed annual coupon payments looks more attractive than a similar (in terms of creditworthiness) bond issued today with lower annual coupon payments. This is why the bond price is more than $100. The bond yield essentially indicates the coupon rate that would be attached to a similar bond if it were issued at par today. Given that the Coca-Cola bond is selling for $107.41, it turns out that buying this bond for that price is just like buying a bond for $100 that pays a coupon rate of 4.67 percent. The final column indicates the change in the price of the bond since the last trading day. The bond has declined in price by $0.13.

6.5.2 Stock Tables

An example of Coca-Cola stock information is presented in Figure 6.3. The first two columns indicate the highest and lowest stock prices in the last 52 weeks. The next column indicates the company name. The fourth column indicates the ticker symbol assigned to Coca-Cola by the New York Stock Exchange. The next column indicates the annual dividend (in dollars). The next three columns relate to the previous day's trading activity. The closing price is indicated, as is the price change (in dollars) since the previous trading day's closing price. The number of shares traded, in hundreds, is indicated in the next column. The current dividend yield is indicated as a percentage in the next-to-last column. It is calculated by taking the current annual dividend of $0.80 divided by the closing stock price of $45.70. The final column indicates the trailing price-earnings ratio: the current price per share divided by the earnings per share over the last year. We can sur-

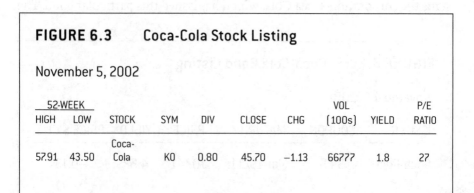

FIGURE 6.3 Coca-Cola Stock Listing

November 5, 2002

52-WEEK		STOCK	SYM	DIV	CLOSE	CHG	VOL (100s)	YIELD	P/E RATIO
HIGH	LOW								
57.91	43.50	Coca-Cola	KO	0.80	45.70	−1.13	66777	1.8	27

mise that the earnings per share for Coca-Cola over the last year have been around $1.69. Thus taking the current price of $45.70 divided by the earnings per share of $1.69 gives us a price-earnings multiple of 27. This is a somewhat unusual situation since historically stocks have traded at average price-earnings ratios of around 15.0.

6.6   Market Efficiency

Market efficiency is an important way of thinking about and comparing the prices for securities in various types of markets such as the bond market or the stock market. A market is said to be efficient if prices fully and immediately reflect all relevant information. In other words, a market is efficient if the price paid for a security is the price that reflects the intrinsic value of that security. The concept of market efficiency is critical to both firms and investors. From a firm's perspective, market efficiency has implications related to the timing of the issuance of securities. From the investor's perspective, efficiency has implications for overall investment strategies.

While the notion of market efficiency is fairly straightforward, it is important to note that market efficiency is not a statement of fact but rather a hypothesis put forward to describe a particular market, such as the U.S. stock market in general. The challenge, faced by countless academic researchers, has been to develop empirical tests such that the results of the tests are either consistent or inconsistent with the notion of market efficiency.

Researchers have developed three categories of hypotheses and tests related to market efficiency: weak form, semistrong form, and strong form. Each form relates to how we define relevant information. The weak form of the efficient market hypothesis (EMH) states that prices fully and immediately reflect all historical price (and trading volume) information. If the weak form of the EMH is deemed to be true (based on empirical tests), then this implies that the current price incorporates any historical prices and volume. Thus knowing the pattern of stock prices (for example, whether the current price is much lower or higher than the price one year ago) does not provide any insight about the future stock price. Thus if the weak form is true, then technical analysis—examining patterns and trends in historical stock prices—is not a fruitful investment strategy.

The semistrong form of the EMH states that prices fully and immediately reflect all public information. If the semistrong form is deemed to be true (again, on the basis of empirical tests), then this implies that trading based on publicly available information in annual reports, in the newspaper, or on the Internet—fundamental analysis of a company—is not a viable strategy as well. (Fundamental analysis often refers to a top-down approach of investigating the economic outlook, the industry prospects, and then the firm-level analysis of growth and risk in order to estimate an intrinsic value of a firm compared to its actual selling price.) If the information is relevant, then it should be immediately incorporated into the stock price, not through a gradual process.

The strong form of the EMH states that prices fully and immediately reflect all information, both public and private. If the strong form is deemed to be true, then this implies that even insiders—senior management, the board of directors, and anyone with private information about a firm—would not be able to benefit from their knowledge.

Empirical tests, which have focused on stock markets, particularly in the United States, have provided mixed results. Many tests attempting to test the weak form by replicating technical analysis strategies have failed to uncover reliable winning strategies able to outperform the market over a long period. However, more recent studies have uncovered some viable strategies related to momentum investing (buying stocks that have done particularly well over the last six months or so and holding them for the next six months). Semi-strong form tests have focused on the immediacy of market reaction to new public information. These event studies have examined good-news announcements, such as an increase in dividends, and have found support for the quickness with which the information has been incorporated into the stock price. Strong form studies have focused on the ability of insiders to capitalize on their ability to buy shares in their company prior to a rise in the stock price and sell prior to a decline. Not surprisingly, these studies have refuted the notion of strong form EMH. In other words, insiders do appear to have the ability to develop superior investment strategies.

The bottom line of these studies appears to suggest that U.S. stock markets are generally efficient (but certainly not in the strong form); however, there may be pockets of inefficiency whereby investors may be able to profit. It should be emphasized that these studies are never free from controversy given the challenges of empirical research and the lack of one agreed-on model related to the determination of stock prices. If stock markets are truly efficient, then managers should be less concerned with the timing of the issuance of securities, and investors should be less concerned with trying to pick one or two winning stocks but rather simply invest in a passive index fund strategy, that is, buy a well-diversified portfolio of stocks and hold them for a long period of time.

6.7 Summary

1. A firm raises long-term financing by issuing securities such as bonds, common shares, or preferred shares.

2. Bonds are usually issued at par value and pay interest or coupons every six months. The principal amount is repaid on the maturity date. The types of features associated with bonds often distinguish them from one another.

3. The credit risk of bonds is assessed by various bond rating agencies. Ratings typically range from AAA (most creditworthy) to C (least creditworthy). Bonds rated BBB and above are said to be investment grade, while bonds rated BB and below are high-yield, or junk, bonds.

4. Common shareholders are the residual claimants of any earnings after other stakeholders, such as bondholders, have been satisfied. Common shareholders are collectively the owners of the firm. Any earnings available to common shareholders are either paid as common dividends or retained in the business in order to generate future profits.

5. Preferred shares represent a hybrid security with some features of both bonds and common stocks. Preferred shares pay regular dividends, but the dividends are not tax deductible from the firm's perspective. Typical preferred shares have no maturity and consequently no principal repayment. Preferred shareholders typically must receive their dividends before any dividends are paid to common shareholders.

6. Capital markets represent the markets in which securities are issued and traded. Markets can be distinguished by the method of issue, either to private investors, such as pension funds and insurance companies, or to the public at large. Some stocks are traded on organized exchanges while others trade over the counter. Intermediaries such as investment dealers play an important role in facilitating the buying and selling process.

7. Markets are said to be efficient if the prices of securities fully and immediately reflect all relevant information.

6.8 Additional Readings

A useful overall investments book is

Sharpe, William, Gordon Alexander, and Jeffrey Bailey. *Investments*. 6th ed. Upper Saddle River, NJ: Prentice-Hall, 1999.

An interesting book focusing on bonds and fixed income securities is

Fabozzi, Frank. *Bond Markets: Analysis and Strategies.* 4th ed. Upper Saddle
River, NJ: Prentice-Hall, 2000.

A classic investment book with an efficient market perspective is

Malkiel, Burton. *A Random Walk Down Wall Street.* 7th ed. New York: Norton, 1999.

6.9 Self-Study Problems

1. All else equal, would you expect to receive a higher or lower interest payment if a bond had a sinking fund? If a bond had a call provision?
2. What factors would impact the price of preferred shares?
3. On the basis of the following bond information, describe the features of the bond and explain the timing of the expected cash flows (assume today is January 1, 2003): coupon = 6.4 percent; maturity date = January 1, 2013; price = $103.42; and yield = 5.94 percent.
4. On the basis of the following stock information, describe the features of the stock and assess its performance: dividends per share = $0.80, current share price = $28.50, current dividend yield = 2.8 percent, current P/E multiple = 24.5, share price one year ago = $24.00, and market total return over the past year = 16.5 percent.
5. Present arguments both for and against why stock markets might be efficient.

7. Assessing the Cost of Capital: What Investors Require

This chapter is the second of three chapters to examine various aspects related to the long-term financing needs of the firm. While the previous chapter provided an overview of various financial instruments such as bonds, preferred shares, and common shares, this chapter focuses on the explicit cost, from the firm's perspective, associated with issuing each type of instrument. The average cost of raising funds is known as the *cost of capital*. The cost of capital is a key driver of the overall value of the firm. If a firm is able to lower its cost of capital, then all potential investments appear more attractive. A simple example of the cost of capital is presented, followed by a more detailed discussion of the cost of each component, with highlights on the risk (from the perspective of the buyer) associated with each instrument. Finally, an actual example of the cost of capital calculation is presented.

7.1   Simple Cost of Capital Example

Suppose an individual wishes to start a new company and has identified the need for a $1 million capital outlay. After much deliberation, it is determined that funds can be raised from three sources, in the following amounts: $200,000 through debt financing (issuing a bond), $100,000 through the issuance of preferred shares, and $700,000 through the issuance of common shares.

Next, we need to determine the cost of each source of financing. Our approach is to think of the terms *cost* and *return* interchangeably. This is because cost to the firm can also be interpreted from a potential investor's perspective. Rather than considering cost, investors consider the potential return on their investments. So to measure the cost to the firm of raising funds, we can instead examine the required return that would entice potential investors to buy a firm's newly issued debt (or bonds), preferred shares, and common equity (or stocks). These relationships are outlined in Figure 7.1.

In this example, it is determined that the bond can be issued to pay interest at a rate of 10 percent, which is the return required by bond investors. However, in the case of bonds, we must make an important distinction between the firm's cost and the investors' required return. Since the debt interest payments are a tax-deductible expense for the firm and since the firm anticipates a tax rate of 50 percent, the effective *after-tax* cost of debt to the firm is 5 percent (or the before-tax cost of 10 percent times 1 minus the tax rate of 0.50). The preferred shares can be issued to pay a dividend of 7 percent, the return required by preferred share investors (since preferred dividends are not tax deductible for the firm). Finally, it is determined that the equity investors expect (or require) a 15 percent return on their investment.

We can now calculate the overall cost of raising capital from these sources by taking a weighted average of the three costs. The calculations are presented in Figure 7.2. The resulting weighted-average cost of capital, also known as the WACC, is 12.2 percent, on an after-tax basis. Note that the weights from all the sources must add up to 1.

We can generalize the previous example with some commonly used notation, whereby the weight of each component is represented by *w* and the cost is represented by *K*. The generalized form of the weighted-average cost of capital is presented in Figure 7.3.

FIGURE 7.1   The Relationship between Firm Costs and Investor Required Returns

FIRM		INVESTORS
Cost of raising funds	=	investor required return
Cost of debt (before tax)	=	required return on bond investment
Cost of preferred	=	required return on preferred shares
Cost of equity	=	required return on equity investment

FIGURE 7.2   Simple Cost of Capital Example

COMPONENT	WEIGHT	COST	WEIGHTED COST
Debt	0.20	$10\% \times (1 - 0.50) = 5\%$	1.0%
Preferred	0.10	7%	0.7%
Common equity	0.70	15%	10.5%
Total weighted cost			12.2%

7.2   Cost of Capital Implications

Now that we have a very basic understanding of how the cost of capital is calculated, before we proceed to a more detailed discussion on the cost of each of the components, it is important to step back and reflect on the importance of the cost of capital to a firm. The cost of capital can be interpreted in a number of ways. It can be thought of as a key value driver: the lower the cost of raising funds, the more valuable the firm will be. This is because the firm is facing a number of potential investments. The lower the cost of undertaking these investments, the more profitable the investments will be. A second interpretation, as described in the previous example, is that the cost of capital is the average cost of financing the various investments or projects facing the firm. A third interpretation, from an investor's perspective, is that the cost of capital represents the rate of return that must be earned on the firm's investments, at a minimum, in order to satisfy all of the investors.

FIGURE 7.3   General Cost of Capital Calculation

COMPONENT	WEIGHT	COST	WEIGHTED COST
Debt	w_d	K_d	$w_d K_d$
Preferred	w_p	K_p	$w_p K_p$
Common equity	w_e	K_e	$w_e K_e$
Total weighted cost		$K_c = (w_d K_d) + (w_p K_p) + (w_e K_e)$	

FIGURE 7.4   Cost of Capital Implications

Earnings before interest and taxes (EBIT)	$1 million × 24.4%	$244,000
Interest	$200,000 × 10%	20,000
Earnings before taxes (EBT)	$244,000 – $20,000	$224,000
Tax (at 50% rate)	$224,000 × 0.50	112,000
Earnings after tax (EAT)	$224,000 – $122,000	$112,000
Preferred dividends	$100,000 × 7%	$7,000
Available to common shareholders	$112,000 – $7,000	$105,000
Common shareholders required return	$700,000 × 15%	$105,000
Residual after required return	$105,000 – $105,000	$0

Suppose we calculate the after-tax cost of capital to be 12.2 percent, as indicated in the example above. On the basis of the $1 million capital outlay, suppose the firm is able to generate a before-tax (and before financing cost) return of 24.4 percent (this number is carefully chosen to be the grossed-up amount of the after-tax cost of capital: 12.2 percent divided by 1 minus the tax rate). The resulting financial situation is presented in Figure 7.4.

This example highlights some important implications related to an understanding of the cost of capital. Note that in this example all of the investors, or stakeholders, are just satisfied with their investments. The bondholders receive their interest payments. The preferred shareholders receive their preferred dividends. And just enough is available to the common shareholders to satisfy their required return of 15 percent. Suppose, however, that the amount available to common shareholders was less than $105,000. While still profitable from an accounting perspective, the firm would not be earning sufficient profits to satisfy all investors, particularly the ultimate owners of the firm, the common shareholders. In other words, the return on equity would be less than the cost of equity. Conversely, if more than $105,000 were available, common shareholders would be more than satisfied since their return on investment would be greater than what they required or expected. This would make their ownership stake more valuable, thus increasing the overall value of their shares. Thus the goal of the firm should be to maximize the value of common shares; this can be achieved in part by minimizing the overall cost of raising funds, or the overall cost of capital.

We have now addressed the important issue related to why the firm should care about the cost of capital. To summarize, we can think of the cost of capital, in general, as the minimum rate of return, on average, on future-oriented investments the firm makes today. The cost of capital will be used to evaluate these future or *incremental* projects or investments. Thus the overall cost of capital impacts on what investments the firm makes.

In these simple examples, we have intentionally glossed over a number of important issues related to the cost of capital. For example, how do we estimate the cost of each of the components? What is the role of risk in the calculation of these costs? Where did the component weights come from? We now address each of these issues.

7.3   Cost of Debt

The calculation of the cost of debt is fairly straightforward. From the potential bond investor's perspective, we begin by asking what the appropriate bond (or more generally, debt instrument) return is. If the firm has existing publicly traded debt, then the current yield represents the before-tax cost of debt. In some cases, the firm may have numerous outstanding bonds with different times to maturity and different yields. If that is the case, a guideline is to attempt to match the bond maturity with the average length of projects that the firm is considering undertaking with any new funds. In almost all situations, firms tend to have long-term projects, so a long-term bond can be used as a match. Once the before-tax cost of debt has been estimated, this estimate is multiplied by 1 minus the estimated (future) tax rate. In most cases, the tax rate can be estimated by examining the amount of taxes currently paid relative to the before-tax earnings. If the firm had unusual losses and did not pay taxes that year, then a simple estimate of future taxes, usually around 35 to 40 percent, will suffice.

If a firm does not have existing publicly traded debt, then an estimate must be made of the appropriate cost of debt. The usual approach is to examine the current yield on risk-free long-term government bonds, then add an appropriate premium. This premium reflects the riskiness of the firm's ability to repay its principal and make its interest payments. The premium is directly related to its bond rating (or its perceived bond rating relative to other similar firms). An AAA firm will have a very small premium, perhaps less than 0.50 percent. A riskier firm rated BB or lower may have a premium of 2 to 3 percent or more.

As was mentioned earlier, a firm often has numerous debt instruments with different maturities, some short term and others long term. Rather than estimating a separate cost associated with each of these, a common approach is to estimate the amount of permanent debt, both short term and long term, and use one long-term yield to estimate the cost of debt. The logic behind this assumption is that while short-term yields may differ from long-term yields (usually lower), over a long period, short-term rates tend to average to be similar to long-term rates.

A final issue concerning the calculation of the cost of debt is the treatment of current liabilities such as accounts payable, which are related to the firm's operating activities. If the typical terms to repay suppliers are 2 percent 10 days, net 30 days, this implies that if the firm pays its suppliers in 10 days, it receives a 2 percent discount. Otherwise, the full amount is due in 30 days. Consider a $1,000 account payable. The firm can repay $980 in 10 days or $1,000 in 30 days. By forgoing the discount, effectively the firm is borrowing the $980 not paid on day 10 and paying interest of an additional $20 for a loan of 20 days (from day 10 to day 30). We estimate the annual cost (or opportunity cost) of this "loan" in Figure 7.5.

Note that, on an annualized basis, this opportunity cost is quite substantial. Should we be incorporating this cost explicitly in our estimate of the cost of debt? The answer is generally no.

Recall our earlier discussion related to the firm's operating activities. There is a flip side to our discussion of accounts payable. On the current asset side, we have accounts receivable. In effect, we can think of current assets and current liabilities as netting out, to form net working capital.

FIGURE 7.5   Opportunity Cost of Missing Account Payable Discount

Account payable terms	2 percent 10 days, net 30 days
Amount of accounts payable	$1,000
Equivalent to borrowing	$980 for 20 days
Annualized cost	$\dfrac{\$20}{\$980} \times \dfrac{365\ \text{days}}{20\ \text{days}} = 0.37$, or 37%

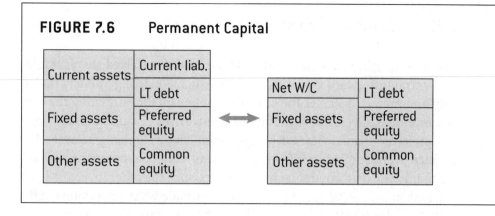

FIGURE 7.6   Permanent Capital

Thus we can think of a revised balance sheet as in Figure 7.6, whereby our costs, associated with the right-hand side of the balance sheet, are related to *permanent capital:* long-term debt, preferred shares, and common equity.

7.4   Cost of Preferred Shares

The calculation of the cost of preferred shares is also relatively straightforward. Many of the principles established in the cost of debt discussion apply to the cost of preferred shares as well. The key question to address is: What yield would the firm need to offer if it were to issue new preferred shares today? If the firm has existing preferred shares, then the estimate of the cost of preferred shares is simply the current yield on existing preferred shares. For example, suppose the firm is paying annual preferred dividends of $2 per share and the preferred shares are currently selling for $29 per share. The current yield is $2 divided by $29, or 6.9 percent. Suppose the firm decided to issue new (perpetual) preferred shares today with a par value of $100 per share. Consequently, the annual dividend on the new preferred shares would be $6.90, for an identical yield of 6.9 percent. Note that, unlike the cost of debt, there is no after-tax adjustment needed since preferred dividends are already paid in after-tax dollars.

If the firm does not currently have any outstanding preferred shares, then the appropriate cost can be estimated by examining the current yield of similar firms. Note that the two main drivers of the current yield on preferred shares are the current level of interest rates (since preferred shares are like bonds but typically with no maturity date) and the perceived riskiness of the firm. Thus an estimate of the cost of preferred shares would be established by examining the preferred stock yield of firms with similar debt ratings.

7.5 Cost of Equity

While estimating the cost of debt and the cost of preferred shares is relatively straightforward, particularly if the firm has existing publicly traded debt and preferred shares, the same cannot be said for estimating the cost of common equity. The estimation problem arises because, unlike bonds and preferred shares, common shares do not have a similar "guarantee," or implicit promise of returns. Instead, common shareholders are the residual claimants and own any remaining earnings once the other investors have been taken care of. We need to somehow estimate what a common equity investor expects or requires when he or she is making the investment. In other words, we need a model of what drives stock prices and hence what drives expected returns.

Researchers have uncovered a number of approaches that provide us with estimates of common equity investor expected returns, and hence estimates of the cost of equity. We examine two well-known approaches here: the dividend model approach and the capital asset pricing model.

7.5.1 Dividend Model Approach

The dividend model approach (also known as the constant growth dividend discount model) is based on the premise that equity investors generally intend to hold a stock for a long period (perhaps even bequeathing it to their children). In this model, what matters to investors is the cash flow or dividends that they expect to receive over the life of owning the stock. Consequently, expected returns are determined by the expected dividend yield as well as the expected growth in dividends over time. The expected growth in dividends can be thought of as the capital gain that investors expect (if they were to sell their stock). As an example, suppose the firm is expected to pay cash dividends of $1.50 per share over the next year. The current stock price is $37.50, so the expected dividend yield is 4 percent. In addition, it is estimated that the dividends will grow, on average, by about 8 percent per year for the foreseeable future. This estimated growth rate of dividends may be determined from the historical growth in dividends or from a current assessment of the firm by analysts. Adding these two components, the estimated required return to equity investors, and hence cost of equity, is 12 percent.

Of course, there are limitations to this model. If a firm does not currently pay dividends, it is difficult to estimate expected future dividends. Even if a firm does pay dividends, if future dividends are not expected to grow at a constant rate, then estimating the cost of equity becomes much more compli-cated. While the dividend yield component is generally easy to estimate, the anticipated growth in dividends is not. Fortunately, we have an alternative (and much more widely used) approach, described in the next section.

7.5.2   Capital Asset Pricing Model

The capital asset pricing model, or CAPM as it is affectionately known (pro-nounced "CAP M"), is an intuitively appealing model developed by Nobel Prize–winning financial economist Bill Sharpe. His work was based on exten-sions of his mentor's work, another Nobel Prize–winning financial econo-mist, Harry Markowitz. Markowitz showed that there were benefits to investing in a well-diversified basket of stocks in terms of enhancing potential rewards relative to risk exposure. Essentially, his key insight was the same as what your mother probably told you: "Don't put all of your eggs in one basket" (unfortunately, no matter how deserving, your mother did not receive a Nobel Prize). Bill Sharpe followed up on this idea and looked specifically at the expected stock returns to an investor who was well diversified among risky securities and had an opportunity to invest in risk-free securities as well.

The intuition behind CAPM (while it is called a "pricing" model, it actu-ally refers to expected returns) is as follows. There are three components to the model. If an investor is considering a risky investment in equities, there is always a risk-free alternative: government bonds. This is a minimum start-ing point for an investor's expected return on an equity investment. The common notation for the return on a risk-free investment is R_f.

Given that stocks, in general, are viewed as riskier than government bonds, investors expect a premium over government bonds. This premium is known as the *market risk premium,* or MRP.

Individual stocks can be viewed as being either more or less risky than the overall market. In order to capture the relative riskiness of a stock rela-tive to the overall market, a stock's *beta,* or β, is estimated. By definition, the market has a beta of 1. Riskier stocks have betas greater than 1, while less risky stocks have betas less than 1. The beta factor then acts as a multiplier for the market risk premium, providing an upward or downward adjust-ment. The overall model is presented in Figure 7.7.

As an example, suppose the risk-free rate is currently 7 percent, the stock's beta is estimated to be 1.2, and the market risk premium is estimated to be 6 percent. The resulting expected return is

$$E(R_s) = K_e = 7\% + 1.2 \times 6\% = 7\% + 7.2\% = 14.2\%$$

FIGURE 7.7   Capital Asset Pricing Model

$$E(R_s) = R_f + \beta_s \times \text{MRP}$$

where $E(R_s)$ = expected return on stock $s = K_e$ = estimated cost of equity
R_f = risk-free rate of return
β_s = beta for stock s
MRP = market risk premium

In terms of operationalizing the model, there are a number of important estimation issues related to each of the three CAPM components. Each is dealt with in turn.

7.5.3   Risk-Free Rate

Clearly, the risk-free rate of return is represented by a government bond yield since we assume that governments generally do not default on their loan obligations. The central question becomes which government security should we choose? Likely candidates include short-term Treasury bills or 1-year, 5-year, 10-year, or 30-year government bonds. Unfortunately, the CAPM is based on theoretical assumptions and thus does not provide a correct answer. Consequently, we must rely on intuition, logic, and best practices among corporations and financial analysts. The general principle is that we should be consistent with our cost of debt. If we are focusing on long-term debt, then we should use a long-term government yield as well. A generally accepted benchmark is the 10-year government bond yield, but sometimes other long-term yields (such as the 30-year yield) are used as well.

7.5.4   Market Risk Premium

The market risk premium represents the expected difference between the return on the stock market investment and the risk-free return. The market return combines capital gains (price appreciation) with any dividends received. In practice, the market is represented by a broad country index such as the S&P 500 Index. Consequently, if we utilize the 10-year government bond as the risk-free rate, then the market risk premium is the expected difference between the return on the stock market index and the long-term government bond return.

We need to address a potentially difficult issue related to the estimation of the market risk premium. We are trying to estimate the *expected* premium. Yet short of surveying all investors and asking them what their long-term stock and bond return expectations are (estimates that might change every day), we have no way of truly capturing expected returns. One way out of this dilemma is to look to the past for our best guess as to what the future may look like. Researchers have done this by examining stock and bond returns as far back as the 1920s. While there are a number of statistical issues that create additional controversy, estimates show that stocks have tended to outperform long-term government bonds by about 5 to 6 percent per year. Thus assuming investors' past expectations have been fulfilled, on average, the average historical market risk premium is a useful estimate of the expected future market risk premium.

7.5.5   Beta

Beta is a relative risk measure. It is estimated by examining the returns in a particular stock over time relative to the return on a market index such as the S&P 500. If a stock is estimated to have a beta of, say, 1.2, this implies that a 1 percent increase in the market, in the absence of any firm-specific news, should coincide with a 1.2 percent increase in the stock, while a 1 percent decline in the market should coincide with a 1.2 percent decline in the stock. Thus, in this example, the stock is riskier than the market. If the beta was estimated at, say, 0.75, then the stock would not be expected to fluctuate as much as the market.

While it is straightforward in a statistical sense to estimate betas (through a technique known as regression analysis), similar issues arise as were encountered in estimating the market risk premium. While we can estimate a historical beta, what we really are interested in is an expected beta. In practice, we can rely on estimates of forward-looking betas provided by well-known financial information firms such as Value Line and Bloomberg.

7.6   Component Weights

At this stage, we have estimated the cost of each component of permanent capital: debt, preferred shares, and common equity. The final step in estimating the overall cost of capital is to assign an appropriate weight to each form of capital and calculate a weighted average. Once again, practice is not nearly as simple as theory. We face our usual issue of knowing what happened in the past but requiring an estimate of what we think is going to happen in the future, namely, how the firm will raise funds in the future.

The simplest approach to estimating component weights is not necessarily the most correct but is certainly the easiest. We can examine the relative weights of the book values based on the most recent financial statements (focusing on the right-hand side of the balance sheet). For example, we could take the book value of any long-term debt (as well as any short-term interest-paying debt that we judge will be rolled over on a "permanent" basis), any preferred shares (assuming the firm has any intention of issuing preferred shares in the future), and any common equity (any common shares plus retained earnings). In practice, we would ignore most other balance sheet items, particularly if they are not material in size (although an argument can be made to include deferred taxes as part of common equity if the firm is assumed to continue to grow).

An alternative approach is similar to the first approach with the exception of estimating market values (instead of book values) for each component. This approach is consistent with our forward-looking assessment since market values represent current investor expectations. This approach is appropriate in the case of a publicly traded firm. With this approach, we need to go beyond information in the annual report to examine the latest market prices for bonds, preferred shares, and common equity. Market values are simply calculated as the price per share of each security times the number of shares outstanding. If such information is not available for a particular component (for example, there is no publicly traded debt), then we often assume that the book values and market values are similar. Usually the biggest difference is related to the common equity component.

In some cases, we can rely on a more direct approach. Ideally, we would like to be able to ask the company's CEO or CFO about how he or she plans to raise capital in the future. Sometimes such information is disclosed publicly through management discussion in the annual report. A firm might indicate a target capital structure that essentially indicates the target component weights. If we have this direct information, then we can use it to estimate component weights. Note also that many firms in a particular industry strive to have very similar capital structures. Thus any information about a representative firm in an industry may be usefully applied to another similar firm.

7.7   Hurdle Rates

Now that we have estimated the overall cost of capital, we need to examine how it is applied internally to the key decisions that a firm's management needs to make. Recall that we have described the overall cost of capital as the minimum rate of return, *on average*, on future-oriented investments the firm makes today. However, not all investments or projects that a firm is presently considering are of equal risk. It is critical that risk is explicitly accounted for in the decision-making process. If not, a firm might be tempted to focus exclusively on potentially high return projects, but if the same projects are the riskiest ones, the firm may end up taking on too much risk. Fortunately, there is a way to incorporate risk through the use of *hurdle rates*.

Typically within a firm, various divisions, or various categories of potential projects, are clearly identified and ranked according to perceived risk. For example, an expansion of an existing facility may be viewed as much less risky than an investment in a new type of business unit. As such, it would be appropriate to require a higher threshold rate of return hurdle for investment in a riskier project. This is the purpose of hurdle rates, as illustrated in Figure 7.8. First, given the perceived riskiness of a division or type of project, a hurdle rate is assigned. Second, if the expected return on a potential project is assessed as being greater than the hurdle rate, then that project is deemed acceptable. Conversely, if the expected return is assessed as being less than the hurdle rate, then the project is rejected.

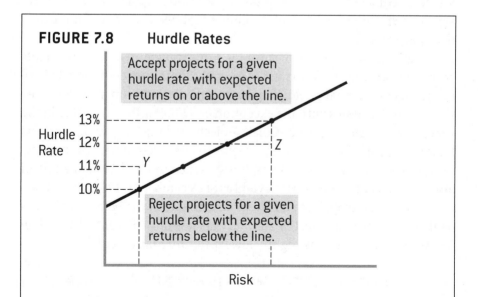

FIGURE 7.8   Hurdle Rates

Accept projects for a given hurdle rate with expected returns on or above the line.

Hurdle Rate: 13%, 12%, 11%, 10%

Z

Y

Reject projects for a given hurdle rate with expected returns below the line.

Risk

In the examples in Figure 7.8, suppose a firm has an overall cost of capital or WACC, of 11.5 percent. Suppose also that a particular project, project Y, is assigned a hurdle rate of 10 percent. Based on an assessment of expected future cash flows from the project, the expected return on the project is actually 11 percent. We would accept, or undertake, project Y. Conversely, suppose a particular project, project Z, is assigned a hurdle rate of 13 percent. Based on an assessment of expected future cash flows from the project, the expected return on the project is actually only 12 percent. We would reject, or not undertake, project Z. Thus we are not basing our decision on the absolute expected return compared to the firm's overall WACC but rather on the expected return, based on the perceived riskiness of the project, relative to the appropriate hurdle rate.

How do hurdle rates relate to the overall cost of capital? In this example, notice that some hurdle rates are below the WACC while others are above the WACC. This is not surprising, since the overall WACC should be related to the types of projects the firm is considering undertaking. For example, suppose the firm had two hurdle rates: 8 percent for type A projects and 12 percent for type B projects. If the firm anticipated accepting a similar number of type A and type B projects, we might expect the WACC to be around 10 percent.

7.8   Coca-Cola Application

We now estimate the cost of capital to Coca-Cola, based on publicly available financial information as of December 31, 1999. The source for much of this analysis is Bloomberg.

Coca-Cola had a variety of short-term and long-term debt instruments with both variable and fixed rates of interest. Short-term debt consisted primarily of commercial paper. Long-term debt ranged primarily from one-year to ten-year notes with the exception of a $116 million note due in the year 2093. Since most of Coca-Cola's projects are long term, we focus on its long-term debt. The ten-year note seems to be representative of the long-term types of Coca-Cola projects. It was issued in April 1999 at a rate of around 6 percent, but its current yield as of December 31, 1999, was 7.4 percent. We therefore use 7.4 percent as an estimate of the before-tax cost of debt. If we incorporate the U.S. statutory tax rate of 35 percent (although in 1999 Coca-Cola's rate was slightly lower), the after-tax cost of debt is

$$K_d = K_d \text{ before tax} \times (1 - \text{tax rate}) = 7.4\% \times (1 - 0.35) = 4.8\%$$

Since Coca-Cola does not have any outstanding preferred shares, we will assume they also have no plans to issue preferred shares in the future, so we will exclude any estimate of the cost of preferred shares.

In order to estimate Coca-Cola's cost of equity, we will rely on the CAPM. As part of this estimation, we need, as of December 31, 1999, the long-term (ten-year) U.S. government bond yield (6.4 percent), an estimate of Coca-Cola's beta (1.03), and an estimate of the market risk premium. On the basis of our earlier discussion, we will assume the latter term is equal to 6 percent. We can combine these terms as follows:

$$K_e = R_f + \beta \times \text{MRP} = 6.4\% + 1.03 \times 6.0\% = 12.6\%$$

We will base the debt and equity component weights on market value weights. We assume that the market value of Coca-Cola's debt is very close to its book value of debt (a reasonable assumption for a firm that is not experiencing any financial distress). Long-term debt refers to Coca-Cola's permanent debt or long-term debt plus any short-term debt that is judged to be of a permanent nature. For Coca-Cola, the long-term debt is $854 million. The current portion of the long-term debt is $261 million. Other current loans and notes payable are $5,112 million. The total permanent debt is estimated as $6,227 million.

As of December 31, 1999, there were approximately 2,471 million common shares of Coca-Cola stock outstanding. At the time, the common share price was $58.25. Thus the market value of equity was 2,471 million $\times$ $58.25 = $143,936 million. The total market value of the capital was $6,227 million + $143,936 million = $150,163 million. Based on these market value weights, the capital structure is 4.2 percent debt and 95.8 percent common equity.

Thus the overall cost of capital for Coca-Cola is estimated as

TYPE OF CAPITAL	COST (AFTER TAX)	WEIGHT	WEIGHTED COST
Debt	$7.4\% \times (1 - 0.35) = 4.8\%$	4.2%	0.2%
Equity	$6.4\% + 1.03 \times 6.0\% = 12.6\%$	95.8%	12.1%
Cost of capital (K_c)			12.3%

7.9   Summary

1. Cost of capital, a key value driver, is the average cost of raising funds. It is also the rate of return that must be earned on the firm's investments, at a minimum, to satisfy all of its investors.

2. The cost of raising funds, from the firm's perspective, is equivalent to investor-required returns.
3. The cost of capital is used to evaluate incremental projects or investments.
4. The cost of debt is measured on an after-tax basis and reflects the rate that the firm would need to offer if it issued new debt today.
5. The cost of preferred shares reflects the rate that the firm would need to offer if it issued new preferred shares today.
6. The cost of equity is usually estimated by either the dividend model or the capital asset pricing model (CAPM).
7. The CAPM incorporates the risk-free rate with the market risk premium and beta, a relative risk measure.
8. Component weights are estimated on the basis of book values, market values, or information related to the target capital structure.
9. Hurdle rates depend on the perceived riskiness of divisions or projects and are used to evaluate different types of potential investments.

7.10   Additional Readings

An article that summarizes the controversies surrounding the calculation of the cost of capital and the generally accepted best practices is

Bruner, Robert, Kenneth Eades, Robert Harris, and Robert Higgins. Best Practices in Estimating the Cost of Capital: Survey and Synthesis. *Financial Practices and Education* (Spring/Summer 1998): 13–27.

7.11   Self-Study Problems

1. Acme Company has a debt rating of A and a tax rate of 40 percent. The current long-term government bond yield is 6.2 percent. The typical spread between long-term government yields and A-rated firms is about 1 percent. Estimate Acme's cost of debt.
2. Acme's preferred shares were issued last year at $30 per share but are now trading at $28.50. Acme pays annual preferred dividends of $2.25 per share. Estimate Acme's cost of preferred shares.
3. The current long-term government bond yield is 6.2 percent. The estimated market risk premium is 6 percent. Acme's beta is estimated to be 1.15. Using CAPM, estimate Acme's cost of common equity.

4. Acme's current balance sheet shows book value weights of 32 percent debt, 11 percent preferred shares, and 57 percent common equity. Acme is not planning to issue preferred shares in the future but anticipates a target capital structure of 40 percent debt and 60 percent common equity. Estimate Acme's WACC.

5. Explain whether Acme would consider investing in *any* project with an expected return of less than the estimated WACC.

8. Designing an Optimal Capital Structure: The Debt-Equity Decision

This chapter is the third of three chapters to examine various aspects related to the long-term financing needs of the firm. The long-term capital structure decision boils down to the firm's decision related to the desired mix of long-term debt and common equity (as well as preferred shares in some cases). The chapter begins with a classic argument, based on some restrictive assumptions, that shows why the capital structure decision might not matter. However, once these restrictive assumptions are removed, then capital structure decisions do matter. The design of an optimal capital structure depends critically on evaluating a number of important trade-offs, including the cost to the firm, the risk, the flexibility of future financing, the impact on control by existing shareholders, and the overall timing. Each of these elements is examined in the chapter, along with an application of a firm's decision to change its capital structure.

8.1 Modigliani-Miller Argument: Why Capital Structure Does Not Matter

In the 1950s, two financial economists, Franco Modigliani and Merton Miller, made a significant contribution to the field of corporate finance and were rewarded decades later with a Nobel Prize in economics. Their simple yet profound contribution was to show that, under certain assumptions (known as the MM assumptions and MM theory), the capital structure, or mix of debt and equity, does not impact on the overall value of a firm. Their argument was as follows.

Suppose we live in a world where there are no taxes and no chance that a firm will go bankrupt or face *financial distress* (sounds like a wonderful world to live in). Suppose, as well, that individuals can borrow (or lend) at the same rate at which a firm can borrow. Given these key assumptions, the value of a firm remains the same regardless of how the assets are financed. In other words, no matter how many slices you cut the pie in, the overall size of the pie remains the same.

The following example is in the spirit of the original MM argument. Consider an all-equity firm with one million shares outstanding and a current stock price per share of $10. The market value of the equity (and hence the value of the all-equity firm) is $10 million (one million times $10). The firm pays all of its operating income to shareholders as a dividend. Its operating income next year, and in all subsequent years as well, is anticipated to be $1.5 million. It is important to note that this is not a guaranteed amount but simply a best guess of what the operating income will be. Since the operating income is not anticipated to grow and since all operating income is paid in dividends, the return to shareholders will be the dividend yield they receive: $1.5 million relative to the $10 million market value of equity, or 15 percent.

Now suppose the firm decided to have a different capital structure, such as an equal amount of debt and equity. One way to accomplish this would be to issue $5 million of debt and use the proceeds to repurchase $5 million of equity. Suppose the debt could be issued at a rate of 10 percent. In such a case, if the anticipated operating income level were achieved, the shareholders would indeed benefit with a higher return on their equity investment, as shown in Figure 8.1.

While it appears that the firm's actions are benefiting the shareholders, we have overlooked an important assumption. Recall that, in this example, individuals can borrow at the same rate as the firm. Thus even without a share repurchase by the firm, an individual shareholder (who owns, say, one share) can borrow $10 to purchase an additional share, as shown in Figure 8.2. Note also that by borrowing, the individual (as well as the firm) has taken on more risk.

Thus as long as the individual can borrow at the same rate as the firm, there is no benefit to the individual of having the firm borrow instead. Therefore, a firm's decision on leverage can be offset by investors through their personal borrowing. Thus the value of the firm remains the same. This is what we mean when we say capital structure doesn't matter, according to the MM assumptions.

FIGURE 8.1 Modigliani-Miller Example 1

	ALL EQUITY	EQUITY AND DEBT
Number of shares	1,000,000	500,000
Price per share	$10	$10
Market value of shares	$10,000,000	$5,000,000
Market value of debt	—	$5,000,000
Anticipated operating income	$1,500,000	$1,500,000
Interest	—	$500,000
Earnings (after interest)	$1,500,000	$1,000,000
Earnings per share	$1.50	$2.00
Return on shares	15%	20%

8.2   Relaxing the Assumptions: Why Capital Structure Does Matter

As you know, the real world is much different than the MM world. In particular, there are two main driving factors that suggest capital structure does matter: taxes and bankruptcy possibilities. Taken separately, corporate tax considerations would result in the firm's taking on huge amounts of debt, while bankruptcy considerations would result in the firm's taking on very little debt. The combination of these two factors result in the idea of an optimal capital structure with just the right amount of debt. We provide an overview of the impact of these two factors here, with more discussion of these and other factors.

FIGURE 8.2 Modigliani-Miller Example 2

Equity investment (one share)	$10
Earnings per share (all equity firm)	$1.50
Total earnings for two shares	$3.00
Less interest on $10 borrowed	$1.00
Net earnings on investment	$2.00
Return on equity investment	20%

8.2.1 Impact of Corporate Taxes

The major real-world benefit of debt is that, unlike dividends, interest payments are a tax-deductible expense. Consider the example in Figure 8.3. Suppose the firm faces a corporate tax rate of 35 percent.

Notice that the combined debt and equity income is always greater in the equity and debt case than in the all-equity case. The difference, in this example $175,000, is equal to the amount of interest times the tax rate ($500,000 times 0.35). This amount is also known as the *interest tax shield*. Notice that the debtholders are assumed to earn the going rate (such as 10 percent) on their debt investment. Consequently, the interest tax shield benefit must accrue directly to the equity shareholders. If we assume that the firm continues to maintain, say, $5 million in debt each year, then the interest tax shield will continue at a rate of $175,000 each year. Thus the value of the firm is now equal to the value of an all-equity firm plus the value of a *stream* of interest tax shields.

Note that in a world of both personal and corporate taxes, individual investors may not be able to get the full advantage of debt by borrowing personally. Corporate versus personal borrowing rates may be different, as well as tax rates.

Recall the key assumption so far: there is no possibility of bankruptcy or financial distress. Without that possibility, our example suggests that a firm should continue to borrow to increase its interest tax shield. Thus an optimal capital structure with corporate taxes appears to be one that includes virtually no equity and huge amounts of debt!

FIGURE 8.3   Impact of Corporate Taxes on Firm Value

	ALL EQUITY	EQUITY AND DEBT
Anticipated operating income	$1,500,000	$1,500,000
Interest	—	$500,000
Earnings before tax	$1,500,000	$1,000,000
Tax at 35%	$525,000	$350,000
Earnings after tax	$975,000	$650,000
Combined debt and equity income (interest plus earnings after tax)	$975,000	$1,150,000

8.2.2   Impact of Bankruptcy

We now relax the key assumption of no bankruptcy or financial distress possibilities. Financial distress occurs when the firm is not in a position to meet its debt obligations, or interest and principal payments. In some cases, a firm needs to rely on the legal mechanism of bankruptcy to reorganize its obligations and repayment terms with its creditors to avoid liquidation.

Bankruptcy and financial distress costs can take two forms: indirect and direct. Direct forms include legal and administrative costs associated with the actual bankruptcy proceedings. Indirect forms occur when a firm faces loss in business due to its circumstances. For example, if it is known that an airline is facing difficulties meeting its credit obligations, potential passengers may avoid booking flights on the airline; this decreases revenue and makes the financial situation worse. Other indirect costs include the time management spends dealing with the financial distress rather than on strategy or looking for ways the firm can add value. As well, there is an increased possibility that management may be forced into a position to gamble what remains of the firm by taking on extremely risky projects in the hopes of having a small chance of avoiding bankruptcy.

8.2.3   Combining Corporate Taxes and Bankruptcy Costs

We can now combine the benefits and costs of debt to present a simple model representing the impact of capital structure on firm value. We can think of the value of the firm as follows:

> Overall market value of the firm = market value of all-equity firm
> + value of interest tax shield – cost of financial distress

We can also represent the value of the firm as in Figure 8.4. As an all-equity firm begins to take on more debt, firm value increases because of the benefits of interest tax deductibility. As the firm takes on a large amount of debt, there is an increased chance that the firm may undergo financial distress and have associated bankruptcy-related costs. At some point, the optimal amount of debt, these bankruptcy costs begin to outweigh the tax-deductibility benefits.

While the benefits of interest tax deductibility and the costs of financial distress are the two main drivers of capital structure, there are also a number of additional considerations for the firm deciding on an optimal capital structure. We examine a number of these considerations below. We begin by exam-

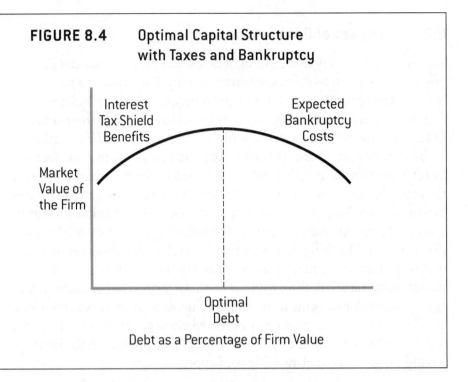

FIGURE 8.4   Optimal Capital Structure with Taxes and Bankruptcy

ining the cost of raising funds as well as the impact on returns to shareholders in firms with different capital structures. We then examine additional considerations of risk, financial flexibility, control, and optimal timing.

8.3   Minimizing Cost

If a firm were simply concerned with minimizing the costs of incremental financing, then the choice would be straightforward. As we examined in chapter 7, the cost to the firm, on an after-tax basis, is much lower for raising debt than for raising common equity. It might appear that a firm would always decide to choose "cheap" debt. However, such an approach would be too narrow given the complexities of the decision.

We can also examine the capital structure decision directly from the perspective of the common shareholder. Again, we need to be careful not to focus too narrowly on returns to investors, but they are certainly an important factor and a good place to start. In order to do so, we first need to introduce a preview of a valuation model we will examine in chapter 10.

8.3.1   A Simple Valuation Model

A simple valuation model (known as the price-earnings valuation model) states that the price per share that an equity investor is willing to pay is based on two components. The first component is the projected earnings per share. The second component is based on a consensus in the marketplace as to how many times the projected earnings a stock is worth. For example, if the projected earnings are $1 per share, the market may deem a fair price to be $15, or 15 times the projected earnings. Such a multiple of earnings depends on two critical factors. The first factor is the perception that future years' anticipated earnings will grow at either a fast or a slow rate. The higher the anticipated growth rate, the greater the price an investor should be willing to pay, all else equal. The second factor is the confidence that the investor has related to how certain the anticipated earnings are. The more confident the investor, the greater the price he or she should be willing to pay, all else equal.

8.3.2   EBIT Break-even: What Leverage Really Means

Now that we understand the basics of this simple valuation model, let's examine an example of a firm with two possible capital structures. Suppose an all-equity firm needs to increase its capital to fund a new major project. We will compare the impact on earnings per share (EPS) in two different scenarios. In the first case, the all-equity firm issues an additional $30,000 in equity (3,000 shares at $10 per share). In the second case, the firm issues $30,000 in debt at an interest rate of 10 percent. We start with the assumption that the type of financing does not impact on the operations of the business. Consequently, the anticipated operating profit, or earnings before interest and taxes (EBIT), will be the same, $10,000, in the all-equity scenario and in the debt-and-equity scenario. Figure 8.5 presents each scenario, including the resulting earnings per share and return on equity.

It appears that if the firm were making the new debt or equity decision on the basis of the information above, the decision would be quite straightforward. Issuing debt results in a higher level of anticipated EPS as well as anticipated ROE. However, we need to address the extent to which the apparently obvious result is specific to this example or whether it can be generalized to all possible scenarios.

In order to explore this issue further, we will examine what happens if the *actual* EBIT is different from the *anticipated* EBIT. To accomplish this, we can start by calculating a break-even EBIT, for which the EBIT level is such that

FIGURE 8.5   Debt versus All-Equity Firm 1

	DEBT FIRM	ALL-EQUITY FIRM
Earnings before interest and taxes (EBIT)	$10,000	$10,000
Interest	3,000	0
Earnings before tax	$7,000	$10,000
Tax at 35%	2,450	3,500
Earnings after tax	$4,550	$6,500
Common shares		
Previous	3,000	3,000
New	0	3,000
Total common shares	3,000	6,000
Earnings per share (EPS)	$1.52	$1.08
Common equity		
Previous	$30,000	$30,000
New	0	30,000
Total common equity	$30,000	$60,000
Return on equity (ROE)	15.2%	10.8%

the EPS for the debt scenario is the same as the EPS for the all-equity scenario. Note that the EPS can be rewritten as

EPS = (EBIT – interest)(1 – tax rate)/number of common shares outstanding

Based on this formulation, calculations for the break-even EBIT are presented in Figure 8.6. The calculations use the simple principles of algebra. (If you aren't mathematically inclined, don't despair. We will be drawing a picture soon to go with the calculations.)

These calculations suggest that if the actual EBIT is $6,000 rather than the anticipated $10,000, then the EPS should be the same under both financing scenarios. This break-even EPS calculation is confirmed in Figure 8.7. If EBIT is $6,000, then EPS is $0.65 in both scenarios. Note also in Figure 8.7 that if EBIT is $3,000, then EPS for the debt firm is zero. Finally, note that if EBIT is zero, then EPS for the all-equity firm is zero as well.

FIGURE 8.6   Break-even EBIT Calculation

	DEBT FIRM	ALL-EQUITY FIRM

$$(EBIT - \$3,000)(0.65)/\$3,000 = (EBIT - 0)(0.65)/\$6,000$$
$$(EBIT - \$3,000)/\$3,000 = EBIT/\$6,000$$
$$(EBIT - \$3,000)(\$6,000)/\$3,000 = EBIT$$
$$(EBIT - \$3,000)2 = EBIT$$
$$2EBIT - \$6,000 = EBIT$$
$$2EBIT - EBIT = \$6,000$$
$$EBIT = \$6,000$$

FIGURE 8.7   Debt versus All-Equity Firm 2

	DEBT FIRM	ALL-EQUITY FIRM
Earnings before interest and taxes (EBIT)	$6,000	$6,000
Interest	3,000	0
Earnings before tax	$3,000	$6,000
Tax @ 35%	1,050	2,100
Earnings after tax	$1,950	$3,900
Common shares		
Previous	3,000	3,000
New	0	3,000
Total common shares	3,000	6,000
Earnings per share (EPS)	$0.65	$0.65
Common equity		
Previous	$30,000	$30,000
New	0	30,000
Total common equity	$30,000	$60,000
Return on equity (ROE)	6.5%	6.5%

FIGURE 8.8   Break-even EBIT: What Leverage Really Means

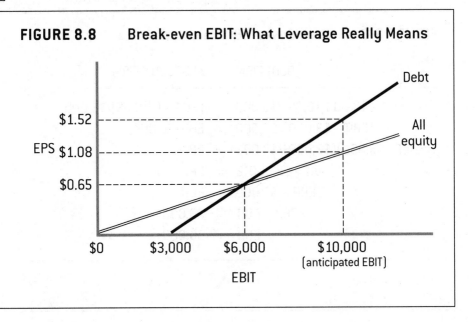

We can combine these observations in order to present a graph with a powerful message. The graph in Figure 8.8 helps us to understand what we really mean by the term *leverage*. Note that if we knew that EBIT was going to be above $6,000, we would issue debt (assuming anticipated EBIT for next year is representative of future year EBITs). Conversely, if we knew EBIT was going to be less than $6,000, we would issue equity.

Now let's return to our simple valuation model. It appears, at first blush, that issuing debt is more attractive because, as was shown in Figure 8.5, we anticipate a higher EPS with that scenario. However, we are ignoring the other crucial part of the valuation model we described earlier. Recall we noted that the earnings multiple depends on risk: the more risk (for example, through financial leverage), the lower the multiple. Consequently, it is not automatically the case that a firm with a higher anticipated EPS will have a higher stock price. It depends, in part, on our assessment of risk. In other words, how confident are we of the anticipated EBIT and what is the impact on EPS if we are wrong?

Look again at Figure 8.8 and think of it as a picture of a seesaw, or teeter-totter, commonly found in a children's playground. Think of the fulcrum (or balancing point) as at the break-even EBIT level of $6,000. We can now visualize what leverage really means. As a firm takes on more debt, it is able to leverage, or increase, the anticipated EPS. However, there is a downside to increased leverage. The higher up on the seesaw, or the more leverage, the greater the risk, or the greater chance that you will get hurt if you fall off the seesaw. Thus our discussion leads naturally to risk, the second major consideration in the capital structure decision.

8.4   Minimizing Risk

From the perspective of the firm, risk is related to the ability to meet debt and interest payment obligations. On the basis of the previous example, we can think of risk as the possibility of deviating from the expected EBIT and hence not being able to meet obligations. Clearly, solely on the basis of the criterion of risk, an all-equity firm does not have to worry about any financial obligations related to creditors (although managers should be concerned with satisfying equityholders). Thus even though the cost of equity is greater, it must be balanced with the lower risk from the firm's perspective. We briefly reexamine two types of risks examined earlier: *business risk* and *financial risk*.

8.4.1   Business Risk

Business risk, or operating risk, refers to the projected variability of the earnings of the firm regardless of how the firm is financed (through equity or debt). Firms in some industries clearly have higher business risk than firms in other industries. For example, firms in regulated industries such as utilities tend to have lower business risk. As well, depending on a firm's competitive position, one firm in a particular industry may have a higher or lower amount of business risk relative to its competitors.

The assessment of business risk relates back to our business size-up analysis in chapter 2. Recall we examined the key success factors, opportunities, and risk of an industry, and then examined the firm to determine its strengths and weaknesses relative to the key success factors. We also relied on historical financial ratios. For the purpose of assessing business risk, we can focus on any trends in changes in revenues as well as the operating margin (EBIT as a percentage of revenues) over time. Higher business risk would be associated with greater variability of revenues as well as a declining operating margin. We would then want to examine whether these risks might increase in the future.

8.4.2 Financial Risk

Financial risk is directly related to the proportional amount of debt in the firm's capital structure. Regardless of the firm's business risk, financial risk is an additional consideration. We examined a number of financial ratios related to financial risk in chapter 3. The debt-to-equity ratio and the long-term-debt-to-capital ratio provided us with such measures. In addition, financial risk was provided by the interest coverage ratio, the amount of EBIT relative to interest expenses.

Other coverage ratios could be estimated, as well, related to cash requirements instead of just interest payments. For example, the cash flow coverage ratio is measured as follows:

$$\text{Cash flow coverage} = \text{EBITDA}/(\text{interest payments} + \text{before-tax cost of debt repayment})$$

Instead of EBIT, the numerator reflects cash flows (by adding back noncash expenses such as depreciation and amortization to give EBITDA), while the denominator includes not only interest but any required principal repayments as well. The before-tax cost of debt repayment is measured as

$$\text{Before-tax cost of debt repayment} = \text{principal repayment}/(1 - \text{tax rate})$$

The latter term reflects the fact that the firm must earn enough income before tax to meet the principal repayment from after-tax earnings. If a firm is raising capital and wishes to compare two alternative capital structures, it could calculate the liquidity and leverage ratios under each scenario and assess the financial risk.

8.5 Maximizing Flexibility

Growing firms often face ongoing external financing. The decision to issue either debt or equity today often impacts on future financing decisions. Depending on the firm's current capital structure, as well as the capital structure subsequent to today's financing decision, the firm may be implicitly deciding on future financing as well.

For example, suppose a firm currently has a long-term-debt-to-capital ratio of 55 percent, above the industry average of 45 percent. If the firm is in need of capital and issues additional debt, its ratio will increase to 65 percent, while an equity issue will decrease its ratio to around the industry average. If the firm chooses to issue debt today, it will almost certainly need to issue equity the next time it needs to raise external funds. Not only would the proportion of debt be at a much higher level than the industry average, but the debt covenants would probably restrict further borrowing. Alternatively, if the firm issues equity today, it still has the choice of issuing debt or equity in the future. In other words, by choosing equity, the firm is maximizing its flexibility related to the future choice of financing.

8.6   Maintaining Control

Ultimate control of a firm depends on who owns the major portion of the common shares. Small businesses often start out with a single owner-manager who has 100 percent control of the firm. As a private business becomes public, the original owner's equity stake is diminished. So long as the original owner has more than 50 percent of the voting common equity, this original owner ultimately controls the decision making of the firm by voting for the board of directors, to whom the managers are responsible.

As a firm grows and needs additional external capital in the form of equity, the firm is owned by a wider base of shareholders. In many widely held firms, it is possible to own a large portion of the common equity, but less than 50 percent, and still maintain effective control. For example, owning 40 percent of a firm with ten million shareholders, with the next-largest shareholder's owning only 12 percent of the common equity, would represent effective control since it is unlikely that over 80 percent of the remaining shareholders would act as a homogeneous group and be able to impact on the board of directors.

Consider a different situation. Suppose the original owner owns 40 percent of the outstanding common shares but is planning a new common equity issue that would see the original owner's stake decrease to 25 percent of the postissue common shares. It may be possible for a new or existing investor to capture a greater stake of the outstanding shares, thereby gaining effective control. In other words, the firm may be taken over by another firm or new investors. The original owner-managers, perhaps including the existing CEO, may be in a position where they would be required to give up management of the firm. Thus each subsequent issue of common equity can change the dynamics of the control of the firm and ultimately change the direction of the firm's business activities.

From an owner-manager's perspective, the choice between debt and equity, based solely on the criteria of control, is a straightforward one: issuing debt does not change the control position. However, the importance of this criterion depends critically on how likely a change of control is.

8.7   Optimal Timing

If a firm has ongoing external financing needs, it is important to examine both the current and expected outlook in capital markets: the bond market and the stock market. Recall our discussion in chapter 6 concerning efficient markets. If bond and stock markets are efficient, then the timing of when to issue debt or equity should not matter. However, if markets are not efficient, there may be an optimal time to issue securities. For example, if a firm perceives the current equity market to be overvalued, then they should consider issuing equity. The intuition is as follows: Suppose the firm is hoping to raise $100 million and the current stock price is $25 per share, but the firm feels the true or intrinsic value of the shares is only $20 (note that if markets are efficient, the market price should always equal the intrinsic price). If the firm issues equity today at the $25 price, it will only need to issue four million shares. However, if the price declines in the near future to the intrinsic value, the firm will need to issue a total of five million shares. In addition, if the stock market has been increasing recently, there might be more of an appetite for new shares. In times when markets have declined significantly, there is often little appetite for new shares at any price.

In terms of debt or bonds, attractiveness from the firm's perspective depends on the current and expected outlook for interest rates. If long-term rates are low, then a bond issue may be attractive. However, if rates are currently high, the firm may want to wait until rates decline.

In some cases, both bond and stock issues are either attractive or unattractive to the firm. For example, often the stock market is performing well at the same time that interest rates are low. In such a case, the firm must make a decision about the relative attractiveness both currently and in the future when the firm might need additional financing.

8.8   Evaluating the Criteria

We have examined five criteria that a firm should use when considering its optimal capital structure decision: cost, risk, flexibility, control, and timing. We summarize our discussion in Figure 8.9.

As we can see from the chart, determining the optimal capital structure involves assessing trade-offs. If cost and control are the most important criteria, then more debt is better. However, if risk and flexibility are the most important, then more equity is better. Managers need to balance all of these

FIGURE 8.9   **Summary of Optimal Capital Structure Choice Criteria**

CRITERIA	DEBT	EQUITY	IDEAL ($\checkmark$)
Cost	Low $\checkmark$	High	Low
Risk	High	Low $\checkmark$	Low
Flexibility	Low	High $\checkmark$	High
Control	High $\checkmark$	Low	High
Timing	Depends	Depends	Depends

factors. While it is often difficult to determine a precise mix of optimal debt and equity, managers should be able to develop a sense of direction, given the existing amount of debt and equity. For example, managers should be able to determine whether the firm needs to issue a lot more debt, a lot more equity, or a similar proportion to the existing mix. Note also that factors are constantly changing, so the decision is not a onetime decision but rather an ongoing decision.

8.9   Application: A Firm's Decision to Change Its Capital Structure

Determining the optimal capital structure involves both quantitative and qualitative analysis. Much of the qualitative analysis was described above. In this section, we focus on the quantitative analysis. Recall that the ultimate goal is to maximize the value of the firm. Alternatively, we can achieve this maximized value by seeking to minimize the cost of financing, or the cost of capital. The cost of capital, and hence the value of the firm, should be different for different levels of debt and equity. Consider the example presented in Figure 8.10.

We start with an all-equity firm with $1,000 in assets. We assume that regardless of the capital structure, the firm is able to earn a 30 percent operating profit on its assets (EBIT/assets). Its cost of debt and equity are presented below, along with a fixed tax rate. On the basis of any interest payments, we can calculate after-tax earnings. We assume that these earn-

FIGURE 8.10   Optimal Capital Structure Example

Assets	$1,000	$1,400	$1,800	$2,200
Equity (book value)	$1,000	$1,000	$1,000	$1,000
Debt (book and market value)	$0	$400	$800	$1,200
Debt/assets (%)	0%	29%	44%	55%
EBIT/assets (%)	30%	30%	30%	30%
K_d (before tax)	10.0%	10.2%	10.3%	11.7%
K_d (after tax)	6.0%	6.1%	6.2%	7.0%
K_e	18%	19%	20%	24%
EBIT	$300	$420	$540	$660
Interest	$0.0	$40.7	$82.7	$140.0
Earnings before tax	$300.0	$379.3	$457.3	$520.0
Tax at 40%	$120.0	$151.7	$182.9	$208.0
Earnings after tax	$180	$228	$274	$312
Equity (market value)	$1,000	$1,198	*$1,372*	$1,300
Shares	100	100	100	100
Price per share	$10.00	$11.98	$13.72	$13.00
EPS	$1.80	$2.28	$2.74	$3.12
Earnings multiple	5.56	5.26	5.00	4.17
K_c (based on BV weights)	18.0%	15.3%	*13.9%*	14.7%

ings will remain constant in perpetuity, given the asset base, and we assume that all earnings are paid out as dividends each year. Consequently, the market value of equity is calculated as the after-tax earnings divided by the cost of equity. Given a fixed number of shares, we can calculate the price per share, the earnings per share (EPS), and the earnings multiple (price per share divided by earnings per share). Finally, we can calculate the cost of capital, or WACC, in the usual manner (in this example, for simplicity, we use book value weights; one of the end-of-chapter questions asks you to recalculate the cost of capital using market value weights).

With the all-equity firm, not surprisingly, the cost of capital is simply the cost of equity. Suppose the firm increases its asset base to $1,400 and decides to add $400 in debt. Notice that both the cost of debt and the cost of equity are assumed to increase, although the cost of debt is lower than the cost of equity. Overall, the cost of capital has declined and the market value of the equity of the firm has increased. As we move to $1,800 in assets and add more debt, the cost of capital continues to decline and the market value of the equity correspondingly increases. However, given the assumptions in this example, as we move to $2,200 in assets and add more debt, the cost of capital increases and the market value of equity decreases. The intuition is that as the firm takes on a substantial amount of debt, lenders are concerned about bankruptcy possibilities and thus demand a huge risk premium and equity-holders require higher returns to compensate for the increased financial risks they face. At this point, the benefits of interest deductibility for tax purposes are outweighed by the potential cost of financial distress. Consequently, for this particular firm, it would appear that the optimal capital structure is around 44 percent debt to assets (on a book value basis).

8.10   Summary

1. Capital structure refers to the mix of debt and common equity (as well as preferred equity) of a firm. Optimal capital structure refers to the debt-equity mix that maximizes the value of the firm's common equity.
2. In a world with no taxes, no risk of bankruptcy, and identical borrowing and lending opportunities for firms and individuals, a firm's capital structure is not related to the value of the firm.
3. In a world with corporate taxes and bankruptcy risk, an optimal capital structure exists as a trade-off between the benefits of interest expense tax deductibility and the potential cost of bankruptcy.
4. The EBIT break-even analysis indicates the projected EBIT level such that EPS is identical under two different debt-equity mix scenarios.
5. Five key criteria for evaluating the optimal capital are cost, risk, flexibility, control, and timing.

8.11   Additional Readings

The classic article related to capital structure is the seminal study

Modigliani, Franco, and Merton Miller. The Cost of Capital, Corporate Finance and the Theory of Investment. *American Economic Review* 48 (June 1958): 261–97.

8.12   Self-Study Problems

1. Calculate the cash flow coverage ratio based on the following information: EBIT = $540,000, depreciation and amortization = $65,000, interest payments = $180,000, principal repayment = $75,000, and tax rate = 35 percent.
2. Calculate an EBIT break-even between a debt firm (DF) and an all-equity firm (EF) based on the following information: DF interest = $40,000, DF number common shares = 6,000, EF number of common shares = 10,000, and tax rate = 35 percent. Check your answer by calculating the EPS for both DF and EF at the break-even EBIT.
3. Repeat cost of capital calculations in Figure 8.10 assuming market value weights instead of book value weights.

9. The Investment Decision and Time Value of Money Concepts

This chapter is the first of two chapters examining the investment decisions of the firm. Earlier, we referred to investment decisions—buying real assets for the firm—as capital budgeting. Assuming the firm is able to manage day-to-day cash flow and has lined up both short-term and long-term financing, the firm can now turn its attention to investment decisions. An analysis of investment decisions involves examining the trade-off between the expected cash flows generated from an investment and the cost of financing the investment. This analysis involves applications of time value of money concepts. We carefully examine the underpinnings of the time value of money. We show how the time value of money relates directly to the valuation of bonds, preferred shares, and common shares. We then examine a variety of well-known investment decision criteria, from the simple payback method to time-value-of-money-based concepts including the *net present value* and the *internal rate of return*.

9.1 Overview of the Decision-Making Process

Business management centers on making decisions. Better managers make better decisions. Throughout this book, we have alluded to numerous types of decisions that financial and nonfinancial managers face. For example, we have examined decisions involving working capital management and long-term financing. Capital budgeting or investments involve yet another type of decision. All of these decisions, including those about the capital budgeting process, can be described within an overall business decision-making framework. The steps of this framework are outlined in Figure 9.1.

The first step involves defining the decision to be made. For example, a firm may need to make a decision about to how to improve the profitability of one division. There may be a number of short-term and long-term issues related to this decision. For example, a related issue may be how to motivate the workers in that division.

The second step involves developing a list of criteria that are used to evaluate any alternative strategies that the firm is considering. For example, one criterion might be maximizing profitability. Another criterion might be minimizing risk. Yet another criterion might be maintaining good relations with the firm's union. It should be recognized that it might not be possible for any one alternative to satisfy every criteria. In such cases, prioritizing criteria is important.

The third step involves generating alternatives. One alternative is invariably the do nothing, or status quo, alternative. Management should typically consider more than two alternatives, so as not to overlook some possible viable solutions, but should not consider so many alternatives that evaluation becomes too time consuming. Usually three to four distinct alternatives are appropriate. For example, in dealing with the issue of raising the profitability of a particular division, alternatives might include deciding whether to purchase a new piece of equipment to replace an existing piece of equipment, deciding whether to upgrade the existing equipment, or deciding whether to outsource and scrap the existing equipment.

The fourth step involves the analysis and assessment of the alternatives. This is usually the most critical and most time consuming step. Note that with each alternative, we should be able to quantify the potential benefits,

---

FIGURE 9.1   **Decision-Making Framework**

1. Definition of decision to be made and related issues
2. Criteria to be used to evaluate alternatives
3. Generation of alternatives
4. Analysis and assessment of alternatives
5. Decision and implementation

such as increased profitability. However, once we are able to quantify these benefits, while we may have a clear "winning" alternative from the perspective of maximizing profitability, we then need to balance this by examining the other criteria. It might be the case that the alternative that maximizes profitability is also the riskiest or involves major layoffs that might damage future relationships with the firm's union.

The final step involves making a decision and developing an implementation plan. The key role that management plays is assessing the trade-offs involved in any decision. For example, quantitative benefits must be weighed against qualitative factors. While developing the numbers cannot answer all questions, it does play an important role by articulating the trade-offs involved.

We can apply the general decision-making process specifically to the capital budgeting, or investment, process. While most of the steps are fairly straightforward, we will concentrate on the analysis step. In terms of the capital budgeting decision, this step invariably involves an assessment of trade-offs: the initial cost of investment versus the expected benefits in terms of additional cash flows and profitability in the future. With capital budgeting decisions, there is always a quantitative component to the analysis. We focus on this quantitative component in this chapter.

The easiest part of the quantitative analysis involves knowing the initial cost of a potential investment, such as new equipment. We can think of this as a cash outflow today when the decision is being made. The next part of the process involves estimating any future costs and benefits, or cash outflows and inflows. It is the net cash flow that is relevant. In addition, we need to examine the *incremental* cash flow compared with that of the do nothing alternative. The final part of the analysis involves comparing the net cash flows and taking into account the timing of the cash flows, or what is known as the time value of money. We first develop the basics related to the time value of money. We then revisit previously introduced financial securities, including bonds, preferred shares, and common shares, to show how these securities' values are determined by time value of money concepts. We then apply time value of money concepts in a capital budgeting setting.

9.2   Time Value of Money Concepts

Simply stated, the time value of money implies that one dollar today is worth more than one dollar tomorrow. While this may seem like a straightforward notion, it is one that is often overlooked. For example, many lotteries boast large prize money, but with payouts over many years. In such cases, winners would have been better off with a smaller nominal prize but with more money up front.

Time value of money concepts are often confused with concepts related to risk and inflation. For example, we often think that the reason we might prefer a dollar today rather than a dollar tomorrow is because either we think prices might rise tomorrow or there is a risk we might not get money back from any investment today. While these are both valid concerns, they obscure the fundamental premise behind the time value of money—the concept of *opportunity cost.*

Consider the following example. You and a friend are passing by the Momma's Homemade Cookie store, a favorite local establishment. Their specialty is huge chocolate chip cookies for five dollars. You happen to have five dollars exactly, but your friend doesn't have any money (sharing a cookie is not an option). Your friend asks to borrow five dollars from you and agrees to pay you back next week. Your friend insists on paying you back a fair amount for agreeing to lend the money today. How much would you require in return?

The answer to this question demonstrates what the time value of money represents—a fair return for the opportunity cost of forgoing consumption today. The only reason that rational individuals would forgo consumption today is if they can consume even more in the future. By giving up the consumption of one cookie today, you should be able to consume more than one cookie in the future. Notice that in this example we have implicitly assumed that cookie prices are not anticipated to increase (that is, there is no inflation) and there is no risk that your friend will not pay you back. If we anticipated either of these events, we would have required a greater payback for lending the money today. However, and fundamentally, we still require an opportunity cost.

9.2.1 Future Values

We begin by examining the concept of future values of single amounts. Suppose you are given $100 today but you are prepared to forgo spending that money. Instead, you choose to invest the money in a safe investment, such as a one-year Treasury bill. The Treasury bill currently yields 7 percent. What is the future value, in one year, of $100 invested in the Treasury bill?

In one year, you will receive the principal you invested plus the interest of 7 percent. The interest on the $100 is $7, so you will receive $107. In other

---

FIGURE 9.2   **Future Value of a Single Amount, One-Period Example**

$$FV = PV(1+r)$$

where FV = future value

PV = present value

r = interest rate or rate of return on the investment

---

words, the future value of $100 invested today for one year at the rate of 7 percent is $107. The specific calculation is

$$\begin{aligned} FV &= \$100(1 + 0.07) \\ &= \$100(1.07) \\ &= \$107 \end{aligned}$$

Note that the 1 in the calculation above represents the principal, while 0.07 represents the interest rate (in decimal form). We generalize this one-period example in Figure 9.2.

Now suppose instead you chose to invest the $100 in a two-year investment certificate that guaranteed an annual return of 8 percent each year. Any interest earned after one year is *compounded*. In other words, you receive interest on any interest earned. In this case, how much money would you receive at the end of two years?

In one year, you would have earned the principal you invested plus the interest of 8 percent. The interest on the $100 is $8, so you would have earned $108. We can now treat this situation as another one-year investment. However, instead of a $100 investment, this is a $108 investment. Consequently, after two years, you would have earned the principal and interest reinvested after one year ($108) plus the interest earned on that full amount in the second year. Eight percent of $108 is $8.64. Thus the amount you receive is $116.64. In other words, the future value of $100 invested today for two years at a rate of 8 percent is $116.64. The specific calculation is

$$\begin{aligned} FV &= \$100(1.08)(1.08) \\ &= \$108(1.08) \\ &= \$116.64 \end{aligned}$$

We generalize this two-period example to a multiperiod example over n years (where n is greater than 1) in Figure 9.3.

FIGURE 9.3   Future Value of a Single Amount, Multiperiod Example

$$FV = PV(1+r)(1+r)\cdots$$
$$= PV(1+r)^n$$

where FV = future value
PV = present value
r = interest rate or rate of return on the investment
n = number of periods

Note that the $(1+r)^n$ calculation can be performed on many calculators with a simple y^x key, where y is $(1+r)$ and x is n.

9.2.2   Time Lines

At this point, it is worthwhile to pause and provide a graphic representation of the concepts covered so far. We can do this through drawings of *time lines*. A time line represents the cash inflows or outflows, the information that we have to solve a particular problem, and the unknown element we are trying to solve for. A time line for the two-period problem is presented in Figure 9.4.

The time line indicates various points in time starting with today at $t = 0$. Two periods are indicated: $t = 1$ at the end of the first period, and $t = 2$ at the end of the second period. In this example, each period is one year, but a period could be any length, such as a week, a month, or six months. Whatever length is chosen, it is assumed that cash flows can only occur at the end of a particular period. The –$100 indicates a cash outflow of $100 today, representing the present value of the investment. The investment interest rate of 8 percent is indicated. The time line indicates that we are trying to solve

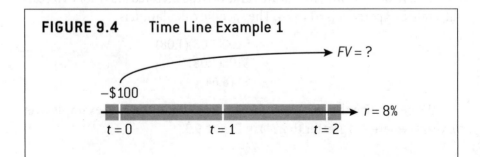

FIGURE 9.4   Time Line Example 1

$FV = ?$

–$100

$r = 8\%$

$t = 0$ $t = 1$ $t = 2$

for the future value of the $100 investment. We can see that the investment is for a two-year period.

While this particular time line is illustrated for a straightforward situation, other time lines can be more complicated depending on the timing and nature of the cash flows. For example, some cash flows might be positive (inflows) in some periods and negative (outflows) in other periods. Some cash flows might occur at the beginning or at the end of periods (most of our examples and the accompanying formulas assume end-of-period cash flows). Thus it is always worthwhile to draw time lines.

9.2.3 Present Values

Now that we have illustrated the concept of future value, the concept of present value is straightforward. We can think of present value as the reverse of future value. Instead of asking what a particular investment today will grow to in the future, we can ask what is the worth, today, of receiving an anticipated cash flow in the future. For example, suppose we require $500 in one year in order to pay for a furniture purchase. If we can earn a return of 9 percent, how much money do we need to set aside today? In other words, what is the present value of $500 received one year from now if the investment rate, or discount rate, is 9 percent?

Today we need to set aside a principal amount that will earn interest of 9 percent a year and be equal to $500 in a year. So instead of starting with a known investment, or present value, and multiplying by 1 + the interest rate, we take the future value and divide by 1 + the interest rate. The specific calculation is

$$PV = \$500/(1 + 0.09)$$
$$= \$500/(1.09)$$
$$= \$458.72$$

To check the calculation, note that 9 percent of $458.72 is $41.28. If we add the principal of $458.72 and the interest of $41.28, we end up with exactly the desired future value of $500. We generalize this one-period example in Figure 9.5.

Now suppose instead you require the $500 in two years. Recall that any interest earned each year is compounded. We work backward from the final period (year 2). One year before, you will need to have an amount such that the amount plus interest will give you $500 in one year. We know from the example above that the amount is $458.72 or $500/(1.09). We are now left with another one-period calculation. We repeat the process to determine

---

FIGURE 9.5   Present Value of a Single Amount, One-Period Example

$$PV = FV/(1 + r)$$

where FV = future value
PV = present value
r = interest rate or discount rate

---

what amount must be invested for one year at 9 percent interest and result in an end-of-period value of $458.72. That amount is $458.72/(1.09), or $420.84. The specific calculation is

$$
\begin{aligned}
PV &= (\$500/1.09)/1.09 \\
&= \$458.72/1.09 \\
&= \$420.84
\end{aligned}
$$

$$
\begin{aligned}
\text{or, } PV &= \$500/[(1.09)(1.09)] \\
&= \$500/1.1881 \\
&= \$420.84
\end{aligned}
$$

Note that the two different representations above result in the same answer (just a different order of operations—one divides each time; the other multiplies the terms in the denominator first and then divides).

We can also describe the two-step process in a time line as shown in Figure 9.6.

We can generalize this two-period example to a multiperiod example over n years (where n is greater than 1) in Figure 9.7.

Note that this general formula for present value is simply a rearrangement of the general formula for future value, as given in Figure 9.3.

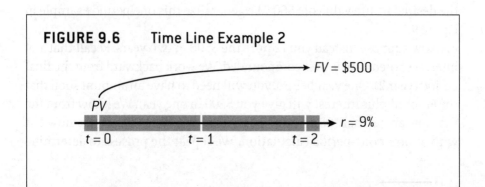

FIGURE 9.6   Time Line Example 2

FV = $500

PV

r = 9%

t = 0   t = 1   t = 2

FIGURE 9.7 **Present Value of a Single Amount, Multiperiod Example**

$$PV = FV/[(1+r)(1+r)\cdots]$$
$$= FV/(1+r)^n$$

where FV = future value

PV = present value

r = interest rate or discount rate

n = number of periods

9.2.4 Using Financial Calculators and Spreadsheets

We can simplify future value and present value calculations by using standard financial calculators. You can tell what type of calculator is a financial calculator (as opposed to either a simple calculator or a scientific calculator) because it has the following keys: PV for present value, FV for future value, i or r for the interest rate or discount rate, n for the number of periods, and PMT for stream of payments.

Before we examine some examples, there are some useful tips that may help you to avoid becoming frustrated with your calculator. While it may ultimately be necessary to read the often-daunting instructions manual, these tips will get you started.

1. It is always a good practice to clear your calculator between calculations, using a Clear, or C, key.
2. Most calculations assume cash flows occur at the end of each period, as in the examples above. Alternatively, if a time value of money problem is such that cash flows occur at the beginning of each period (for example, if you invested in a retirement fund at the start of each year), most financial calculators can be set to deal with this by pressing a Begin, or BGN, key.
3. Some cash flows are inflows while others are outflows. In some applications, it is critical to distinguish between inflows and outflows. For example, if you are making an investment today (PV) and wish to calculate what the investment will grow to in several years (FV), the initial investment represents a cash outflow while the amount in the future is like a cash inflow. With many calculators, it is important to enter the PV amount as a negative number (an outflow) so that the FV amount is positive (an inflow). In order to do this, you need to use the plus/minus (+/–)

key. For example, type 100, then press the +/– key (–100 should now appear), then press *PV*.

4. When entering a percentage in a time value calculation, most financial calculators require you to enter the actual number in conjunction with the i or r key. For example, 8 percent is entered as 8. However, with some calculators, you may need to enter .08.

5. Some calculators allow you to display a different number of digits to the right of the decimal point. For most calculations, rounding is not critical so it does not matter if your calculator displays 150.27 or 150.26666667.

6. Some financial calculators are preset on the basis of monthly compounding (i.e., 12 payments per year), often indicated as "$P/Y = 12$." You may need to reset this to "$P/Y = 1$," or regular annual compounding.

Now let us reexamine some of the future value and present value examples presented earlier, but with financial calculators or spreadsheets. Recall the example above investing $100 today in a two-year certificate that guaranteed an annual return of 8 percent per year. In order to calculate the money you would receive at the end of two years, enter the following information into your calculator (after you have cleared it), using the appropriate keys, as indicated in Figure 9.8.

In order to perform this calculation using a spreadsheet such as Excel, it is often fairly straightforward to simply insert an existing function such as the *FV* function. In Excel, select "Insert" from the menu, then "Function," then function category "Financial," then "FV." Note that the form of this function is *FV*(rate, nper, pmt, *PV*, type). Using our notation, rate is the interest rate, or *r*, *in decimal form*; nper is the number of periods, or *n*; pmt is the annuity amount (if applicable), and *PV* is the present value amount. Type is optional and performs the same function as the BGN key on a calculator. If type is set as 1, then it is assumed that any cash flow occurs at the beginning of the period. If type is set as 0 or if it is not included, then it is assumed

---

FIGURE 9.8   Financial Calculator Future Value Example

PV	→	–100	Type 100, then press +/–, then press PV.
r	→	8	Type 8, then press r.
n	→	2	Type 2, then press n.
Compute *FV*.			Press COMP, then press *FV*.
Answer is		116.64	This answer should appear.

FIGURE 9.9   Spreadsheet Future Value Example

	A	B	C	D	E
1	rate	.08			
2	nper	2			
3	pmt	0	=FV(B1,B2,B3,B4)	⟶	116.64
4	PV	−100			

that any cash flow occurs at the end of the period. In the example above, choose a particular cell and enter the following information:

$$=FV(.08,2,0,-100,0) \quad \text{or} \quad =FV(.08,2,0,-100)$$

The same answer, 116.64, should appear.

Alternatively, to create a more transparent and general function, enter the information separately from the function, as indicated in Figure 9.9.

Recall the present value example above. We require $500 in two years. If we can earn a return of 9 percent each year, how much money do we need to set aside today?

In order to calculate the money you would receive at the end of two years, enter the following information into your calculator (after you have cleared it), using the appropriate keys, as indicated in Figure 9.10.

In order to perform this calculation using a spreadsheet such as Excel, we would insert an existing *PV* function. In Excel, select "Insert" from the menu, then "Function," then function category "Financial," then "*PV*." Note that the form of this function is *PV*(rate, nper, pmt, *FV*, type). Using our notation, rate is the interest rate, or *r in decimal form*; nper is the number of periods, or *n*; pmt is the annuity amount (if applicable); and *FV* is the future value amount. Type is optional and performs the same function as the BGN key on a calcu-

**FIGURE 9.10   Financial Calculator
Present Value Example**

FV	→	500	Type 500, then press FV.
r	→	9	Type 9, then press r.
n	→	2	Type 2, then press n.
Compute *PV*.			Press COMP, then press PV.
Answer is		−420.84	This answer should appear.

FIGURE 9.11   Spreadsheet Present Value Example

	A	B	C	D	E
1	rate	.09			
2	nper	2			
3	pmt	0	=PV(B1,B2,B3,B4)	→	−420.84
4	FV	500			

lator. If type is set as 1, then it is assumed that any cash flow occurs at the beginning of the period. If type is set as 0 or if it is not included, then it is assumed that any cash flow occurs at the end of the period. In the example above, choose a particular cell and enter the following information:

$$=PV(.09,2,0,500,0) \quad \text{or} \quad =PV(.09,2,0,500)$$

The same answer, −420.84, should appear.

Alternatively, to create a more transparent and general function, enter the information separately from the function, as indicated in Figure 9.11.

9.2.5   Annuities

In many situations, cash flows occur in an equal stream. This stream of equal cash flows is known as an *annuity*. We can examine both the future value of annuities and the present value of annuities.

Consider the following example of an annuity. Suppose you plan to invest $1,000 each year, starting one year from now, in a retirement fund. You plan to retire in four years. You invest in a guaranteed certificate that promises to pay 7 percent each year. How much money will you have in four years (just after making your fourth $1,000 investment)?

We can start by drawing a time line, as in Figure 9.12.

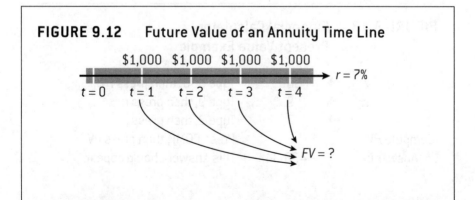

FIGURE 9.12   Future Value of an Annuity Time Line

FIGURE 9.13 Future Value of Annuity Formula

$$FVA = PMT[(1+r)^n - 1]/r$$

where FVA = future value of annuity
PMT = annuity payments
r = interest rate or rate of return on the investment
n = number of periods

The actual formula, as indicated in Figure 9.13, looks rather complex. Rather than trying to solve for this algebraically, it is much simpler to use a financial calculator or spreadsheet function.

In order to calculate the money you would receive at the end of four years, enter the following information into your calculator (after you have cleared it), using the appropriate keys, as indicated in Figure 9.14.

In order to perform this calculation using a spreadsheet such as Excel, we would insert the existing *FV* function. In Excel, select "Insert" from the menu, then "Function," then function category "Financial," then "FV." Recall that the form of this function is *FV*(rate, nper, pmt, *PV*, type). In the example above, choose a particular cell and enter the following information:

=FV(.07,4,–1000,0,0)   or   =FV(.07,4,–1000,0)

The same answer, 4,439.94, should appear.

Alternatively, to create a more transparent and general function, enter the information separately from the function, as indicated in Figure 9.15.

The present value of an annuity follows a similar construct. Consider the following example. Suppose you plan to withdraw $1,000 each year for the next four years, starting one year from now, from a retirement fund. How

---

FIGURE 9.14 Financial Calculator
Future Value of Annuity Example

PMT	→	–1,000	Type 1,000, then press +/–, then press pmt.
r	→	7	Type 7, then press r.
n	→	4	Type 4, then press n.
Compute FV.			Press COMP, then press FV.
Answer is		4,439.94	This answer should appear.

FIGURE 9.15   **Spreadsheet Future Value
of Annuity Example**

	A	B	C	D	E
1	rate	.07			
2	nper	4			
3	pmt	−1000	=FV(B1,B2,B3,B4) ⟶		4439.94
4	PV	0			

much money do you need to invest today in a guaranteed certificate that promises to pay 7 percent each year? We can start by drawing a time line, as in Figure 9.16.

FIGURE 9.16   **Present Value of an Annuity Time Line**

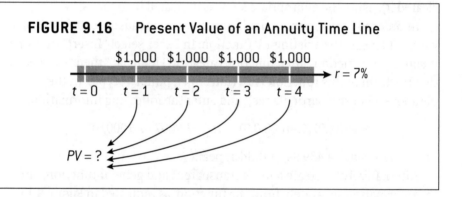

The actual formula looks rather complex, as indicated in Figure 9.17. Rather than trying to solve for this algebraically, it is much simpler to use a financial calculator or spreadsheet function.

FIGURE 9.17   **Present Value of Annuity Formula**

$$PVA = PMT[1 - 1/(1+r)^n]/r$$

where PVA = present value of annuity
PMT = annuity payments
r = interest rate or rate of return on the investment
n = number of periods

FIGURE 9.18   Financial Calculator
Present Value of Annuity Example

PMT	→	1,000	Type 1,000, then press pmt.
r	→	7	Type 7, then press r.
n	→	4	Type 4, then press n.
Compute *PV.*			Press COMP, then press PV.
Answer is		−3,387.21	This answer should appear.

In order to calculate the money you would need to invest today, enter the following information into your calculator (after you have cleared it), using the appropriate keys, as indicated in Figure 9.18.

In order to perform this calculation using a spreadsheet such as Excel, we would insert the existing *PV* function. In Excel, select "Insert" from the menu, then "Function," then function category "Financial," then "PV." Recall that the form of this function is *PV*(rate, nper, pmt, *FV*, type). In the example above, choose a particular cell and enter the following information:

$$=PV(.07,4,1000,0,0) \quad \text{or} \quad =PV(.07,4,1000,0)$$

The same answer, −3387.21, should appear.

Alternatively, to create a more transparent and general function, enter the information separately from the function, as indicated in Figure 9.19.

If you do not have access to a financial calculator or a spreadsheet, present value and future value calculations for most problems can be solved using tables such as those found in Appendix C. The four tables calculate the relevant time value factors under the following scenarios: the present value of $1 (table 1), the future value of $1 (table 2), the present value of an

FIGURE 9.19   Spreadsheet Present Value
of Annuity Example

	A	B	C	D	E
1	rate	.07			
2	nper	4			
3	pmt	1000	=PV(B1,B2,B3,B4) ⟶		−3387.21
4	FV	0			

annuity stream of $1 per period (table 3), and the future value of an annuity stream of $1 per period (table 4). Interest rates of 1 to 15 percent and 1 through 20 periods are presented. In order to estimate, say, the present value of $100 to be received in ten years, assuming a discount rate of 10 percent, first find the relevant factor in table 1: 0.386. Since we wish to find the present value of $100, we would multiply $100 by 0.386, getting $38.60.

9.3   Time Value of Money Applications

Now that we have an understanding of time value concepts, we can reexamine our discussion of previous financial securities since bond, preferred share, and common equity prices all represent the present value of expected cash flows to the relevant investors. Recall in chapter 6 we discussed the features and markets for these securities. Now we can focus on the pricing of each.

9.3.1   Bond Example

From an investor's perspective, bonds represent a form of lending to a firm. In time value of money terminology, the amount lent to the firm today is the present value (*PV*). The length of maturity is represented by the number of periods (*n*). Bonds are a combination of single amounts and annuities. The single amount is the principal amount that is lent and will be repaid in the future (*FV*). The interest payments represent annuity streams (*PMT*). The discount rate (*r*) used to calculate the present value of the interest (or coupon) payments and the principal amount is known as the *yield to maturity*, or YTM. Recall that bonds are typically issued with a par value, or face value, of $1,000. At the time of issue, the coupon rate, which is the percentage of the par value of the bond paid annually as interest, is equal to the yield to maturity (recall also that most bonds pay interest on a semiannual basis). However, after the issue, the general level of interest rates may change; this would cause the yield to maturity to change as well. As the yield to maturity changes, so does the price of the bond. The yield to maturity is the most widely used benchmark to summarize the current-expected bond return.

Now consider the following bond example. A three-year bond is issued. The face value (and future value *FV*) is $1,000. The coupon rate is 8 percent. This implies annual payments of $80 (8 percent of $1,000), or more specifically six (*n*) payments of $40 (*PMT*) every six months. While the coupon rate is 8 percent, the initial *semiannual* yield to maturity (*r*) is simply the

FIGURE 9.20   Bond Valuation Time Line

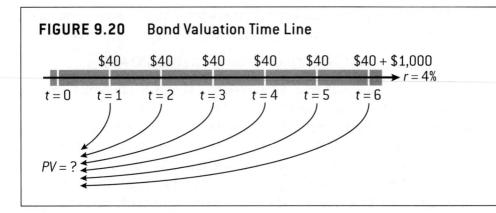

coupon rate divided by two (the number of six-month periods in a year), or 4 percent. We can apply our time value of money concepts to calculate the present value (*PV*) of the cash flow streams, which should initially equal the par value of the bond, or the amount of $1,000 originally lent to the firm. Let us begin by drawing a time line as in Figure 9.20.

We can proceed in two steps. First, we can calculate the present value of the principal, $1,000, to be repaid in six (six-month) periods, discounted at the semiannual rate of 4 percent. Second, we can calculate the present value of an annuity of $40 for six periods, also discounted at the semiannual rate of 4 percent. The sum of these two amounts is the present value, or the price we should be willing to pay for the bond.

With a financial calculator or spreadsheet, we can combine the two steps since we have the same number of periods and the same discount rate for each step. Calculations are presented in Figure 9.21.

In order to perform this calculation using a spreadsheet such as Excel, we would insert the existing *PV* function. In Excel, select "Insert" from the menu, then "Function," then function category "Financial," then "PV." Recall

FIGURE 9.21   Financial Calculator Bond Value Example

PMT	→	40	Type 40, then press PMT.
r	→	4	Type 4, then press r.
n	→	6	Type 6, then press n.
FV	→	1,000	Type 1000, then press FV.
Compute PV.			Press COMP, then press PV.
Answer is		−1,000	This answer should appear.

that the form of this function is PV(rate, nper, pmt, *FV*, type). In the example above, choose a particular cell and enter the following information:

$$=PV(.04,6,40,1000,0) \quad \text{or} \quad =PV(.04,6,40,1000)$$

Not surprisingly, the present value is $1,000, which is the initial amount lent (i.e., –1,000 represents the cash outflow, or purchase price of the bond). Now suppose interest rates change the day after you purchased the bonds (i.e., when you lent the $1,000 to the firm). Suppose new information about the economy was released that suggested inflation was going to be much lower than investors had expected. For a bond with this particular risk, investors would now be willing to accept a yield to maturity of, say, 7 percent (or 3.5 percent on a semiannual basis) instead of 8 percent as in the example above. If the firm were to issue the bond today (instead of yesterday), a bond with a $1,000 face value issued at par would pay semiannual interest of only $35 instead of $40. What impact will this have on the price of the bond that you purchased *yesterday?* We can recalculate the price, as above, except use an interest rate (or yield to maturity) of 3.5 percent instead of 4 percent. When we make this one change, the price of the bond goes *up* to $1,026.64! Other investors would be willing to pay more for your bond since it has more attractive coupons than similar bonds issued today. This highlights the most fundamental concept related to bonds: *When interest rates go down, bond prices go up (and vice versa).* Just as investors would ideally like to buy bonds when interest rates are high (especially when they feel interest rates might decline), conversely firms would like to issue bonds when interest rates are low (especially when they feel interest rates might rise).

9.3.2 Preferred Share Example

Recall that (perpetual) preferred shares provide preferred shareholders with a steady stream of dividends. Consider a preferred shareholder who buys a preferred share, when it is issued, for $50 (the par value). In return, the shareholder expects to receive a preferred dividend of $2.50 each year (in this example, we will assume the dividends are paid annually starting in one year, although preferred dividends are usually paid quarterly). Note that the dividend is specified as 5 percent of the par value (or $2.50/$50). This is also known as the *initial* preferred dividend yield.

We can draw a time line to demonstrate that the initial price represents the present value of anticipated dividends, as shown in Figure 9.22.

Suppose we were to apply our annuity formula to calculate the present value of the first five dividends. Using our spreadsheet function PV(rate,

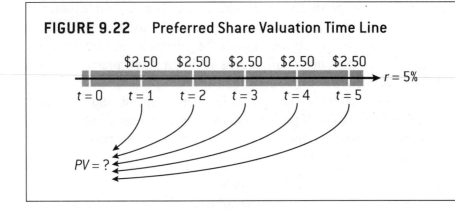

FIGURE 9.22   Preferred Share Valuation Time Line

nper, pmt, *FV*, type), where rate is 0.05, nper is 5, pmt is $2.50, and *FV* and type are zero gives a present value of $10.82. As we change the number of periods, the present value increases. For example, as we increase nper to 10, 20, 50, 100, and 150, we obtain present values of $19.30, $31.16, $45.64, $49.62, and $49.97, respectively. Thus when nper is very large, we have an approximate present value for our perpetuity, which we know should be $50.

Fortunately, there is an easier way to calculate the present value of a perpetuity, or the value of a perpetual preferred share, as shown by the formula in Figure 9.23. Thus the value of the preferred share is simply equal to $2.50/0.05, or $50.

There are two major factors that influence the price of preferred shares, both of which impact on interest rates or yields. From an investor's perspective, the dividend yield should be appropriate given the risk of the investment as well as other opportunities the investor faces. When considering preferred share investments, investors consider alternative investments such as long-term corporate bonds. Investors also consider the riskiness of the corporation since, if the firm is forced into bankruptcy, preferred shareholders may no longer receive their dividends. These factors combine to

FIGURE 9.23   Present Value of a Perpetuity Formula

$$PV = CF/r \quad \text{or} \quad PV = DIV/r$$

where CF = perpetual cash flow or preferred dividend (DIV)
r = rate of return on the investment or preferred dividend yield

determine an appropriate dividend yield. Just as a bond's yield to maturity can change on a day-to-day basis, so can a preferred's dividend yield.

Consider the example above. Suppose the general level of interest rates goes up. As a consequence, similar firms are issuing new preferred shares with initial dividend yields of 6 percent instead of 5 percent. If the dividend yield increases (i.e., investors demand a higher yield), this should have a negative impact on the value of preferred shares, just as increasing interest rates had a negative impact on the value of bonds. We can recalculate the new price of the preferred shares.

$$
\begin{aligned}
PV &= DIV/r \\
&= \$2.50/0.06 \\
&= \$41.67
\end{aligned}
$$

Note that the amount of dividends has not changed (since it remains the same for these types of preferred shares) but, since the required dividend yield has increased, the price must decrease. Now investors are indifferent between buying the existing preferreds at a lower price and buying the new preferreds.

9.3.3 Common Equity Example

Consider an investor in a common share that pays a dividend. This investor plans to buy and hold the security. What should this investor be willing to pay for the security? The answer depends on a number of factors. First, the investor must anticipate the expected future stream of dividends. Second, the investor must estimate the present value of that stream of dividends based on discounting the anticipated cash flows at an appropriate discount rate. That discount rate should reflect the riskiness of the anticipated cash flows, or dividends, and should therefore represent the investor's required return for investing in such a stock. In chapter 7 we described the CAPM as a way of estimating a common equity investor's required return. We can use that model as a method of specifying a discount rate. In general, we can represent the value of a common share as the present value of dividends, as indicated in the time line in Figure 9.24. We can formalize the present value calculation as in Figure 9.25.

We could estimate the value of the common share if we could estimate the anticipated dividend stream. However, similar to the challenge we faced with the perpetual preferred, we would need to calculate the present value of each cash flow or dividend. What is more complicating in the current situation is the fact that firms tend to increase their common share dividend

FIGURE 9.24 Common Share Valuation Time Line

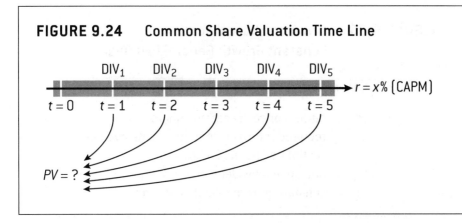

over time. Consequently, we could not rely on the annuity formula presented above. Fortunately, there is a solution to make our calculations a lot easier. If we are willing to make an assumption that dividends grow at a constant rate g, then we can reestimate our general formula. While DIV_1 remains the same, we replace DIV_2 with $DIV_1(1 + g)$. For example, suppose next year's dividend was anticipated to be one dollar and the dividend was anticipated to grow at a rate of 5 percent forever. Then DIV_2 would be estimated as $1.00(1.05) = $1.05; DIV_3 would be $DIV_1(1 + g)(1 + g)$, or $DIV_1(1 + g)^2$. The actual amount would be $1.00(1.05)(1.05) = $1.1025. The general formula would be as in Figure 9.26.

While the above formulation does not appear to be any simpler, it turns out that many years ago a clever mathematician was able to show that a growing perpetuity simplifies to the formula in Figure 9.27.

Continuing with the previous example, DIV_1 is estimated to be $1.00 and g is estimated to be 5 percent (or 0.05). Suppose r is estimated to be 12 per-

FIGURE 9.25 Common Share Valuation, General Formula

$$PV = DIV_1/(1 + r) + DIV_2/(1 + r)^2 + DIV_3/(1 + r)^3 + DIV_4/(1 + r)^4 + \cdots$$

where PV = current price of common share

r = required return by common share investor (estimated by the CAPM)

DIV_t = anticipated dividend in t periods

FIGURE 9.26 Common Share Valuation,
Constant Growth General Formula

$$PV = DIV_1/(1+r) + DIV_1(1+g)/(1+r)^2 + DIV_1(1+g)^2/(1+r)^3 + \cdots$$

where PV = current price of common share
 r = required return by common share investor
 (estimated by the CAPM)
 DIV_1 = anticipated dividend in one period
 g = constant growth rate of dividends

---

cent (or 0.12); then the stock price should be $1.00/(0.12 – 0.05) = $1.00/0.07 = $14.29. (Note that this formulation only makes sense if r is greater than g, but this is a reasonable assumption.)

This simple-looking formula provides some powerful insights into why stock prices go up or down each day. The price of a stock depends on two, and only two, simple factors: the anticipated growth rate of dividends and the perceived riskiness of the dividend stream. An easy way to remember these factors is

Growth is good!
Risk is rotten!

Notice that when we increase the anticipated growth of dividends, g (g as in *Growth is good!*), investors would be willing to pay more for the stock. Conversely, if we increase the anticipated risk of the future cash flows, as

---

FIGURE 9.27 Common Share Valuation,
Constant Growth Simplified Formula

$$PV = DIV_1/(r-g)$$

where PV = current price of common share
 r = required return by common share investor
 (estimated by the CAPM)
 DIV_1 = anticipated dividend in one period
 g = constant growth rate of dividends

captured by the higher required return, r (r as in *Risk is rotten!*), investors would only accept a lower stock price.

For example, if g is 6 percent instead of 5 percent (growth is good), then the value of the stock is $\$1.00/(0.12 - 0.06) = \$1.00/0.06 = \$16.67$. Alternatively, if the required return is only 11 percent instead of 12 percent (risk is rotten), then the value of the stock is $\$1.00/(0.11 - 0.05) = \$1.00/0.06 = \$16.67$. If the growth rate is at the higher level of 6 percent but the riskiness has also increased such that the required return is now 13 percent instead of 12 percent, then the value of the common stock is $\$1.00/(0.13 - 0.06) = \$1.00/0.07 = \$14.29$. In this example there was an offsetting trade-off between growth and riskiness.

9.4   Capital Budgeting Techniques

Now that we have an appreciation of time value of money concepts and understand their applications to the valuation of bonds, preferred shares, and common shares, we are finally in a position to appreciate the various capital budgeting techniques, since many of them rely on time value of money concepts. We begin with the simplest technique, the payback method, which does not rely on time value of money concepts (which is the major weakness of this technique). We then examine the related techniques of net present value and internal rate of return.

9.4.1   Payback

Recall the capital budgeting process described earlier. We begin by determining the initial cost of the investment. This is the cash outflow today when the decision is being made. We then estimate any future costs and benefits, or cash outflows and inflows, focusing on the net cash flows. On average, these net cash flows should be cash *in*flows; otherwise the investment would certainly not be worthwhile. We then compare the net cash flows relative to the initial investment.

The payback method is the simplest method for assessing capital budgeting decisions. For projects with an up-front investment and smooth annual cash flows, the *payback period* is estimated as shown in Figure 9.28.

Consider the following example. Suppose a firm is considering a project that requires an initial investment of $\$100,000$. The project is expected to generate average annual net cash flows of $\$20,000$ for the next eight years.

FIGURE 9.28 Payback Method, Simple Example

$$\text{Payback period} = \frac{\text{initial investment}}{\text{average annual net inflow}}$$

The payback period is calculated as \$100,000/\$20,000 = five years. In general, the payback period represents the length of time to repay the initial investment. In a sense, the payback method attempts to capture the riskiness of the project. If the payback period is very short, then the project is less risky. Some firms have project guidelines such as only accepting projects with payback periods of, say, three years or less.

Given our knowledge of the time value of money, we can identify the major deficiency with this method. There is no attempt to distinguish between cash flows in the earlier years and cash flows in the later years; all are treated the same. Any guideline measure of a desired payback period is arbitrary. As well, there is no incorporation of an opportunity cost.

9.4.2 Net Present Value

Net present value (NPV) attempts to capture the net value added to the firm by taking on any particular project. In its simplest form, consider a project with a cash outflow today and one with an anticipated cash inflow in one year. In this one-period example, NPV is calculated as in Figure 9.29.

Suppose the initial outlay (C_0) is \$80,000, the project net cash inflow in one year (C_1) is \$100,000, and the appropriate discount rate (r) is 10 percent. Note that the discount rate is directly related to the cost of capital described in chapter 7. If the project has the same risk as the overall firm, then the dis-

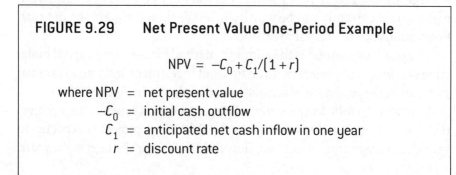

FIGURE 9.29 Net Present Value One-Period Example

$$\text{NPV} = -C_0 + C_1/(1 + r)$$

where NPV = net present value
$-C_0$ = initial cash outflow
C_1 = anticipated net cash inflow in one year
r = discount rate

FIGURE 9.30   Net Present Value Multiperiod Example

$$NPV = -C_0 + C_1/(1+r) + C_2/(1+r)^2 + C_3/(1+r)^3 + \cdots$$

where NPV = net present value

$-C_0$ = initial cash outflow

C_t = anticipated net cash inflow at time t

r = discount rate

---

count rate should be closely related to the cost of capital. If the project is more or less risky than the average firm project, then an appropriate hurdle rate that reflects the project riskiness, is used.

The net present value is calculated in two stages. First, the present value of the expected cash flow is calculated on the basis of the time value of money concepts described earlier in this chapter. The present value is $90,909. Second, the initial investment is subtracted from this amount, leaving $10,909, or the net present value of the investment.

The net present value rule states that a firm (that is not facing any capital constraints) should accept any project with a net present value greater than or equal to zero. Note that the special case of a zero NPV project results from a project that provides just enough compensation for the riskiness of the project.

We can generalize the net present value calculation to situations with cash flows in more than one period as in Figure 9.30.

Suppose a firm is considering an investment of $300,000 and anticipates net cash inflows in the next three years of $100,000, $150,000, and $200,000. The appropriate discount rate is assumed to be 10 percent. What is the net present value of this project?

First, calculate the present value of each of the three cash flows. The present values are $90,909, $123,967, and $150,263, respectively. Second, calculate the sum of the three present values: $365,139. Third, subtract the initial investment of $300,000, getting a net present value of $65,139. On the basis of the NPV rule, the project should be accepted.

The net present value can also be calculated using a spreadsheet NPV function. In Excel, select "Insert" from the menu, then "Function," then function category "Financial," then "NPV." Note that the form of this function is PV(rate, value1, value2, ...). Using our notation, rate is the discount rate, or r, *in decimal form;* value1 is the net cash flow one year from now; value2 is

FIGURE 9.31   Spreadsheet Net Present Value Example

	A	B	C	D	E
1	rate	.10			
2	initial investment	−300			
3	value1	100	=B2+NPV(B1,B3,B4,B5) ⟶		65.139
4	value2	150	or =B2+NPV(B1,B3:B5)		
5	value3	200			

the net cash inflow two years from now; and so on. In the example above, chose a particular cell and enter

$$=-300+\text{NPV}(.10,100,150,200)$$

The same answer as above (in thousands of dollars), 65.139, should appear.

Alternatively, to create a more transparent and general function, enter the information separately from the function, as indicated in Figure 9.31.

The greatest challenges with the net present value rule are determining realistic cash flow estimates and determining an appropriate hurdle rate.

9.4.3   Internal Rate of Return

While the net present value method has tremendous intuitive appeal, a related measure is often more popular in practice. The internal rate of return (IRR) measure is actually similar to the yield to maturity measure for bonds. The technique solves for the discount rate that results in a zero NPV project. Unlike the NPV method that gives a dollar value for the amount of value added, the IRR method gives a percentage return to assess the viability of the project. While the NPV rule states that a firm (not facing any capital constraints) should accept any project with a net present value greater than or equal to zero, the IRR rule states that a firm should accept any projects with an internal rate of return greater than or equal to a prespecified hurdle rate. Note that the hurdle rate should be the same as the discount rate used in the NPV assessment. Consequently, both NPV and IRR decisions should be consistent (at least for most straightforward situations with an initial cash outflow and subsequent cash inflows).

In the example described above, the firm is considering an investment of $300,000 and anticipates net cash inflows in the next three years of $100,000,

$150,000, and $200,000. The appropriate *hurdle* rate is assumed to be 10 percent. What is the internal rate of return of this project and should it be accepted?

For a multiperiod problem, it turns out that there is no easy method to calculate the IRR by hand or even using many standard financial calculators (except for a brute-force trial-and-error process). However, the process is quite straightforward using spreadsheets (as well as some more-advanced calculators).

In Excel, select "Insert" from the menu, then "Function," then function category "Financial," then "IRR." Note that the form of this function is IRR(values, guess). The values must be specified in a very particular manner. The first value is the initial cash outflow, expressed as a negative number, such as –300. The subsequent values represent the net cash flows, first starting one year from now (100), then two years from now (150), then three years from now (200). This process would continue for as many years as appropriate. The guess represents a guess of what the IRR might be (in fact, the spreadsheet function is based on an iterative trial-and-error process and needs a reasonable place to start for some complex problems). In most cases, simply starting with the hurdle rate or even 0.10 should suffice. In the example above, choose a particular cell and enter

$$=IRR(-300,100,150,200,.10)$$

The answer 20.61% should appear.

Alternatively, to create a more transparent and general function, enter the information separately from the function, as indicated in Figure 9.32.

In this example, consistent with our NPV analysis, the IRR of 20.61 percent is above the hurdle rate of 10 percent, so the project should be accepted.

FIGURE 9.32   Spreadsheet Internal Rate of Return Example

	A	B	C	D	E
1	guess	.10			
2	initial investment	–300			
3	value1	100	=IRR(B2,B3,B4,B5,B1)	→	20.61%
4	value2	150	or =IRR(B2:B5,B1)		
5	value3	200			

There is one major cautionary note related to the IRR method. An implicit assumption is that any cash inflows generated in the earlier years can be reinvested (for example, in other new projects) at the rate of the IRR. In many cases, this is not a realistic assumption. While it does not impact on the accept or reject decision in our example, the resulting rate of return should be interpreted cautiously.

9.5   Summary

1. The business decision-making framework involves five steps: definition of decision to be made, determination of criteria to be used to evaluate alternatives, generation of alternatives, analysis and assessment of alternatives, and decision and implementation.
2. The time value of money implies that one dollar today is worth more than one dollar tomorrow due primarily to the opportunity cost of forgoing consumption today.
3. A time line is an essential tool in analyzing time value of money problems.
4. Basic time value of money concepts include present values and future values of single amounts, and present values and future values of annuities.
5. Bond valuation, preferred share valuation, and common share valuation all represent applications of the time value of money.
6. A fundamental bond valuation concept is that bond prices move inversely to changes in yields (or interest rates).
7. The constant growth dividend discount model highlights the importance of growth and riskiness as stock valuation drivers.
8. The payback method is the simplest capital budgeting technique but ignores the time value of money.
9. Net present value estimates the net addition to the firm by accepting a project with a particular initial investment and projected net cash flows.
10. The internal rate of return method estimates the discount rate such that the net present value of a project is just equal to zero.

9.6   Additional Readings

See any of the corporate finance textbooks listed at the end of chapter 1.

9.7   Self-Study Problems

1. Calculate the future value (FV) in three years of a cash outflow of $100 today and a cash outflow of $150 in one year, assuming an investment rate of 9 percent.
2. Calculate the present value (PV) of a cash inflow of $500 in one year and a cash inflow of $1,000 in five years, assuming a discount rate of 15 percent.
3. Calculate the future value (FV) in five years of an annuity stream of five annual cash flows of $1,200, with the first cash flow received in one year, assuming a discount rate of 10 percent.
4. Calculate the present value (PV) of an annuity stream of five annual cash flows of $1,200, with the first cash flow received in one year, assuming a discount rate of 10 percent.
5. This chapter has described the fundamental bond relationship between interest rates and bond prices. Two other relationships are "For a given change in interest rates, long-term bond prices fluctuate more than short-term bond prices" and "For a given change in interest rates, low coupon bond prices fluctuate more than high coupon bond prices." Present numerical examples of each of these concepts.

10. Valuation: Measurement and Creation of Value

This chapter is the second of two chapters examining the investment decisions of the firm. It focuses specifically on the measurement and creation of value for the firm as a whole (as opposed to an individual project) and integrates many of the concepts examined earlier in this book. Traditional firm valuation techniques are presented, such as discounted cash flow analysis and price-earnings analysis. As well, the concept of value-based management and the measurement of economic value added (EVA) are addressed. Essentially, such approaches attempt to measure the ability of management to increase value for common shareholders. One attempt to increase value is often through the firm merger or acquisition process. Other methods of corporate restructuring are also available.

10.1 Valuation Overview

We encounter valuation issues in numerous business settings. For example, a private firm may be considering going public through the IPO process. Alternatively, management of an existing public company may be considering taking the firm private through a management buyout (MBO) or a leveraged buyout (LBO). A firm may be considering divesting itself of or spinning-off one of its divisions. Finally, a firm may be considering acquiring another firm or merging with it. In each case, it is critical to be able to measure the value of the firm (or part of the firm) to establish a fair price at which to buy or sell.

Measurement of value is only part of the story. Once we have a handle on what we feel an existing business is worth, we are in a better position to assess how additional value can be created. For example, if a firm is determined to be at a nonoptimal capital structure level, then by changing the capital structure, value may be created. Alternatively, increased efficiencies or partnerships may reduce costs, thereby increasing cash flows and firm value.

If a firm is publicly traded, then one can argue that its value (or specifically its market value of equity) is simply the current stock price times the number of shares outstanding. While this is clearly an important and straightforward measure of value, the appropriateness of this measure depends on your belief in the efficiency of markets. In addition, in the case of a potential acquisition, hidden value may be unlocked by utilizing existing assets in a manner different from their current use. Thus we begin by focusing on the first challenge of simply measuring value, then turn our attention to the issue of creating additional value.

10.2 Measuring Firm Value

There are a number of techniques for measuring firm value. Probably the most important and certainly the most conceptually appealing is the discounted cash flow approach that relies on the time value of money concepts described in chapter 9. However, there are a number of alternative techniques as well. The price-earnings approach provides a shorthand assessment of how many times projected earnings an investor should be willing to pay for a stock. Alternative approaches focus on cash or revenues rather than earnings. We investigate each of these approaches.

10.2.1 Discounted Cash Flow Analysis

Discounted cash flow (DCF) analysis is an extension of previously introduced time value concepts. While there are a number of different approaches, the essential elements involve projecting cash flows, estimating the present value of those cash flows, and adding them together to estimate value. When we discuss value, we ultimately tend to refer to the value of the *common equity* of the firm. Note that this is quite different from the value of the firm's assets since assets are equal to both the liabilities of the firm as well as the equity of the firm. There are two different approaches to valuing the equity of the firm. One is a direct approach that estimates the cash flows available directly to the shareholders. We are going to focus on the indirect (but generally more popular) approach that focuses first on the overall value of the firm and second on the value of its equity. The intuition behind this approach is to think of the value of a firm's equity as the value of the entire business less the claims by other investors such as creditors and preferred shareholders. We begin with an overview of the process, then outline five steps involved in the calculations, and then present a numerical example.

We begin with the concept of *free cash flows* (FCF). Free cash flows are the cash flows available (or free) to all stakeholders (including bondholders, preferred shareholders, and common shareholders) after accounting for operating expenses, taxes, provisions for capital expenditures, and provisions for changes in working capital requirements. The actual calculation is presented in Figure 10.1 and described in more detail below.

Cash flows after operating expenses are what we referred to earlier as earnings before interest and taxes, or EBIT. At this point, we have accounted for all costs associated with producing the good or providing the service but we have not yet accounted for taxes or any financing charges such as the interest on any money borrowed. We must then account for the taxes on these operating earnings. For example, if the tax rate is 35 percent (or 0.35), we would take 65 percent (or 0.65) of the before-tax earnings to estimate the after-tax earnings, or in other words we would multiply EBIT by (1 − tax rate).

In most situations, we assume a business is growing over time. If this is the case, then most firms need to invest to grow. For example, if a firm has depreciating assets such as a plant and equipment, at a minimum the firm will need to replace these depreciating assets. If a firm were not growing, we would expect capital expenditures to approximately offset the amount of depreciation. If the business were growing over time, then we would expect capital expenditures to exceed depreciation.

FIGURE 10.1   Free Cash Flow Formula

FCF = EBIT(1 − tax rate) + noncash expenses − capital expenditures
− net increases in working capital

Finally, recall our examination of working capital needs in chapter 4. If a business is growing, it may be experiencing an increasing gap (in dollar terms) between current assets, such as accounts receivable, and inventory and current liabilities, such as accounts payable. Just as a growing firm must be prepared to set aside money for increased capital expenditures, it must also be prepared to set aside money for increased working capital needs.

Note that free cash flows appear to be ignoring any financing costs such as the interest expense on borrowing. We are not ignoring such financing issues but rather incorporating them into the discount rate we will use to discount any future cash flows. The discount rate is equivalent to the cost of capital we estimated previously, which incorporates the cost of the various forms of financing, including debt, preferred shares, and common equity.

Our approach focuses on estimating the value of the firm as a whole or the value of the firm's assets. Since we are ultimately interested in the value of the firm's common equity, we need to subtract the value of any of the firm's debt and preferred equity outstanding.

We now outline the five-step process to estimating the value of a firm's equity in Figure 10.2. Some new terms, such as *terminal value* are described below.

Step 1 involves estimating the cost of capital, as described in chapter 7. Recall that the weighted average cost of capital is estimated as $K_c = w_d K_d + w_p K_p + w_e K_e$, where the w's represent the weights and the K's represent the cost of debt, preferred shares, and common equity. This cost of capital will be used as the discount rate for calculating the present value of future cash flows.

Step 2 involves estimating future annual free cash flows. Many of the components of the free cash flow estimate have been described above, includ-

FIGURE 10.2   Discounted Free Cash Flows Approach

1. Estimate the cost of capital.
2. Estimate annual free cash flows.
3. Calculate the present value of the free cash flows for the next number of years.
4. Estimate a terminal value and a present value of the terminal value and add the latter to the other cash flow present values.
5. Subtract the value of any debt and other noncommon equity sources of capital.

ing taking the after-tax amount of the operating (EBIT) profits and subtracting both capital expenditures and net increases in working capital. The
remaining items relate to dealing with noncash items such as depreciation
and amortization. These items are added back since they do not affect the
cash position of the firm.

An important issue relates to the number of years of free cash flow estimates that need to be estimated. While there is no set rule, industry practice suggests five to ten years is a reasonable amount of time. Most firms
have a reasonable idea of projected revenues and any major expenditures
in the next five to ten years. A guiding principle is that you should project
out a number of years until you are willing to make an assumption that free
cash flows will grow at a constant rate beyond that time.

Step 3 involves calculating the present value of the anticipated free cash
flows for the next five to ten years using the cost of capital as the discount
rate. We are assuming that the cost of capital will remain the same throughout the entire estimation period. The discounting process is the same as
described in chapter 9. It is always worthwhile to draw a time line as in
Figure 10.3 to visualize the task at hand. We will refer to this time line as
part 1 since we have not yet dealt with cash flows beyond the five- to ten-
year period. Note that we are implicitly assuming that any cash flows are
occurring at the end of each year.

Step 4 involves estimating a terminal value (*TV*) and then calculating
its present value. The terminal value represents the value, as of the last year
of annual forecasts, of all free cash flows beyond that point in time. In other
words, the terminal value represents the value of a perpetuity of cash flows.
There are a number of approaches to deal with a terminal value. One method
would be to simply estimate what the firm might be worth at some future
point in time (say in five years) and then take the present value of that

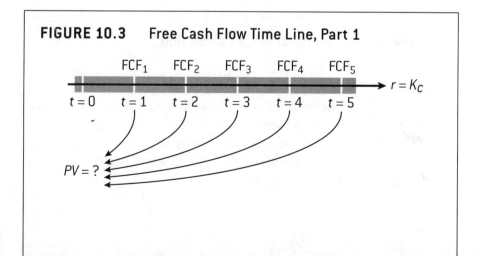

FIGURE 10.3   Free Cash Flow Time Line, Part 1

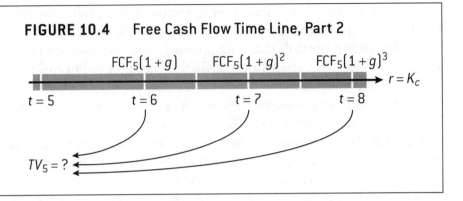

FIGURE 10.4 Free Cash Flow Time Line, Part 2

amount. A more common method is to make an assumption that free cash flows will grow at a constant rate beyond that point in time.

Suppose we have specified five years of projected free cash flows and have calculated the present value of those free cash flows as in Figure 10.3. Consider, for now, an extended time line that starts at $t = 5$ instead of the usual $t = 0$. The reason we are going to do this is because we wish to determine the value, *at time* $t = 5$, of all cash flows beyond $t = 5$. In other words, consider free cash flows at $t = 6$, $t = 7$, and so on. Recall our assumption that these free cash flows will grow at a constant rate in perpetuity starting at this point. Recall our constant growth approach to valuing a dividend-paying stock as present in Figures 9.26 and 9.27. Our new extended time line is present in Figure 10.4.

We know from chapter 9 that the value of the future cash flows, as of $t = 5$ (or TV_5), will be as in Figure 10.5.

The final part of step 4 involves calculating the present value of the terminal value. This is a straightforward calculation.

$$PV \text{ of } TV_5 = TV_5/(1 + K_c)^5$$

FIGURE 10.5 Terminal Value Calculation

$$TV_5 = [FCF_5(1+g)]/(K_c - g)$$

where TV_5 = terminal value of free cash flows as of $t = 5$
K_c = cost of capital
FCF_5 = estimated free cash flow as of $t = 5$
g = anticipated constant growth rate of free cash flows beyond $t = 5$

FIGURE 10.6   Free Cash Flow Time Line, Parts 1 and 2 Combined

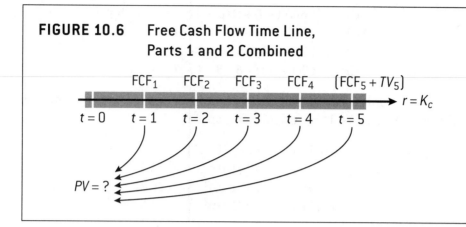

We can combine the two time lines as in Figure 10.6. We have now estimated the overall value of the firm (V_F), or the value of the firm's assets.

Step 5 involves simply subtracting any debt and other related obligations (V_D) in order to arrive at the value of the firm's equity (V_E), which is our ultimate goal.

$$V_E = V_F - V_D$$

Note that throughout this process, we have been focusing on free cash flows available to all stakeholders: bondholders, preferred shareholders, and common equity shareholders. Since we are focusing on the value to the common shareholders, we subtract the value of claims by those other stakeholders. This would include the value of debt and any preferred shares outstanding.

Consider the following numerical example of the discounted free cash flow process. Suppose a firm is anticipated to earn before interest and taxes (EBIT) $40,000, $50,000, and $60,000 in each of the next three years. Depreciation is estimated to be $4,000, $5,000, and $6,000 in each of the next three years. Capital expenditures are estimated to be $6,000, $7,000, and $8,000 in each of the next three years. Incremental increases in working capital requirements are estimated to be $2,000, $3,000, and $4,000 in each of the next three years. The tax rate is 40 percent, while the cost of capital is estimated to be 10 percent. Free cash flows beyond year 3 are estimated to grow at an annual rate of 3 percent. The current value of existing debt is $100,000. What is an estimate of the value of the equity?

Since step 1 is completed and we know the cost of capital is 10 percent, we can proceed directly to step 2 and estimate the annual free cash flows. The calculations are

$$\begin{aligned}
\text{FCFs} &= \text{EBIT}(1-t) + \text{Dep} - \text{CapEx} - \text{WCchg} \\
\text{FCF}_1 &= 40(1-0.4) + 4 - 6 - 2 = 20 \\
\text{FCF}_2 &= 50(1-0.4) + 5 - 7 - 3 = 25 \\
\text{FCF}_3 &= 60(1-0.4) + 6 - 8 - 4 = 30
\end{aligned}$$

Step 3 involves calculating the present value of the free cash flows for the next three years. Those calculations are

$$\begin{aligned}
PV \text{ of } FCF_t &= FCF_t/(1+K_c)^t \\
PV \text{ of } FCF_1 &= 20/(1.10) &= 18.2 \\
PV \text{ of } FCF_2 &= 25/(1.10)^2 &= 20.7 \\
PV \text{ of } FCF_3 &= 30/(1.10)^3 &= \underline{22.5} \\
& & 61.4
\end{aligned}$$

Step 4 involves estimating a terminal value, calculating the present value of the terminal value, and adding it to the present value of the other free cash flows in order to estimate the value of the firm. The calculation is

$$\begin{aligned}
TV_t &= [FCF_t(1+g)]/(K_c - g) \\
PV \text{ of } TV_t &= TV_t/(1+K_c)^t \\
TV_3 &= 30(1.03)/(0.10 - 0.03) &= 441.4 \\
PV \text{ of } TV_3 &= 441.4/(1.10)^3 &= 331.6 \\
V_F &= \text{sum of all FCFs} &= 61.4 + 331.6 = 393.0
\end{aligned}$$

Finally, step 5 involves subtracting any debt obligations from the value of the firm in order to estimate the value of equity. The calculation is

$$\begin{aligned}
V_E &= V_F - V_D \\
&= 393.0 - 100.0 = 293.0
\end{aligned}$$

There are some final observations related to the discounted free cash flow approach. In practice, it is often challenging to estimate many of the parameters related to the discounted free cash flow process. For example, in a merger or acquisition situation one must carefully assess the resulting business risk to determine an appropriate cost of capital. In general, annual free cash flow estimates are often based on projected revenues as a starting point but projected capital expenditures and working capital changes are more difficult to estimate. As well, the appropriate tax rate is not necessarily based on the previous year's tax rate (particularly if the year was not a typical one in terms of tax payments) but rather based on the anticipated tax rate. Finally, care must be taken in terms of determining the appropriate point at which to estimate a terminal value.

10.2.2   Price-Earnings and Comparable Analyses

Recall in chapter 8 we briefly introduced the price-earnings valuation model. According to the model, the amount common share investors are willing to pay for a share is based on two components. The first component is the projected earnings per share. The second component is a consensus in the marketplace as to how many times the projected earnings a stock is worth. We formalize the model in Figure 10.7 and then describe the components in more detail.

Once the common share price is estimated, the overall value of the firm's common equity is estimated by multiplying the value of a common share times the number of common shares outstanding. Note that this method values the common equity directly.

The forecasted earnings per share estimate is usually based on the subsequent year provided that year is representative of future years (that is, there are no extraordinary gains or losses or an unusual impact on revenues). For publicly traded companies, such information has become more readily available through consensus forecasts by analysts and provided through various financial information services. If such information is not available or if the firm is private, then we can rely on the forecasted income statement analysis presented in chapter 5.

Determining an appropriate price-earnings multiple is more challenging. The process often involves *comparable analysis* of other similar companies in the same industry. The approach involves examining similar firms and estimating their average price-earnings multiple. A similar company is one that experiences similar growth, risk, financial leverage, and dividend payout, although the two primary factors are growth and riskiness. Since the price-earnings multiple reflects the growth prospects and riskiness of the firm, a related approach estimates a simple industry-wide price-

---

FIGURE 10.7   **Price-Earnings Valuation Model**

$$P_0 = \text{appropriate } P/\mathcal{E} \text{ multiple} (EPS_1)$$

$$
\begin{aligned}
\text{where } P_0 &= \text{estimated price per share today} \\
\text{appropriate } P/\mathcal{E} \text{ multiple} &= \text{number based on comparables} \\
&\quad\ \text{assessment} \\
EPS_1 &= \text{projected earnings per share} \\
&\quad\ \text{next year}
\end{aligned}
$$

earnings average, then adjusts that amount either upward or downward depending on the perceived growth prospects and riskiness of the firm. For example, if the firm is deemed to have greater growth prospects than the industry average, then (all else equal) it should be assigned a higher multiple (recall "Growth is good"). Alternatively, if the firm is deemed to have more risk than the industry average, then (all else equal) it should be assigned a lower multiple ("Risk is rotten"). In many situations, assigning a multiple becomes as much an art as a science in attempting to balance growth and risk considerations. It is important to highlight that, at any point in time, we would expect to see average industry multiples vary considerably. Similarly, even within an industry, we would expect to see average multiples vary over time as overall industry (and market) conditions change. As a rough guideline, historically in North America, market-wide price-earnings multiples have averaged around 15 to 17.

While apparently very different looking, the price-earnings model is actually strongly connected to the constant growth dividend discount model presented in chapter 9. Recall the formulation $P_o = DIV_1/(r-g)$, where P_o is the current price of the common share, r is the required return by common share investor, DIV_1 is the anticipated dividend in one period, and g is the constant growth rate of dividends. If we assume a constant payout K of dividends from earnings, we can rewrite the formula to incorporate earnings per share.

$$P_o = KEPS_1/(r-g)$$

Rearranging, we can solve for the price-earnings multiple.

$$P_o/EPS_1 = K/(r-g)$$

Thus, this analysis confirms that the price-earnings multiple is directly related to growth and inversely related to risk.

Some final comments related to price-earnings multiples are in order. Do not confuse these multiples with the price-earnings multiples often reported in the financial press. While we have focused on *forward-looking* multiples based on the future prospects of the firm, the financial press reports *trailing* multiples: the current stock price divided by the earnings over the past year. Also, most analysts do not rely on one single valuation method. However, a second (or third) measure should act as a check on other measures. If assumptions are consistent, alternative approaches should result in similar valuation results. If you use two different methods and come up with large valuation variations, then you should reexamine the assumptions you have made.

10.2.3 Other Valuation Methods

Although the price-earnings approach is generally the most common valuation multiple technique, in some industries other multiples are more appropriate. For example, in many resource-based industries as well as telecommunications industries price-to-cash flow multiples are most popular. A related measure examines the ratio of share price to earnings before interest, taxes, depreciation, and amortization, or EBITDA. The EBITDA measure is often a simple proxy for cash flows. If a firm is in a very early industry life-cycle stage and has not generated a consistent stream of earnings, the price-to-sales ratios are often more relevant. In general, the valuation process is as in Figure 10.8.

Conglomerates often pose an interesting challenge from a valuation perspective as they involve a number of different business groups. As such, one valuation technique focuses on assessing the breakup value of these conglomerates, or the value that might be captured if each division were sold separately.

Whatever valuation technique is used, it must be recognized that any results, either through simple calculations or through more elaborate spreadsheets, are only as good as the assumptions that underlie the models.

10.3 Value Creation and Value-Based Management

Up to this point, we have focused on the measurement of the value of a firm. This was a critical first step before examining management in order to create value. There is a growing trend among corporations to fulfill their mandate

---

Figure 10.8   Other Valuation Models

$$P_0 = (\text{appropriate } P/\text{variable multiple})\text{variable}_1$$

where P_0 = estimated value per share today

appropriate $P/$variable multiple = number based on comparables assessment

variable_1 = projected variable per share next year

Variables may include sales, cash flows, or EBIT.

to maximize shareholder value by implementing value-based management programs. Probably the most popular is the *economic value added*, or EVA, approach instituted by the Stern Stewart consulting group. We examine the EVA approach as well as related value-based management programs. We also examine the special case of mergers and acquisitions, as well as other corporate restructurings, which attempt to add value as well.

10.3.1 The EVA Approach

Economic value added is an overall approach to the measurement of value creation as well as a process for attempting to create value. The idea is that managers cannot add value until they know where and how value can be created. Thus EVA is often viewed as both a measurement tool and a management process.

The EVA concept is fairly simple. It suggests that in order to make relevant business decisions, we must consider all costs associated with those decisions. Typical financial statements, while extremely useful for many purposes, have shortcomings related to business decision making. Financial statements do not present all relevant information related to the economic costs associated with generating revenues. In particular, the cost of raising equity and the return required by equity shareholders does not appear on the income statement. Yet we know from our discussion of the cost of capital, equity is not free. The EVA approach attempts to measure "true" economic profit. As such, proponents of EVA claim that the EVA measure is more closely related to changes in shareholder value (i.e., changes in stock prices) than changes in accounting measures such as earnings per share.

The underlying assumptions related to EVA are similar to the assumptions presented earlier related to the discounted cash flow (DCF) approach to firm valuation. A business is worth the present value of anticipated net cash flows discounted at the cost of capital, less the amount invested to generate future cash flows. Thus there are three key value drivers: net operating profits after tax (NOPAT), which are similar to part of the free cash flow concept, $EBIT(1 - t)$; the investment in capital; and the cost of capital. The EVA approach helps to carefully define the first two value drivers by starting with accounting statements and making adjustments where appropriate to reflect true profits and investments and incorporates the third value driver by accounting for all forms of financing, including equity financing.

The EVA is a one-period measure of true economic performance just as earnings after tax are a one-period measure of accounting profit. The EVA is defined for a particular period, such as a year, as in Figure 10.9.

FIGURE 10.9   Economic Value Added 1

$$EVA = EBIT(1-t) - \text{invested capital}(K_c)$$
$$= NOPAT - \text{invested capital}(K_c)$$
$$= NOPAT - \text{capital charge}$$

where EVA = economic value added
EBIT = earnings before interest and taxes
t = tax rate
NOPAT = net operating profit after taxes
invested capital = amount of permanent financing (debt and equity)
K_c = cost of capital

We can interpret EVA in a number of ways. Based on the formulation above, EVA is the net operating profit less an opportunity cost for *all* invested capital. This idea was first introduced in chapter 7, particularly in the example presented in Figure 7.4. Note that traditional financial statements include only interest costs associated with any debt and not the return required or expected by equityholders. The EVA can also be interpreted as the amount by which profits exceed (or fall short of) the required minimum rate of return investors could receive by investing in other securities of comparable risk.

We can also represent EVA in a slightly different (but equivalent) manner, as in Figure 10.10. In this formulation, we reinterpret NOPAT as the return on capital employed (ROCE) times the amount of capital invested or employed. The ROCE is also referred to as the return on net assets, or RONA.

Figure 10.10   Economic Value Added 2

$$EVA = NOPAT - K_c(\text{invested capital})$$
$$= ROCE(\text{invested capital}) - (K_c)(\text{invested capital})$$
$$= (ROCE - K_c)\text{invested capital}$$

where EVA = economic value added
NOPAT = net operating profit after taxes
ROCE = return on capital employed
invested capital = amount of permanent financing (debt and equity)
K_c = cost of capital

FIGURE 10.11   NOPAT Calculation Example

Revenue	$45m
Operating expenses	$30m
Operating profit	$15m
Taxes (at 40%)	$6m
NOPAT	$9m

We can now focus on what factors drive EVA. We can clearly see that EVA depends on both the amount of capital employed as well as the *spread* between ROCE and K_c. Thus one key to creating value is to identify opportunities or market segments where a firm has a competitive advantage and is able to earn a positive spread or where the market structure is such that the overall sector is profitable. Identifying such opportunities or markets relates back to our discussion of business size-up in chapter 2.

Consider the following simple example. Suppose a firm generates revenues of $45 million, incurs operating expenses of $30 million, has a tax rate of 40 percent, and has a capital structure consistent with $50 million in debt and $50 million in common equity. The cost of debt (before tax) is 8 percent while the required return on equity is 12 percent. What is the EVA for the year?

The first step is to calculate NOPAT as described in Figure 10.11.

The second step is to calculate the total amount of capital employed. In this situation it is a straightforward addition of the debt of $50 million and the equity of $50 million, for a total amount of capital of $100 million.

The third step is to calculate the cost of capital. The familiar calculation is described in Figure 10.12.

FIGURE 10.12   Cost of Capital Calculation Example

TYPE OF CAPITAL	COST (AFTER TAX)	WEIGHT	WEIGHTED COST
Debt	8%(1 − 0.4) = 4.8%	50%	2.4%
Equity	12%	50%	6.0%
Cost of capital (K_c)			8.4%

FIGURE 10.13   EVA Calculation Example

$$
\begin{aligned}
\text{EVA} &= \text{NOPAT} - \text{capital charge} \\
&= \$9m - \$100m(8.4\%) \\
&= \$9m - \$8.4m \\
&= \$0.6m
\end{aligned}
$$

The final step is to calculate EVA as in Figure 10.13. Thus in this example, the firm is creating value for its shareholders by providing its equity shareholders with a return that exceeds the required return of the shareholders.

In this simple example we have assumed that the accounting measures truly reflected economic realities. In most situations, this is not the case. As such we need to make adjustments to both NOPAT and capital. For example, if a firm buys another business and pays more than the book value of that business, goodwill is created. Standard accounting practices suggest that a portion of the goodwill should be written off as an annual expense. However, the EVA approach suggests that investors expect a return on the goodwill amount, which is why the firm was willing to pay such a price initially. As such, NOPAT should be adjusted by adding goodwill expenses, and capital should be adjusted by adding accumulated goodwill. While Stern Stewart has identified more than one hundred possible adjustments, for most firms only a handful of adjustments are required.

One criticism of EVA is that it is simply a one-period performance measure and it is historical. As a response to this criticism, Stern Stewart created a related measure known as *market value added*, or MVA, defined in Figure 10.14.

The market value of the firm is the market value of the firm's debt plus preferred shares plus common equity. Invested capital is the total amount invested initially by the various stakeholders. A positive MVA indicates the market believes the firm has created value for its stakeholders. An alternative interpretation of MVA is that it represents the present value of anticipated EVAs, discounted at the appropriate cost of capital. Thus while a firm might

---

FIGURE 10.14   Market Value Added

$$\text{MVA} = \text{market value of the firm} - \text{invested capital}$$

have had a negative EVA last year, it still might have a positive MVA if the market anticipates future EVAs to be positive.

Given our discussion of EVA, how can a firm hope to create value? One way is to improve the rate of return on the existing capital base, or increase the NOPAT relative to the current amount of capital employed. This could result from either increased revenues or decreased costs. Another method is for the firm to invest more capital in attractive projects with positive spreads or with returns that exceed the cost of capital. Yet another method is for a firm to stop investing in unattractive projects that have returns less than the appropriate cost of capital.

The EVA can be used in a variety of ways. It can be used to set goals and to gauge performance against competitors. It can be used for capital budgeting decisions. It can also be used as a measure to develop compensation incentives. The EVA has the benefit of being conceptually simple, applicable to business units (in addition to the firm as a whole), and correlated with stock price performance. There are, however, a number of limitations. Much training and education is required at all levels within an organization to use it. Commitment is required from top management. An appropriate cost measurement system is required. Compensation plans may need to be amended. Employees need to maintain a forward-looking outlook despite the backward-looking nature of the measure.

10.3.2 Mergers and Acquisitions and Other Restructuring

An important way that many firms attempt to add value is through mergers and acquisitions (M&As). Such M&As have long played an important role in the growth of firms. Firms can either grow internally, through retained earnings, or externally, through additional financing or through M&As. A merger involves a transaction that forms a new economic unit from two or more units. Mergers usually imply the melding of firms of similar size. An acquisition has a similar outcome but usually involves a much larger firm acquiring control of a smaller firm.

There are many reasons why one firm might wish to merge with or acquire another firm. One reason is the possibility of lowering costs, for example, through stronger purchasing power or greater management efficiency. Thus through synergies, the combined entity should be worth more than the value of each firm as a separate entity. This is the "two plus two equals five" argument.

A related reason, aside from pure synergies such as economies of scale or the ability to increase profits through cross-selling, is that one firm's management team perceives the current management of another firm to be inefficient in its operations of that firm and feels they could do a better job. "Agency problems" can arise since management is acting as agents on behalf of the principals, the shareholders. If management is more concerned with their own well-being or perks of the job, then shareholders may ultimately suffer. An acquisition can alleviate agency problems.

Often M&A activity occurs in cycles and is concentrated in certain industries at various times. In order to be successful, a firm's corporate strategy must be appropriate, funding must be available, new value must be identified, and the economic environment must be positive. If success is defined from the perspective of shareholder returns before and after the merger, not all mergers are successful. Sometimes, firms overpay relative to the actual value of the acquired firm due to overoptimistic assumptions. For example, forecasted economic conditions and synergistic gains may not be reasonable. Postintegration may be more problematic than anticipated. As well, in the heat of the battle, a firm may simply overpay.

In many ways, valuation in a M&A situation is similar to other valuation situations. For example, discounted cash flows can be estimated and comparable analysis can be performed. However, there are some unique considerations. For example, the value placed on a target firm by a potential buyer may differ from the value placed on the firm by the potential seller. The potential seller looks at the business from the perspective of running it as is while the potential buyer looks at it from the perspective of any value added through synergies as well as increased management efficiencies.

Consider the framework in Figure 10.15. This framework addresses the issue of how much a target buyer should be willing to pay. The first component, value to (potential) seller, represents the current value of the firm to the present owners. This is what value the current owners can derive on the basis of the existing or planned operations of the business. This amount can be estimated by the DCF process described above.

FIGURE 10.15   Acquisition Valuation Model

Maximum value of
target firm to buyer = value to seller
                        + value added by buyer
                        + change in value to buyer if target
                           firm acquired by competitor

The second component, value added by (potential) buyer, consists of several components. One part is the present value of any estimated synergies such as cost savings by combining the two entities or other methods of running the operation more efficiently. A second part is the value added by the potential buyer through a new strategy from the acquisition such as taking advantage of new market opportunities that were not possible by the existing owners. The third part incorporates the value of any sale of redundant assets after the acquisition, such as the sale of property or buildings that are not required to run the combined entity. The fourth part is the present value of any financial benefits resulting from a revised credit rating or availability of funds.

The third and final component, change in value to buyer if target firm acquired by competitor, is very difficult to calculate but often quite important in some (but not all) situations. Quite frequently, a number of mergers and acquisitions take place in one industry among the largest competitors. For example, the second and third largest firms in the industry might announce a merger to become the largest firm in the industry, only to have this announcement followed by a reaction of the largest firm that it is acquiring another firm in order to remain the largest. Thus a potential acquirer must consider the implications if a potential target is acquired by a direct competitor.

By combining the three components, we have an estimate of the maximum value the buyer should be willing to pay. Quite clearly, this amount will be more than the current value to the seller. This difference demonstrates why a premium of 20 to 30 percent above the current target share price is often offered in acquisition situations.

While mergers and acquisitions are the most dramatic attempt at value creation, there are other forms of corporate restructuring. For example, a firm may decide to either sell or *spin off* one of its divisions. If the firm sells a division, it is simply attempting to get cash for the assets. It might feel that it can create more value by redeploying assets elsewhere within the firm. Alternatively, a spin-off involves creating a new entity, still owned by existing shareholders but run separately from the old firm. The general notion is that, particularly in a large conglomerate, sufficient attention or management incentives might not be in place to ensure shareholder value maximization. Additionally, analysts might undervalue the existing firm if some of the divisions are in very different businesses since it is often difficult to place one multiple on the cash flows from different businesses. Thus by spinning off a division, value creation often occurs. The combined value of old and new shares is usually worth more than the previous value of the shares.

10.4   Summary

1. The discounted cash flow (DCF) method is one of the most common valuation techniques. The cost of capital is estimated. Free cash flows are estimated by anticipating operating profits, capital expenditures, and working capital needs. Present values are estimated and the value of debt and related obligations are subtracted to obtain an estimate of the value of the firm's equity.

2. The price-earnings (*P/E*) approach estimates the value of equity (on a per-share basis) directly by forecasting expected earnings per share, then multiplying that amount by an appropriate *P/E* multiple. The multiple should reflect both the growth prospects as well as the perceived riskiness of the firm, particularly relative to other firms in the industry.

3. Economic value added (EVA) is a value-based management process and tool that attempts to measure value added and enhance the value creation process. The EVA is a measure of true economic profit and reflects the amount by which a firm's profits exceed the required minimum rate of return investors could receive by investing in other securities of comparable risk.

4. Valuation is important in a merger and acquisition (M&A) context whereby one firm acquires the assets of another firm. During this process, value is often created through synergies between the two firms.

10.5   Additional Readings

A thorough book on valuation is
Copeland, Tom, Tim Koller, and Jack Murrin. *Valuation: Measuring and Managing the Value of Companies.* 3rd ed. New York: Wiley, 2000.

Stern Stewart's economic value added approach is described in
Ehrbar, Al. *Stern Stewart's EVA: The Real Key to Creating Wealth.* New York: Wiley, 1998.

10.6   Self-Study Problems

1. Consider the following information. A firm is anticipated to make earnings before interest and taxes (EBIT) of $30,000, $40,000, and $50,000 in

each of the next three years. Depreciation is estimated to be $3,000, $3,500, and $4,000 in each of the next three years. Capital expenditures are estimated to be $8,000, $9,000, and $10,000 in each of the next three years. Incremental increases in working capital requirements are estimated to be $2,500, $3,000, and $3,500 in each of the next three years. The tax rate is 35 percent while the cost of capital is estimated to be 9 percent. Free cash flows beyond year 3 are estimated to grow at an annual rate of 4 percent. The current value of existing debt is $150,000. What is an estimate of the value of the equity?

2. A firm is expected to have before-tax earnings of $2.5 million next year. The tax rate is 35 percent. There are one million common shares outstanding. Comparable firms in the same industry are estimated to have price-earnings multiples of 10 to 16. Estimate the intrinsic value of the firm's share price using the price-earnings method.

3. A firm has EBIT of $1.5 million. The tax rate is 35 percent. The firm has debt of $2.5 million and common equity of $5 million. The firm's cost of capital is estimated to be 11 percent. Calculate the firm's EVA.

11. Comprehensive Case Study: Wal-Mart Stores

11.1 Putting It All Together

We now near the end of our journey through the world of finance. Before the journey ends, we can reflect on where we have come from and how each chapter has related to other pieces of the overall puzzle.

Recall our original goal: to acquire an understanding of key financial concepts. Three chapters (2, 3, and 4) were devoted to assessing the *current* business through a business size-up, performance measurement related to financial statement analysis, and day-to-day cash management. One chapter (5) was devoted to assessing *future* financing requirements through financial statement projections. Three chapters (6, 7, and 8) were devoted to making long-term financing decisions by understanding capital markets, determining the cost of capital, and examining issues related to raising long-term capital. Finally, two chapters (9 and 10) were devoted to understanding issues related to investments such as time value of money, as well as measuring and adding value.

The first part of the book laid the groundwork and established the importance of assessing a business from a variety of financial as well as non-financial perspectives. If we don't understand the industry and the business, then we are at a disadvantage when we try to interpret a firm's financial information. We are also at a disadvantage if we hope to be able to create value for the firm's common equity shareholders.

The second part of the book used the understanding of a firm's current position as a springboard to project a firm's future financial position. The understanding of financial ratios is crucial to the development of projected financial statements. Knowing the projected financial situation of the firm allows managers to take action today related to the need for any additional external financing such as bank loans.

The third part of the book turned the focus from short-term financing issues to long-term financial issues and from internal financing (through retained earnings) to external debt and equity financing. Various financial instruments and markets were described followed by an examination of the costs associated with each type of financing. The importance of determining an appropriate mix of financing was highlighted.

Finally, the fourth part of the book examined the assessment of investments, both in individual projects and in the firm as a whole. The measurement of value relied critically on an understanding of the firm's cost of capital as developed in the third part of the book. This last part examined ways that both financial and nonfinancial managers can attempt to add value for equity shareholders.

11.2   Wal-Mart Case Study

We are now in a position to apply our frameworks and techniques to a comprehensive case study of the world's largest retailer (as measured by revenues), Wal-Mart Stores. Based in Arkansas and founded by the legendary Sam Walton, Wal-Mart is the world's largest retailer and has over 4,000 stores worldwide, including stores in all 50 states as well as in Argentina, Brazil, Canada, Germany, Korea, Mexico, Puerto Rico, the United Kingdom; joint venture agreements in China; and a stake in a leading Japanese retail chain. Wal-Mart is best known for its discount stores (Wal-Mart Stores) but also runs combined discount and grocery stores (Wal-Mart Supercenters), membership-only warehouse stores (SAM's Club), and smaller grocery stores (Neighborhood Markets). In the spring of 2002, Wal-Mart had just released its results for the fiscal year ending January 31 and its shares were selling for around $60. How can we use the frameworks and techniques described in previous chapters to understand Wal-Mart's position in the industry and assess Wal-Mart's financial performance as well as its financial outlook in order to ultimately determine the appropriateness of the value of its shares?

The first step is to gather information. Major sources include the firm's annual report, as well as its Securities Exchange Commission (SEC) form

10-K filing (available through the SEC's Electronic Data Gathering, Analysis, and Retrieval system, or EDGAR). Additional sources of analysis include investment firm research reports. Basic financial information and links to additional data sources are available through many financial and information online Web sites, including reuters.com, bloomberg.com, moneycentral.msn.com, yahoo.com, and quicken.com. The second step is to perform an analysis of the gathered data.

11.2.1 Wal-Mart Size-up

We begin by assessing the current business of Wal-Mart through a business size-up of external factors, including an assessment of the economy and the industry. We continue our assessment of Wal-Mart by examining its internal strengths and weaknesses in the areas of operations, marketing, and management. We can identify both opportunities and risks facing Wal-Mart and the financial implications of each and assess the financial health of the firm through an analysis of financial ratios. One goal of the size-up is to be in a better position to meaningfully interpret Wal-Mart's financial information.

From an economic perspective, despite a mild recession in the United States in 2001, the outlook in 2002 was better than expected, although a number of uncertainties remained. Traditional economic indicators such as housing starts, auto purchases, new orders by manufacturers, and employment looked mildly positive. Much of the positive outlook had been attributed to the consumer segment. Consumers had benefited from lower taxes as well as lower interest rates. For example, between the first quarter of 2001 and the first quarter of 2002, 90-day T-bill rates dropped dramatically from around 6 percent to under 2 percent, and as lending rates also dropped, borrowing was much more affordable for consumers. Businesses substantially cut inventories in the fourth quarter of 2001, leaving firms poised for increases in production. The outlook was for real GDP growth above 3 percent annually with controlled inflation and increasing corporate profits. Interest rates were forecast to rise gradually but not dramatically.

In order to perform an industry assessment, we must first define the relevant industry or industries of interest. The broad industry category is retail sales, with five subindustries (Wal-Mart's largest product categories by sales) of grocery (including candy and tobacco), hardgoods (such as major appliances), softgoods (including garments and apparel), pharmacy, and electronics. From a life-cycle perspective, a strong case can be made that the overall retail industry, as well as most of the subindustries, are in a phase of stabilization. It is anticipated that any long-term growth in industry revenues will tend to occur at a similar rate to the overall economy. Thus the overall industry outlook can be described as neutral—not a growth industry but not one expected to be in decline in the near future either. The industry is anticipated to remain profitable.

Each country in which Wal-Mart competes has unique factors, but the general competitive environment is similar. Recall the five factors identified as the key contributors to the intensity of competition: ease of entry, availability of substitute products, the power of suppliers, the power of customers, and the extent of rivalry among current competitors. The retail industry is not particularly easy to enter given the many barriers, including large capital expenditures in plant and equipment and investments in distribution channels. There is a steady demand for both groceries and nonfood retail products, with no likely emergence of major substitute products. Suppliers appear to be numerous and thus do not appear to be a threat to profitability. Similarly, customers are individual consumers who do not wield major power. The largest impact on profit margins is related to the intensity of existing rivalries. In the general merchandise area, Wal-Mart's competitors include Sears and Target, with specialty apparel retailers including Gap and Limited. Department store competitors include Dillard, Federated, and J. C. Penney. Grocery store competitors include Kroger, Albertson, and Safeway. The major membership-only warehouse competitor is Costco Wholesale. While many of these competitors are formidable, Wal-Mart dominates due to its ability to achieve many of the industry key success factors described below. On the basis of net sales, the Wal-Mart Stores segment was the largest among all retail department and discount department store chains, and SAM's was number one among the warehouse club industry.

In order to succeed in the retail industry, firms need to strive to be the lowest cost producer or alternatively to be able to differentiate their products. In terms of groceries, given the commodity-based nature of the industry, product differentiation is difficult. In other retail areas, product differentiation may be possible, but price (and hence low costs) are a key success factor. Another key success factor is the ability of firms to deliver quality products. Both price and quality can be combined into value. Service is another important factor, including availability of products and postpurchase satisfaction. Developing a strong brand through marketing is also crucial. All of these key success factors have important financial implications. The pricing strategy of a firm impacts on its profitability. Management of cash flows is crucial to operate efficiently. Capital expenditures are required to maintain facilities and provide growth. Marketing expenditures need to be maintained.

An internal analysis of Wal-Mart's strengths and weaknesses in the areas of operations, marketing, and management will help us to examine Wal-Mart's ability to achieve the industry key success factors and better understand the financial analysis. In terms of its operations, Wal-Mart has a clear strategy of being the lowest-cost and lowest-priced competitor in the industry. By reducing costs, Wal-Mart can maintain its profit margin even with lower prices, thereby increasing market share and increasing overall profitability. Wal-Mart is renown for its efficiency of centralized distribution and inventory control. Its clearly stated objective is to maximize sales volume and inventory turnover while minimizing expenses. In terms of distribution, approximately 84 percent of Wal-Mart's discount stores' and Supercenters' merchandise purchases were shipped from Wal-Mart's 72 distribution centers.

Wal-Mart attempts to have a special relationship with its customers from the time they walk through the doors and are met by the famous Wal-Mart greeters until they make their purchases. Marketing emphasizes the everyday low prices of Wal-Mart and attempts to capture a local connection with customers in particular communities. In order to meet competitive pressures, Wal-Mart employs many programs, including Everyday Low Prices and Price Rollbacks.

The Walton family's Wal-Mart presence is felt through Sam Walton's son S. Robson Walton, who is the chair of the board. Insiders, including Walton family members, own 40 percent of outstanding shares. A major strength has been the Wal-Mart culture.

In terms of overall opportunities, Wal-Mart's size and dominant position give it tremendous clout relative to its competitors and allow it to pursue its successful low-cost and low-price strategy. In the United States, Wal-Mart has the opportunity to increase its market share relative to its competitors. Internationally, Wal-Mart has made great inroads in selective global locations but still has room to grow.

Risks can generically be described as factors outside of Wal-Mart's direct control. The 10-K form lists factors that could materially affect Wal-Mart's financial performance, which include changes in the cost of goods, expenses such as electricity, competitive pressures, inflation, consumer debt levels, currency exchange fluctuations, trade restrictions, unemployment levels, and interest rate fluctuations. Most likely risks include a slowdown in consumer spending, particularly on higher-margin products, and increased price competition, forcing Wal-Mart to sacrifice margin.

Wal-Mart's 2002 financial statements are presented in the figures. The income statement is presented in Figure 11.1, the balance sheet is presented in Figure 11.2, and the cash flow statement is presented in Figure 11.3. Net sales in fiscal year ending January 31, 2002, grew by almost 14 percent, while net income, as well as earnings per share, grew by 6 percent. Part of this difference in growth rates is attributable to the changing mix of Wal-Mart's sales, with an increase in the lower-margin grocery sector. Assets grew by 7 percent. Cash provided by operating activities also grew by 7 percent. Wal-Mart continued to invest heavily in capital expenditures (i.e., property, plant, and equipment). Wal-Mart's cash provided by operating activities exceeded its cash requirements for investing, allowing it to use cash to pay down debt and also buy back some shares.

FIGURE 11.1   Wal-Mart Income Statements

FOR YEAR ENDED JANUARY 31 (IN $MILLIONS)	2002	2001
Revenues		
Net sales	217,799	191,329
Other income, net	2,013	1,966
Total revenues	219,812	193,295
Cost of goods sold	171,562	150,255
Gross profit	48,250	43,040
Expenses		
Operating, selling, and general and administrative expenses	36,173	31,550
Interest expenses, net	1,326	1,374
Total expenses	37,499	32,924
Earnings (income) before taxes and minority interest	10,751	10,116
Income tax	3,897	3,692
Earnings (income) before minority interest	6,854	6,424
Minority interest	(183)	(129)
Earnings after tax (net income)	6,671	6,295
Average number of shares outstanding (millions)	4,465	4,465
Net income per share	$1.49	$1.41

SOURCE: Adapted from 2002 *Wal-Mart Annual Report*.

FIGURE 11.2   Wal-Mart Balance Sheets

AS OF JANUARY 31 (IN $MILLIONS)	2002	2001
Assets		
Current assets		
Cash and cash equivalents	2,161	2,054
Accounts receivable	2,000	1,768
Inventories	22,614	21,442
Prepaid expenses and other	1,471	1,291
Total current assets	28,246	26,555
Property, plant, and equipment (PPE)		
Land (property)	10,241	9,433
Plant and equipment (PE)	48,377	43,000
Less accumulated depreciation	12,868	11,499
Net PPE	45,750	40,934
Goodwill and intangible assets	8,595	9,059
Other assets	860	1,582
Total assets	83,451	78,130
Liabilities and Equity		
Current liabilities		
Commercial paper	743	2,286
Accounts payable	15,617	15,092
Accrued liabilities and income tax	8,517	7,196
Current maturities of long-term debt	2,405	4,375
Total current liabilities	27,282	28,949
Long-term debt	18,732	15,655
Deferred income taxes	1,128	1,043
Minority interest	1,207	1,140
Shareholders' equity	35,102	31,343
Total liabilities and equity	83,451	78,130

SOURCE: Adapted from 2002 *Wal-Mart Annual Report*.

FIGURE 11.3 Wal-Mart Cash Flow Statements

FOR YEAR ENDED JANUARY 31 (IN $MILLIONS)	2002	2001
Operating Activities		
Net income	6,671	6,295
Depreciation and amortization	3,290	2,868
Deferred taxes	185	342
Net change in operating assets and liabilities	48	(145)
Other, net	66	244
Net cash provided by operating activities	10,260	9,604
Investing Activities		
Purchases of property, plant, and equipment (PPE)	(8,383)	(8,042)
Investment in international operations	—	(627)
Proceeds from termination of net investment hedges	1,134	—
Other investing activities	103	(45)
Net cash used in investing activities	(7,146)	(8,714)
Financing Activities		
Issuance of debt	4,591	3,778
Payments of debt	(5,219)	(3,714)
Issuance of stock	—	581
Purchases of stock	(1,214)	(193)
Dividends	(1,249)	(1,070)
Other financing activities	113	176
Net cash used in financing activities	(2,978)	(442)
Effect of exchange rate changes	(29)	(250)
Cash		
Net increase during year	107	198
Balance at beginning of year	2,054	1,856
Balance at end of year	2,161	2,054

SOURCE: Adapted from 2002 *Wal-Mart Annual Report*.

Wal-Mart financial ratios are presented in Figure 11.4. Return on equity in 2002 was 19 percent, only slightly off of 2001's pace of 20 percent. A decomposition of the ROE presented in Figure 11.5 shows that Wal-Mart's profit margin slipped (from our previous discussion, due to a change in the product mix). As well, Wal-Mart's financial strategy was slightly more conservative, with a decline in its financial leverage ratio, indicating proportionately less debt relative to equity in its capital structure. Offsetting these factors, Wal-Mart was able to "sweat its assets" better, increasing its revenue substantially more than the increase in its asset base. The increase in the asset turnover measure suggests more effective resource management. In the other ratios in Figure 11.4, the expense ratio was steady and the gross margin down only slightly, reflecting subtle changes in product mix. Inventory management improved in 2002. Consequently, the overall financing gap (as measured by the difference between the age of inventory plus receivables minus the age of payables) declined slightly. The long-term-debt-to-capital ratio declined slightly from 42 to 38 percent. This ratio is "in line with management's objective to maintain a debt to total capitalization of approximately 40 percent" (2002 *Wal-Mart Annual Report*). Interest coverage remained strong and improved to over nine times.

FIGURE 11.4   Wal-Mart Financial Ratios

PERFORMANCE MEASURE	NUMERATOR	DENOMINATOR
Return on equity	Net income	Equity
Profitability		
Gross margin	Gross profit	Revenue
Expense ratio	Expenses	Revenue
Resource Management		
Age of inventory	Inventory	Avg. daily cost of goods
Age of receivables	Accounts receivable	Average daily sales
Age of payables	Accounts payable	Avg. daily purchases
Liquidity and Leverage		
Current ratio	Current assets	Current liabilities
Acid test	Cash + acc. receivable	Current liabilities
Debt to equity	Total debt	Common equity
Long-term debt to capital	Long-term debt	LTD + equity
Interest coverage	EBIT	Interest expenses

FIGURE 11.4 Wal-Mart Financial Ratios (*continued*)

(IN $MILLIONS OR % AS INDICATED) PERFORMANCE MEASURE	2001			2002		
	NUM-ERATOR	DENOM-INATOR	MEASURE	NUM-ERATOR	DENOM-INATOR	MEASURE
Return on equity	6,671	35,102	19.0%	6,295	31,343	20.1%
Profitability						
Gross margin*	48,250	217,799	22.2	43,040	191,329	22.5
Expense ratio*	37,499	217,799	17.2	32,924	191,329	17.2
Resource Management						
Age of inventory	22,614	470	48.1	21,442	412	52.1
Age of receivables*	2,000	597	3.4	1,768	524	3.4
Age of payables†	15,617	470	33.2	15,092	412	36.7
Liquidity and Leverage						
Current ratio	28,246	27,282	1.04	26,555	28,949	0.92
Acid test	4,161	27,282	0.15	3,822	28,949	0.13
Debt to equity‡	46,014	35,102	1.31	44,604	31,343	1.42
Long-term debt to capital§	21,880	56,982	0.38	22,316	53,659	0.42
Interest coverage	12,077	1,326	9.11	11,490	1,374	8.36

*Based on net sales.
†Based on cost of goods sold.
‡Current and long-term liabilities.
§Includes commercial paper.

11.2.2 Assessing Wal-Mart's Future Performance

Now that we better understand the impact of key economic factors, the industries in which Wal-Mart competes, Wal-Mart's competitive position, and Wal-Mart's strengths and weaknesses, we can examine Wal-Mart's future financing requirements through pro forma financial statements or projections. Understanding Wal-Mart's current financial position is a springboard to being able to project its future financial position.

According to the 2002 *Wal-Mart Annual Report*, "Management believes the cash flows from operations and proceeds from the sale of commercial paper will be sufficient to finance any seasonal buildups in merchandise inventories and meet other cash requirements. If the operating cash flow we generate is not sufficient to pay dividends and to fund all capital expenditures, the Company anticipates funding any shortfall in these expendi-

FIGURE 11.5 Wal-Mart ROE Decomposition

	2002	2001
Net income ($millions)	6,671	6,295
Revenues	219,812	193,295
Profit margin (PM) = net income/revenues	3.0%	3.3%
Revenues	219,812	193,295
Assets	83,451	78,130
Asset turnover (AT) = revenues/assets	2.63	2.47
Assets	83,451	78,130
Equity	35,102	31,343
Financial leverage (FL) = assets/equity	2.38	2.49
Return on equity = ROE = $PM \times AT \times FL$	19.0%	20.1%

tures with a combination of commercial paper and long-term debt." We can perform our own pro forma analysis to determine Wal-Mart's anticipated borrowing needs.

The pro forma income statement for the year ended January 31, 2003, is presented in Figure 11.6, along with the relevant assumptions. Given the previous year's revenue growth of 14 percent and accounting for the industry and company size-up analysis, revenues are anticipated to grow by 14 percent again. The anticipated gross margin is similar to recent gross margins and reflects a trade-off between a trend toward lower margin products and improved prices from suppliers. Operating expenses (excluding depreciation) are anticipated to remain in the 15 percent range. Depreciation is anticipated to increase to reflect increases in capital expenditures. Interest expenses are anticipated to be around 6 percent of interest-bearing debt (commercial paper and long-term debt, including any debt due within one year). Taxes are anticipated to remain as last year, around 36 percent. Dividends reflect management's announced 7 percent increase for fiscal year 2003, consistent with the company's history of increasing its dividend in every year since its first dividend in 1974. Consequently, Wal-Mart is antic-

FIGURE 11.6   Wal-Mart Pro Forma Annual Income Statement

	ASSUMPTION	JANUARY 31, 2002 ($MILLIONS)
Revenues		
Net sales	14% growth	248,290.9
Other income	14% growth	2,294.8
Total revenues		250,585.7
Costs of goods sold		192,425.4
Gross profit	0.225 fraction of net sales	55,865.4
Operating expenses		
Selling, general, and administrative	0.15 fraction of net sales	37,243.6
Depreciation	Higher on the basis of increased capital expenditures	3,800.0
Total operating expenses		41,043.6
Earnings before interest and taxes		14,821.8
Interest expenses	Anticipated average = 6% debt	1,847.7
Earnings before tax (EBT)		12,974.1
Taxes	0.36 fraction of EBT	4,670.7
Earnings after tax (EAT)		8,303.4
Dividends	$0.30 × number of shares	1,339.5
Change in retained earnings		6,963.9

ipated to achieve after-tax earnings of $8.3 billion and an increase of retained earnings (after common share dividends) of $6.9 billion. On the basis of 4.465 million shares outstanding, Wal-Mart is anticipated to have earnings per share of $1.86.

The pro forma balance sheet as of January 31, 2003, is presented in Figure 11.7. Cash is anticipated to be at a similar level as the previous year. Age of accounts receivable is anticipated to be at a similar level as the previous years. Age of inventory is anticipated to continue its decline, to 45 days. Property, plant, and equipment reflect management's anticipated increase in capital expenditures (as indicated in the 2002 annual report). Accounts payable days are anticipated to be similar to the past few years, around 35 days. Equity is increased to reflect the anticipated increase in retained earnings from the pro forma income statement. The balancing item is the long-term debt, which includes commercial paper as well as the current portion of any long-term debt, and is anticipated to increase by about $9 billion.

We can now perform sensitivity analysis on some of the key variables. We first examine the impact of net sales. Suppose net sales increase by only 10 percent instead of 14 percent. Earnings after tax are 5 percent lower at $7.88 billion. However, despite lower earnings, loan requirements remain similar because of lower working capital needs. If interest on debt is 7 percent rather than 6 percent, interest expenses increase by over $300 million, and the loan requirement increases by over $200 million. If Wal-Mart continues its inventory management improvement and is able to decrease its age of inventory slightly to 43 days instead of 45 days, it can reduce its loan requirements by over $1.1 billion. The likelihood of each of these outcomes and the particular variables on which to focus should relate back to our size-up analysis.

11.2.3 Wal-Mart's Long-Term Financing

We now examine issues related to Wal-Mart's need to raise long-term capital. As management notes in their discussion as part of the 2002 annual report, "We plan to finance expansion primarily through a combination of commercial paper and the issuance of long-term debt." If our assumptions are reasonable (note that generating reasonable assumptions is one of the most critical aspects of pro forma analysis), we anticipate that Wal-Mart will generate substantial earnings, most of which will be retained in the business, but will also need to rely on external funding. As Wal-Mart looks beyond the next year, it will probably need to tap into capital markets on a regular

FIGURE 11.7 **Wal-Mart Pro Forma Balance Sheet**

		AS OF JANUARY 31, 2003 ($MILLIONS)	
		2002	2003
Assets			
Cash	Assumed minimum	2,161.0	2,200.0
Accounts receivable	3.4 days	2,000.0	2,312.8
Inventory	45.0 days	22,614.0	23,723.7
Prepaid and other current	Same as previous year	1,471.0	1,471.0
Property, plant, and equipment	10,200 new assets (before depreciation)	45,750.0	52,150.0
Other (including goodwill)	Same as previous year	9,455.0	9,455.0
Total assets		83,451.0	91,312.5
Liabilities			
Accounts payable	35.0 days	15,617.0	18,451.8
Accrued liabilities and taxes	Same as previous year	8,517.0	8,517.0
LTD (including the current portion and commercial paper)	Balancing amount	21,880.0	**30,794.8**
Deferred income taxes	Same as previous year	1,128.0	1,128.0
Minority interest	Same as previous year	1,207.0	1,207.0
Total liabilities	Total liability and equity – equity	48,349.0	49,246.6
Equity	Beginning + change in retained earnings	35,102.0	42,065.9
Total liabilities and equity	Same as total assets	83,451.0	91,312.5

basis. As such, we need to determine Wal-Mart's cost of capital of raising funds from various sources.

Our analysis of Wal-Mart in 2002 indicated a long-term-debt-to-total-capital ratio of 38 percent. Based on our pro forma analysis, that ratio is antic-ipated to increase to about 42 percent. The two-year average is very close to Wal-Mart's publicly stated target capital structure of 40 percent (based on book value amounts). If Wal-Mart management had not provided us with such direction, we could have examined the current capital structure (based on either book or market values) or we could have examined the industry average, as proxies for Wal-Mart's target capital structure.

We next need to estimate Wal-Mart's cost of debt and cost of equity. Given the long-term nature of Wal-Mart's capital expenditures (primarily in long-term assets such as new stores), it is most appropriate to estimate a long-term cost of debt. If Wal-Mart did not have any existing public debt, we could examine the current yield on long-term Treasury notes and then add a risk premium related to the bond rating of similar firms. (The U.S. Treasury notes with approximately ten years to maturity were yielding 4.9 percent.) How-ever, since Wal-Mart already has existing debt (rated AA), we can examine the current yield on that debt, which is 6.0 percent for bonds maturing in 2013. Our assumption is that if Wal-Mart were to issue new bonds, the yield on the new bonds would be similar to the yield on the existing bonds (assum-ing similar bond features). Since any interest payments are tax deductible, we need to calculate Wal-Mart's after-tax cost of debt. Given our assumed tax rate of 36 percent for Wal-Mart, the after-tax cost of debt (K_d) is

$$K_d = K_d \text{ before tax}(1 - \text{tax rate}) = 6.0\%(1 - 0.36) = 3.8\%$$

On the basis of the capital asset pricing model, we can estimate Wal-Mart's cost of equity (K_e). According to Bloomberg, Wal-Mart's beta is esti-mated to be 0.90 (on the basis of a comparison of Wal-Mart's weekly returns over the last two years compared to the S&P 500 return over the same period). Assuming a market risk premium (MRP) of 6 percent, the cost of equity is

$$K_e = R_f + \beta\text{MRP} = 4.9\% + 0.90(6.0\%) = 10.3\%$$

Based on the assumed target capital structure of 40 percent debt (w_d) and 60 percent equity (w_e), the overall cost of capital (K_c) for Wal-Mart is esti-mated as

$$K_c = w_d K_d + w_e K_e = 0.40(3.8\%) + 0.60(10.3\%) = 7.7\%$$

11.2.4 Wal-Mart Valuation

We can now measure our assessment of the value of Wal-Mart and also examine Wal-Mart's ability to add value for its shareholders. For our assessment of value added, we can measure Wal-Mart's most recent year EVA. For an overall assessment of value, including our expectation for the future, we rely on the discounted cash flow analysis presented in chapter 10.

Recall that EVA is a period measure that attempts to capture a firm's ability to add value for shareholders, after accounting for the requirements of other stakeholders. We can use the EVA approach to examine Wal-Mart's true economic profit in 2002. We can estimate Wal-Mart's net operating profit after tax, or NOPAT, as EBIT(1 – tax rate). Note that we have implicitly assumed that the accounting costs are reflective of economic costs. For 2002, Wal-Mart's EBIT was $12,077 million. Based on a 36 percent tax rate, Wal-Mart's NOPAT is $7,730 million. On the basis of book values of debt and equity, we can estimate Wal-Mart's invested capital. (For simplicity, we measure capital and cost of capital as of the end of the period, although an alternative measure could examine an average.) The total of debt (including commercial paper, the current portion of long-term debt, and the remaining long-term debt) is $21,880 million. The book value of equity is $35,102 million, for a total invested capital of $56,982 million. The capital charge, estimated as the product of the invested capital and the cost of capital of 7.7 percent, is $4,388 million. Finally, EVA is calculated as the difference between NOPAT and the capital charge, or $3,342 million. Thus for the fiscal year ending January 31, 2002, Wal-Mart added considerable value to shareholders, far in excess of required or expected returns.

As our last task, we can apply the discounted cash flow analysis to determine the per-share value of Wal-Mart stock based on our assumptions. Note that if our valuation assumptions are identical to the implicit prevailing market assumptions, then our estimate of the intrinsic value of Wal-Mart shares should be identical to the prevailing market value. If the resulting intrinsic value estimate is greater than the market value, then we can conclude that the shares are undervalued. The analysis is presented in Figure 11.8. We recap the cost of capital estimation. We next estimate annual cash flows for the next five years, using similar assumptions to our one-year pro forma financial statement analysis. We assume annual revenue growth of 14 percent, an EBIT margin of 6 percent (a slight improvement relative to the past few years), 3 percent growth in capital expenditures for 2003 as anticipated by management (assuming more efficient utilization of assets), and 5 percent growth in depreciation for 2003 as estimated in the pro forma

FIGURE 11.8   Wal-Mart Discounted Cash Flow Analysis

DISCOUNT RATE WACC (K_c) ASSUMPTIONS	
Weight of debt w_d	0.40 Wal-Mart target
Weight of equity w_e	0.60 Wal-Mart target
Cost of debt K_d (before tax)	6.0% long-term bond yield
Cost of debt K_d (after tax)	3.8% K_d before tax$(1-t)$
Risk-free rate R_f	4.9% long-term government bond yield
Beta β	0.90 Bloomberg estimate
Market risk premium (MRP)	6.0% assumed
Cost of equity K_e	10.3% CAPM: $R_f + \beta*MRP$
WACC K_c	7.7% $w_d K_d + w_e K_e$

CASH FLOW ASSUMPTIONS	EXPLANATION
Revenues[†]	14.0% growth/year over '02 of 219.8 (billions of $)
EBIT margin (% of revenue)	6.0% slight improvement from recent past
Depreciation	5.0% increase/year over '03 of 3.8 (billions of $)
Working capital change as a % change in revenue[‡]	5.0% based on '02 percentage
Capital expenditures	3.0% increase/year over '03 of 10.2 (billions of $)
Tax rate	36.0% based on '02 percentage

TERMINAL VALUE (*TV*) ASSUMPTIONS	
Free cash flow (FCF) terminal growth	6.0% assumed

[†]Revenues = net sales + other income.
[‡]Working capital = difference between current assets and liabilities (excluding current portion of long-term debt).

FIGURE 11.8 **Wal-Mart Discounted Cash Flow Analysis** (*continued*)

CASH FLOWS ($BILLIONS)

YEAR§	TIME	REVENUES	EBIT	EBIT (1 − t)	+DEP	−CAP EX	−WCCHG	FCF	TV*†	FCF + TV	PV
2003	1	250.6	15.0	9.6	3.8	10.2	1.5	1.7		1.7	1.6
2004	2	285.7	17.1	11.0	4.0	10.5	1.8	2.7		2.7	2.3
2005	3	325.7	19.5	12.5	4.2	10.8	2.0	3.9		3.9	3.1
2006	4	371.3	22.3	14.3	4.4	11.1	2.3	5.2		5.2	3.9
2007	5	423.2	25.4	16.3	4.6	11.5	2.6	6.8	419.5	426.3	294.0

Present value (*PV*) of assets = 304.9

PV of assets	304.9	*TV:* PERPETUITY CALCULATION ASSUMPTIONS	
Less debt#	21.9	WACC	K_c = 7.7%
PV of equity	283.0	FCF terminal growth	g = 6.0%
Shares outstanding	4.47	FCF08 = FCF07(1 + g)	FCF08 = 7.2
Price/share	$63.38	→ $TV = FCF08/(K_c − g)$	

§Fiscal year ending January 31.
#As of January 31, 2002; includes commercial paper and all long-term debt.

analysis, working capital increases at a rate of 5 percent of the change in revenues (similar to 2002), and a tax rate of 36 percent (incorporating the United States and other countries). After five years, we assume a constant growth in free cash flows of 6 percent, used to calculate a terminal value (representing the value of all free cash flows beyond the fifth year).

This terminal value growth estimate is meant to be conservative relative to the five-year growth estimate and assumes Wal-Mart will then grow only marginally above long-term nominal growth in the United States. Our resulting analysis estimates a value of Wal-Mart's assets of just over $300 billion. Given the current interest-bearing debt of just under $22 billion, the resulting estimate of the value of the equity is just over $283 billion. Given 4.465 billion shares, the estimated intrinsic value per share is just over $63, slightly greater than the spring of 2002 price, suggesting the shares are appropriately valued, on the basis of our assumptions. Of course, as new information arrives in the marketplace causing a reassessment of the assumptions, we can expect the value of Wal-Mart shares to fluctuate as well. However, rather than focusing on the price of the shares per se, the real value in this exercise is in the analysis, which forces us to reflect on the key assumptions and what factors might impact on those assumptions. If investors had performed a similar analysis on many of the technology firms that were hot in the late 1990s and invested accordingly, these stocks may not have experienced the dramatic run-ups and collapses that they did.

11.3   Final Comments

Our journey through the wonderful world of finance is now complete. Now that you have a better appreciation for the workings of a business from a financial perspective, it will allow you to better communicate with financial managers as well as assist in maximizing shareholder value.

APPENDIX A Glossary

The following terms are listed (by chapter) in the order in which they appear. Complete definitions of each are presented in the alphabetical listing below.

CHAPTER 1

real assets
common shareholders
profits
investing
capital budgeting
dividends
retained earnings
working capital
assets
liabilities
capital structure
balance sheet
income statement

CHAPTER 2

gross domestic product
business cycle
recession

initial public offering

CHAPTER 3

book value
current assets
marketable securities
accounts receivable
inventory
prepaid expenses
depreciation
goodwill
accounts payable
notes payable
bond
deferred income taxes
equity
preferred shares
common equity
bankruptcy

revenues
cost of goods sold
gross profit
net income
earnings per share
accrual
ratio analysis
return on equity
market value
profit margin
asset turnover
financial leverage
vertical analysis
gross profit margin
inventory turnover
collection period
payable period
current ratio
acid test

debt to equity

interest coverage

CHAPTER 4

statement of change in financial position

sources and uses statement

line of credit

sustainable growth rate

retention ratio

dividend payout ratio

CHAPTER 5

variable costs

fixed costs

iteration method

cash budget

prime rate

LIBOR

CHAPTER 6

financial instruments

capital markets

principal

bondholders

securities markets, see capital markets

par value

face value

maturity date

coupon rate

sinking fund

variable rate

call provisions

covenants

default

dividend payout

private placement

public offering

initial public offering

seasoned equity offering

over the counter

financial intermediaries

underwriting

CHAPTER 7

cost of capital

permanent capital

market risk premium

beta

hurdle rates

CHAPTER 8

financial distress

interest tax shield

CHAPTER 9

net present value

internal rate of return

yield to maturity

payback period

CHAPTER 10

free cash flows

terminal value

comparable analysis

economic value added

spin-off

market value added

Alphabetical Listing

accounts payable (payables) Money owed to suppliers and trade creditors.

accounts receivable (receivables) Money owed by customers.

accrual accounting A method of accounting recognizing revenues when earned and expenses when incurred, regardless of the time of cash flows.

acid test (quick ratio) A measure of a firm's liquidity: the ratio of current assets, excluding inventories, to current liabilities.

asset turnover A measure of the firm's ability to generate revenue from its asset base: the ratio of net sales to total assets.

assets Tangible or intangible items of value to a firm.

balance sheet A financial statement reflecting the value of a firm's assets, liabilities, and net worth at a particular point in time.

bankruptcy A legal process of disposing of the assets, or the reorganization of a firm to satisfy creditor claims, and protecting the firm from further legal actions.

beta (β) A measure of the riskiness of a firm's common equity relative to the risk of the overall stock market.

bond A financial instrument issued by a firm, representing long-term debt.

bondholders Owners of bonds.

book value The value of an item as recorded on financial statements.

business cycle Changes in countrywide economic activity reflecting expansions, or increases in real (inflation-adjusted) output, versus contractions, or decreases in economic real output.

call provisions A description of terms under which a firm may redeem all or part of a bond or preferred share issue.

capital budgeting The process of selecting investment projects.

capital markets Markets for long-term financing such as issuing bonds or equity.

capital structure The mix of debt and equity that a firm uses to finance its operations.

cash budget A plan or projection of cash inflows and outflows over a specified period.

collection period A measure of the average number of days over which accounts receivable are outstanding.

common equity (common stock) Securities representing the direct ownership of a firm, or the residual claims on the assets.

common shareholders Owners of common shares, or common equity.

common stock, see *common equity*.

comparable analysis Comparison of the assets or businesses of selected firms, often for the purpose of establishing a fair market value.

cost of capital (weighted-average cost of capital) The weighted average of the cost to a firm of all the forms of long-term financing, including debt, preferred shares, and common shares.

cost of goods (services) sold (cost of sales) The total of all costs, excluding selling and administrative expenses, required to acquire or prepare goods or services for sale.

coupon rate The specified rate of interest on interest coupons attached to bonds.

covenants Provisions in a bond or debt agreement specifying restrictions or requirements on the borrower.

current assets Assets such as accounts receivable and inventory that can be turned into cash within one year.

current ratio A measure of a firm's liquidity: the ratio of current assets to current liabilities.

debt to equity A measure of financial leverage: the ratio of a firm's debt to shareholders' equity.

default Failure to make debt obligation payments.

deferred income taxes A provision for future income taxes arising from timing differences between the recognition of tax liabilities for tax purposes versus a firm's accounting system.

depreciation The periodic decline in the value of an asset, recognized for accounting or tax purposes.

dividend payout The amount of dividends distributed to shareholders.

dividend payout ratio A ratio of the amount of dividends distributed to shareholders relative to the amount of after-tax earnings.

dividends A share of the profits of the firm distributed to shareholders.

earnings, see *net income*.

earnings per share (EPS) A measure of the claim on earnings for each common share: earnings after tax, less any preferred dividends, divided by the number of outstanding common shares.

economic value added (EVA) A firm's or business unit's after-tax operating profit less a charge for the capital employed.

equity (shareholders' equity, net worth) The ownership interest of preferred and common shareholders. Also, the difference between a firm's assets and liabilities.

face value The principal amount due to an investor in securities on the maturity of the security, such as a bond.

financial distress Difficulties experienced by firms in attempting to meet commitments to their creditors.

financial instruments Securities such as bonds and stocks that represent claims on the assets of a firm.

financial intermediaries Stock exchanges, investment banks, or investment dealers that attempt to facilitate the buying and selling of securities, first between firms and investors and second among investors.

financial leverage The use of debt to increase the firm's return on equity, while increasing risk exposure.

fixed costs Costs that do not vary over a period with changes in the volume of operations.

free cash flows The cash flow available to a firm after providing for all acceptable investments: after-tax operating income plus noncash items (such as depreciation) less capital expenditures and working capital increases.

goodwill The value of a business paid by a purchaser above its asset book value.

gross domestic product (GDP) The total value of the output of goods and services produced or offered by a country over a period of time.

gross margin percentage The difference between revenues and the cost of goods sold, divided by revenue.

gross profit (gross margin) The difference between revenues and the cost of goods sold.

hurdle rates The minimum acceptable rate of return for investments, depending on the nature and risk of the investment.

income statement A financial statement indicating a firm's revenues, expenses, and resulting income over a period of time.

initial public offering (IPO) The initial sale of stock of a firm to the public.

interest coverage A measure of a firm's ability to meet its debt obligations: the ratio of operating income before tax to interest expenses.

interest tax shield The value of tax savings resulting from the tax deductibility of interest payments.

internal rate of return (IRR) The discount rate at which a project's net present value is exactly equal to zero.

inventory Goods or materials available to be sold or to be used to manufacture products.

inventory turnover A measurement of a firm's control of its investment in inventory: the ratio of the cost of goods sold to (ending or average) inventory.

investing The process of committing funds for the purpose of obtaining a return over a particular period of time.

iteration method A trial and error process for solving particular mathematical problems.

liabilities Obligations to pay a specified amount or perform a particular service.

LIBOR (London Interbank Offered Rate) The rate at which banks offer to lend in the London interbank market; often used as the basis for floating-rate loans.

line of credit An agreement between a lender and a firm in which the firm can borrow up to a maximum amount at any time during a specified period.

market risk premium The difference between the expected return on a stock investment in the market and the expected return on a risk-free investment.

market value The value at which an asset can actually be sold.

market value added (MVA) The difference between the market value of common equity and the book value.

marketable securities Securities that are expected to be converted into cash within a one-year period.

maturity date The date at which an obligation or claim is to be paid.

net income (earnings, profits, net profit) The difference between revenue and all associated expenses over a particular period.

net present value (NPV) The difference between the present value of cash inflows and cash outflows from investments or projects.

net worth, see *equity*.

notes payable Short-term obligations, such as a written promise to repay short-term bank loans or promissory notes.

over-the-counter (OTC) market A market network among security dealers that allows the trading of securities not listed on organized exchanges.

par value An arbitrary amount set as the face value of a security.

payable period A measure of the average number of days over which accounts payable are outstanding.

payables, see *accounts payable*.

payback period A crude measure of the time it takes for an investor to recover his or her initial investment.

permanent capital The amount of interest-bearing debt plus preferred and common equity.

preferred shares (preferred stock) A class of stock, typically dividend bearing, that has preference over common stock in terms of both dividend payments as well as claim on assets.

prepaid expenses A short-term expense expected to yield benefits in the near term.

prime rate The rate offered by lending institutions such as banks to their most creditworthy customers.

principal The original or face amount of a loan on which interest is paid.

private placement The sale of securities to a selected group of well-informed investors.

profit margin The ratio of net income to revenues.

profits, see *net income*.

public offering (public issue) The sale of newly issued securities to the public.

quick ratio, see *acid test*.

ratio analysis The use of financial statement–related ratios to analyze the performance of the firm.

real assets Assets used to produce goods and services.

receivables, see *accounts receivable*.

recession A downturn in a country's economic activity, typically measured as two consecutive quarters of decline in real (or inflation-adjusted) gross domestic product.

retained earnings The cumulative amount of earnings retained or reinvested in the firm and not paid out as dividends.

retention ratio The proportion of earnings reinvested in the firm and not paid out as dividends.

return on equity (ROE) A measure of the effectiveness of the utilization of common shareholders' equity: the ratio of net income, less preferred dividends, to common shareholders' equity.

revenues (sales) The resource inflow to a firm through the sale of goods or the provision of services.

sales, see *revenues*.

seasoned equity offering (SEO) The additional sale of equity securities to the public by an already-public firm.

securities markets, see *capital markets*.

shareholders' equity, see *equity*.

sinking fund A cash fund set aside by the firm in order to meet future debt obligations.

sources and uses statement A financial statement that documents all fund inflows and outflows over a period of time, based on changes in balance sheet item amounts.

spin-off The divestiture of part of a firm by separating a subsidiary from the parent firm and distributing stock in the newly independent firm to shareholders of the parent firm.

statement of change in financial position A financial statement that documents all sources and uses of working capital over a period of time.

sustainable growth rate The rate of growth in revenue that a firm can sustain without changing its profit margin, asset turnover, financial leverage, or dividend payout ratio.

terminal value The value of assets either at the end of their economic life or at an arbitrary point of time in the future.

underwriting The process, initiated by investment banks, of marketing new security issues to the public.

variable costs Costs that vary over a period with changes in the volume of operations.

variable rate A floating or nonfixed loan rate, often tied to changes in the prime rate or LIBOR.

vertical analysis The creation and interpretation of ratios of each item on the income statement as a percentage of revenues.

weighted-average cost of capital, see *cost of capital*.

working capital The difference between current assets and current liabilities on the balance sheet.

yield to maturity (YTM) The internal rate of return (IRR) of a bond when held to maturity.

APPENDIX B Solutions to Selected Self-Study Problems

Chapter 3

1.

Beginning retained earnings	$450
Net income	$35
− Preferred dividend	$5
Available to common shareholders	$30
− Regular dividend	$6
− Special dividend	$10
Change in retained earnings	$14
Ending retained earnings	$464

2.

	2001 ($MILLIONS)	2000 ($MILLIONS)
Net income	3,979	2,177
Revenues	20,374	19,699
Profit margin (PM) = net income/revenues	19.5%	11.1%
Revenues	20,374	19,699
Assets	22,417	20,834
Asset turnover (AT) = revenues/assets	0.91×	0.95×
Assets	22,417	20,834
Equity	11,366	9,316
Financial leverage (FL) = assets/equity	1.97×	2.24×
Return on equity = ROE = $PM \times AT \times FL$	35.0%	23.4%

3.

(IN $MILLIONS UNLESS OTHERWISE NOTED)	2001			2000		
	NUM-ERATOR	DENOM-INATOR	MEASURE	NUM-ERATOR	DENOM-INATOR	MEASURE
Performance Measure						
Return on equity	3,979	11,366	35.0%	2,177	9,316	23.4%
Profitability						
Gross margin*	14,330	20,092	71.3%	13,495	19,889	67.9%
Expense ratio*	8,660	20,092	43.1%	10,096	19,889	50.8%
Resource Management						
Age of inventory	1,055	17	63.7 days	1,066	17	62.7 days
Age of receivables*	1,882	55	34.2	1,757	54	32.2
Age of payables[†]	3,679	17	222.2	3,905	17	229.7
Liquidity and Leverage						
Current ratio	7,171	8,429	0.9×	6,620	9,321	0.7×
Acid test	3,816	8,429	0.5	3,649	9,321	0.4
Debt to equity[‡]	10,609	11,366	0.9	11,160	9,316	1.2
Long-term debt to capital	1,375	12,741	0.1	856	10,172	0.1
Interest coverage	n.m.[§]	n.m.	n.m.	3,501	102	34.3

*Based on operating revenues.
[†]Based on cost of goods sold.
[‡]Current, long-term, and other liabilities.
[§]"n.m." not meaningful.

Chapter 4

3.   Sustainable growth rate = return on equity × retention ratio

$$\begin{aligned}
\text{Return on equity} &= \text{profit margin} \times \text{asset turnover ratio} \\
&\quad \times \text{financial leverage ratio} \\
&= 0.05 \times 3.1 \times 1.5 \\
&= 0.2325
\end{aligned}$$

$$\begin{aligned}
\text{Retention ratio} &= 1 - \text{dividend payout ratio} \\
&= 1 - 0.4 \\
&= 0.6
\end{aligned}$$

$$\begin{aligned}
\text{Sustainable growth rate} &= 0.2325 \times 0.6 \\
&= 0.1395, \quad \text{or} \quad 13.95\%
\end{aligned}$$

Chapter 5

1.

	ASSUMPTION	($THOUSANDS)
Sales	Given	150.0
Costs of goods sold		
Beginning inventory	Last year's ending inventory	12.0
+ Purchases	C.G.S. + ending inventory – beginning inventory	120.7
Costs of goods avail.		132.7
– Ending inventory	60 days of cost of sales	18.7
Costs of goods sold		114.0
Gross profit	0.24 fraction of sales	36.0
Total operating expenses	0.14 fraction of sales	21.0
Earnings before tax (EBT)		15.0
Taxes	0.35 fraction of EBT	5.3
Earnings after tax (EAT)		9.8
Dividends	0.00 fraction of EAT	0.0
Change in retained earnings		9.8

2.

	ASSUMPTION	YEAR 0 ($THOUSANDS)	YEAR 1 ($THOUSANDS)
Assets			
Cash	Assumed minimum		10.0
Accounts receivable	30.0 days of accounts receivable		12.3
Inventory	60.0 days of cost of sales		18.7
Fixed assets	Assumed amount		60.0
Total assets			101.1
Liabilities			
Accounts payable	35.0 days of payables		11.6
Long-term debt	Balancing amount		***29.7***
Total liabilities	Total liabilities and equity – equity		41.3
Equity	Beginning + change in retained earnings	50.0	59.8
Total liabilities and equity	Same as total assets		101.1

3.

	ASSUMPTION	YEAR 0 ($THOUSANDS)	YEAR 1 ($THOUSANDS)
Sales	Given		200.0
Costs of goods sold			
Beginning inventory	Last year's ending inventory	12.0	
+ Purchases	C.G.S. + ending inventory – beginning inventory	165.0	
Costs of goods avail.		177.0	
– Ending inventory	60 days of cost of sales	25.0	
Costs of goods sold			152.0
Gross profit	0.24 fraction of sales		48.0
Total operating expenses	0.14 fraction of sales		28.0

3. (*continued*)

Earnings before tax (EBT)		20.0
Taxes	0.35 fraction of EBT	7.0
Earnings after tax (EAT)		13.0
Dividends	0.00 fraction of EAT	0.0
Change in retained earnings		13.0
Assets		
Cash	Assumed minimum	10.0
Accounts receivable	30.0 days of accounts receivable	16.4
Inventory	60.0 days of cost of sales	25.0
Fixed assets	Assumed amount	60.0
Total assets		111.4
Liabilities		
Accounts payable	45.0 days of payables	20.3
Long-term debt	Balancing amount	***28.1***
Total liabilities	Total liabilities and equity – equity	48.4
Equity	Beginning + change in retained earnings 50.0	63.0
Total liabilities and equity	Same as total assets	111.4

4.

	ASSUMPTION	YEAR 0	YEAR 1	YEAR 2
Sales	15% increase in year 2		150.0	172.5
Costs of goods sold				
Beginning inventory	Last year's ending inventory		12.0	18.7
+ Purchases	C.G.S. + ending inventory − beginning inventory		120.7	133.9
Costs of goods avail.			132.7	152.7
− Ending inventory	60 days of cost of sales		18.7	21.6
Costs of goods sold			114.0	131.1
Gross profit	0.240 fraction of sales		36.0	41.4
Total operating expenses	0.14 fraction of sales		21.0	24.2
Earnings before tax (EBT)			15.0	17.3
Taxes	0.35 fraction of EBT		5.3	6.0
Earnings after tax (EAT)			9.8	11.2
Dividends	0.00 fraction of EAT		0.0	0.0
Change in retained earnings			9.8	11.2
Assets				
Cash	Assumed minimum		10.0	10.0
Accounts receivable	30.0 days of accounts receivable		12.3	14.2
Inventory	60.0 days of cost of sales		18.7	21.6
Fixed assets	Assumed amount		60.0	60.0
Total assets			101.1	105.7
Liabilities				
Accounts payable	35.0 days of payables		11.6	12.8
Long-term debt	Balancing amount		**29.7**	**21.9**
Total liabilities	Total liabilities and equity − equity		41.3	34.8
Equity	Beginning + change in retained earnings	50.0	59.8	71.0
Total liabilities and equity	Same as total assets		101.1	105.7

Chapter 6

3. Coupon rate = 6.40%
   Semiannual coupons = $3.20
   Time to maturity (years) = 10
   Time to maturity (periods) = 20
   Payments of $3.20 every six months for ten years, then $100 in ten years

4. Current dividend yield = dividends per share/current share price
   $$= 0.80/\$28.50$$
   $$= 0.02807, \text{ or } 2.807\%$$

   Dividend per share = current share price × current dividend yield
   $$= \$28.50 \times 0.028$$
   $$= \$0.80$$

   P/E = current price/past four quarter earnings per share (EPS)
   EPS = current price/(P/E)
   $$= \$28.50/24.5$$
   $$= \$1.16$$

   Stock total return (over past year) = (current price − year ago price
   $$+ \text{ dividend})/\text{year ago price}$$
   $$= (\$28.50 - \$24.00)/\$24.00$$
   $$= 0.188, \text{ or } 18.8\%$$

   The stock has outperformed the market's return of 16.5%.

Chapter 7

1. K_d = (long-term government yield + spread) × (1 − tax rate)
   $$= (6.20\% + 1.00\%) \times (1 - 0.40)$$
   $$= 0.0432, \text{ or } 4.32\%$$

2. K_p = current preferred yield = annual dividend/current price
   $$= \$2.25/\$28.50$$
   $$= 0.07895, \text{ or } 7.89\%$$

3. $K_e(\text{CAPM method}) = R_f + \beta \times \text{MRP}$
$$= 6.20\% + 1.15 \times 6.00\%$$
$$= 13.10\%$$

4. WACC is based on the target capital structure of 40% debt and 60% equity.

TYPE	COST	WEIGHT	WEIGHTED COST
Debt	4.32%	0.40	1.73%
Equity	13.10%	0.60	<u>7.86%</u>
			9.59%

Chapter 8

1. Cash flow coverage = EBITDA/(interest payments
                            + before-tax cost of debt repayment)

Before-tax cost of debt repayment = principal repayment/(1 − tax rate)
$$= \$75,000/(1 - 0.35)$$
$$= \$115,385$$

EBITDA = EBIT + depreciation and amortization
$$= \$540,000 + \$65,000$$
$$= \$605,000$$

Cash flow coverage = $605,000/$115,385
$$= 5.24 \text{ times}$$

2.

DEBT FIRM	ALL-EQUITY FIRM
(EBIT − $40,000) × 0.65/6,000	= (EBIT − $0) × 0.65/10,000
(EBIT − $40,000)/6,000	= (EBIT − $0)/10,000
(EBIT − $40,000) × (10,000)/6,000	= EBIT
(EBIT − $40,000) × 1.6666667	= EBIT
1.666667 EBIT − EBIT	= $66,666.67
0.666667 EBIT	= $66,666.67
EBIT	= $100,000.00

Debt firm EPS = $6.50
All-equity firm EPS = $6.50

3.

CASE	1	2	3	4
Equity	$1,000	$1,198	$1,372	$1,300
Debt	$0	$400	$800	$1,200
Equity/assets	100.00%	74.97%	63.17%	52.00%
Debt/assets	0.00%	25.03%	36.83%	48.00%
K_e	18.0%	19.0%	20.0%	24.0%
K_d (after tax)	6.0%	6.1%	6.2%	7.0%
WACC	18.0%	15.8%	14.9%	15.8%

Chapter 9

1. $PV_{a0} = \$100$ Investment rate = 9% $FV_{a3} = 129.503$
   $PV_{b1} = \$150$ Investment rate = 9% $+ FV_{b3} = 178.215$

   Future value = 307.718

2. $FV_{a1} = \$500$ Discount rate = 15% $PV_{a0} = 434.783$
   $FV_{b5} = \$1,000$ Discount rate = 15% $+ PV_{b0} = 497.177$

   Present value = 931.959

3. $i = 10\%$
   $n = 5$
   $PMT = (1,200)$
   $FVA = \$7,326.12$

4. $i = 10\%$
   $n = 5$
   $PMT = \$1,200$
   $PVA = (4,548.94)$

5.(a) Consider five-year and ten-year bonds, with a 10 percent coupon,
   YTM of 10 percent (5 percent every six months).

$i = 5\%$	$i = 5\%$
$n = 10$	$n = 20$
$PMT = \$50$	$PMT = \$50$
$FV = \$1,000$	$FV = \$1,000$
$PVA = (\$1,000.00)$	$PVA = (\$1,000.00)$

Now suppose rates decline to 9 percent (4.5 percent every six months).

$i = 4.5\%$ $i = 4.5\%$
$n = 10$ $n = 20$
$PMT = \$50$ $PMT = \$50$
$FV = \$1,000$ $FV = \$1,000$
$PVA = (\$1,039.56)$ $PVA = (\$1,065.04)$

5.(b) Consider five-year bonds with zero and 10 percent coupons, and a YTM of 10 percent (5 percent every six months).

$i = 5\%$ $i = 5\%$
$n = 10$ $n = 10$
$PMT = \$50$ $PMT = \$0$
$FV = \$1,000$ $FV = \$1,000$
$PVA = (\$1,000.00)$ $PVA = (\$613.91)$

Now suppose rates decline to 9 percent (4.5 percent every six months).

$i = 4.5\%$ $i = 4.5\%$
$n = 10$ $n = 10$
$PMT = \$50$ $PMT = \$0$
$FV = \$1,000$ $FV = \$1,000$
$PVA = (\$1,039.56)$ $PVA = (\$643.93)$

Chapter 10

1.   Tax rate = 35%, $K_c = 9\%$, $g = 4\%$

TIME	EBIT	EBIT$(1-t)$	+DEP	−W/CCHG	SUBTOTAL	TERM VALUE*	TOTAL	DISC VALUE
1	$30,000	$19,500	$3,000	$2,500	$20,000		$20,000	$18,349
2	$40,000	$26,000	$3,500	$3,000	$26,500		$26,500	$22,305
3	$50,000	$32,500	$4,000	$3,500	$33,000	$686,400	$719,400	$555,509

Value of firm = $596,162
− Value of debt = $150,000
Value of equity = $446,162

Terminal value: perpetuity calculation assumptions:
$FCF_4 = FCF_3(1+g) = \$34,320$
Term value $= FCF_4/(K_c - g) = \$686,400$

2.

EBT	$2.500
−Tax (35%)	0.875
EAT	$1.625
Shares outstanding (m)	1.000
EPS	$1.625
Average comparable multiple	13.000×
Intrinsic value = EPS × multiple =	21.125

3. $EVA = EBIT(1-t) - \text{invested capital}(K_c)$

EBIT	$1.500
−Tax (35%)	$0.525
EBIT$(1-t)$	$0.975
Debt	$2.500
Equity	$5.000
Invested capital =	$7.500
$K_c =$	11%

$EVA = \$0.975 - \$7.500(11\%)$
$\quad = \$0.150$

APPENDIX C Present Value and Future Value Tables

TABLE 1   Present Value of $1 Received in n Periods

$PV = 1/(1 + r)^n$

INTEREST RATE r

n	1%	2%	3%	4%	5%	6%	7%	8%	9%	10%	11%	12%	13%	14%	15%
1	0.990	0.980	0.971	0.962	0.952	0.943	0.935	0.926	0.917	0.909	0.901	0.893	0.885	0.877	0.870
2	0.980	0.961	0.943	0.925	0.907	0.890	0.873	0.857	0.842	0.826	0.812	0.797	0.783	0.769	0.756
3	0.971	0.942	0.915	0.889	0.864	0.840	0.816	0.794	0.772	0.751	0.731	0.712	0.693	0.675	0.658
4	0.961	0.924	0.888	0.855	0.823	0.792	0.763	0.735	0.708	0.683	0.659	0.636	0.613	0.592	0.572
5	0.951	0.906	0.863	0.822	0.784	0.747	0.713	0.681	0.650	0.621	0.593	0.567	0.543	0.519	0.497
6	0.942	0.888	0.837	0.790	0.746	0.705	0.666	0.630	0.596	0.564	0.535	0.507	0.480	0.456	0.432
7	0.933	0.871	0.813	0.760	0.711	0.665	0.623	0.583	0.547	0.513	0.482	0.452	0.425	0.400	0.376
8	0.923	0.853	0.789	0.731	0.677	0.627	0.582	0.540	0.502	0.467	0.434	0.404	0.376	0.351	0.327
9	0.914	0.837	0.766	0.703	0.645	0.592	0.544	0.500	0.460	0.424	0.391	0.361	0.333	0.308	0.284
10	0.905	0.820	0.744	0.676	0.614	0.558	0.508	0.463	0.422	0.386	0.352	0.322	0.295	0.270	0.247
11	0.896	0.804	0.722	0.650	0.585	0.527	0.475	0.429	0.388	0.350	0.317	0.287	0.261	0.237	0.215
12	0.887	0.788	0.701	0.625	0.557	0.497	0.444	0.397	0.356	0.319	0.286	0.257	0.231	0.208	0.187
13	0.879	0.773	0.681	0.601	0.530	0.469	0.415	0.368	0.326	0.290	0.258	0.229	0.204	0.182	0.163
14	0.870	0.758	0.661	0.577	0.505	0.442	0.388	0.340	0.299	0.263	0.232	0.205	0.181	0.160	0.141
15	0.861	0.743	0.642	0.555	0.481	0.417	0.362	0.315	0.275	0.239	0.209	0.183	0.160	0.140	0.123
16	0.853	0.728	0.623	0.534	0.458	0.394	0.339	0.292	0.252	0.218	0.188	0.163	0.141	0.123	0.107
17	0.844	0.714	0.605	0.513	0.436	0.371	0.317	0.270	0.231	0.198	0.170	0.146	0.125	0.108	0.093
18	0.836	0.700	0.587	0.494	0.416	0.350	0.296	0.250	0.212	0.180	0.153	0.130	0.111	0.095	0.081
19	0.828	0.686	0.570	0.475	0.396	0.331	0.277	0.232	0.194	0.164	0.138	0.116	0.098	0.083	0.070
20	0.820	0.673	0.554	0.456	0.377	0.312	0.258	0.215	0.178	0.149	0.124	0.104	0.087	0.073	0.061

TABLE 2   Future Value of $1 Received by the End of *n* Periods

$FV = (1 + r)^n$

INTEREST RATE *r*

n	1%	2%	3%	4%	5%	6%	7%	8%	9%	10%	11%	12%	13%	14%	15%
1	1.010	1.020	1.030	1.040	1.050	1.060	1.070	1.080	1.090	1.100	1.110	1.120	1.130	1.140	1.150
2	1.020	1.040	1.061	1.082	1.103	1.124	1.145	1.166	1.188	1.210	1.232	1.254	1.277	1.300	1.323
3	1.030	1.061	1.093	1.125	1.158	1.191	1.225	1.260	1.295	1.331	1.368	1.405	1.443	1.482	1.521
4	1.041	1.082	1.126	1.170	1.216	1.262	1.311	1.360	1.412	1.464	1.518	1.574	1.630	1.689	1.749
5	1.051	1.104	1.159	1.217	1.276	1.338	1.403	1.469	1.539	1.611	1.685	1.762	1.842	1.925	2.011
6	1.062	1.126	1.194	1.265	1.340	1.419	1.501	1.587	1.677	1.772	1.870	1.974	2.082	2.195	2.313
7	1.072	1.149	1.230	1.316	1.407	1.504	1.606	1.714	1.828	1.949	2.076	2.211	2.353	2.502	2.660
8	1.083	1.172	1.267	1.369	1.477	1.594	1.718	1.851	1.993	2.144	2.305	2.476	2.658	2.853	3.059
9	1.094	1.195	1.305	1.423	1.551	1.689	1.838	1.999	2.172	2.358	2.558	2.773	3.004	3.252	3.518
10	1.105	1.219	1.344	1.480	1.629	1.791	1.967	2.159	2.367	2.594	2.839	3.106	3.395	3.707	4.046
11	1.116	1.243	1.384	1.539	1.710	1.898	2.105	2.332	2.580	2.853	3.152	3.479	3.836	4.226	4.652
12	1.127	1.268	1.426	1.601	1.796	2.012	2.252	2.518	2.813	3.138	3.498	3.896	4.335	4.818	5.350
13	1.138	1.294	1.469	1.665	1.886	2.133	2.410	2.720	3.066	3.452	3.883	4.363	4.898	5.492	6.153
14	1.149	1.319	1.513	1.732	1.980	2.261	2.579	2.937	3.342	3.797	4.310	4.887	5.535	6.261	7.076
15	1.161	1.346	1.558	1.801	2.079	2.397	2.759	3.172	3.642	4.177	4.785	5.474	6.254	7.138	8.137
16	1.173	1.373	1.605	1.873	2.183	2.540	2.952	3.426	3.970	4.595	5.311	6.130	7.067	8.137	9.358
17	1.184	1.400	1.653	1.948	2.292	2.693	3.159	3.700	4.328	5.054	5.895	6.866	7.986	9.276	10.761
18	1.196	1.428	1.702	2.026	2.407	2.854	3.380	3.996	4.717	5.560	6.544	7.690	9.024	10.575	12.375
19	1.208	1.457	1.754	2.107	2.527	3.026	3.617	4.316	5.142	6.116	7.263	8.613	10.197	12.056	14.232
20	1.220	1.486	1.806	2.191	2.653	3.207	3.870	4.661	5.604	6.727	8.062	9.646	11.523	13.743	16.367

TABLE 3 Present Value of Annuity: $1 Received Each Period for n Periods

$PVA = 1/r - 1/r(1+r)^n$

INTEREST RATE r

n	1%	2%	3%	4%	5%	6%	7%	8%	9%	10%	11%	12%	13%	14%	15%
1	0.990	0.980	0.971	0.962	0.952	0.943	0.935	0.926	0.917	0.909	0.901	0.893	0.885	0.877	0.870
2	1.970	1.942	1.913	1.886	1.859	1.833	1.808	1.783	1.759	1.736	1.713	1.690	1.668	1.647	1.626
3	2.941	2.884	2.829	2.775	2.723	2.673	2.624	2.577	2.531	2.487	2.444	2.402	2.361	2.322	2.283
4	3.902	3.808	3.717	3.630	3.546	3.465	3.387	3.312	3.240	3.170	3.102	3.037	2.974	2.914	2.855
5	4.853	4.713	4.580	4.452	4.329	4.212	4.100	3.993	3.890	3.791	3.696	3.605	3.517	3.433	3.352
6	5.795	5.601	5.417	5.242	5.076	4.917	4.767	4.623	4.486	4.355	4.231	4.111	3.998	3.889	3.784
7	6.728	6.472	6.230	6.002	5.786	5.582	5.389	5.206	5.033	4.868	4.712	4.564	4.423	4.288	4.160
8	7.652	7.325	7.020	6.733	6.463	6.210	5.971	5.747	5.535	5.335	5.146	4.968	4.799	4.639	4.487
9	8.566	8.162	7.786	7.435	7.108	6.802	6.515	6.247	5.995	5.759	5.537	5.328	5.132	4.946	4.772
10	9.471	8.983	8.530	8.111	7.722	7.360	7.024	6.710	6.418	6.145	5.889	5.650	5.426	5.216	5.019
11	10.368	9.787	9.253	8.760	8.306	7.887	7.499	7.139	6.805	6.495	6.207	5.938	5.687	5.453	5.234
12	11.255	10.575	9.954	9.385	8.863	8.384	7.943	7.536	7.161	6.814	6.492	6.194	5.918	5.660	5.421
13	12.134	11.348	10.635	9.986	9.394	8.853	8.358	7.904	7.487	7.103	6.750	6.424	6.122	5.842	5.583
14	13.004	12.106	11.296	10.563	9.899	9.295	8.745	8.244	7.786	7.367	6.982	6.628	6.302	6.002	5.724
15	13.865	12.849	11.938	11.118	10.380	9.712	9.108	8.559	8.061	7.606	7.191	6.811	6.462	6.142	5.847
16	14.718	13.578	12.561	11.652	10.838	10.106	9.447	8.851	8.313	7.824	7.379	6.974	6.604	6.265	5.954
17	15.562	14.292	13.166	12.166	11.274	10.477	9.763	9.122	8.544	8.022	7.549	7.120	6.729	6.373	6.047
18	16.398	14.992	13.754	12.659	11.690	10.828	10.059	9.372	8.756	8.201	7.702	7.250	6.840	6.467	6.128
19	17.226	15.678	14.324	13.134	12.085	11.158	10.336	9.604	8.950	8.365	7.839	7.366	6.938	6.550	6.198
20	18.046	16.351	14.877	13.590	12.462	11.470	10.594	9.818	9.129	8.514	7.963	7.469	7.025	6.623	6.259

TABLE 4   Future Value of Annuity: $1 Received Each Period for *n* Periods

$FVA = [(1 + r)^n - 1]/r$

INTEREST RATE *r*

n	1%	2%	3%	4%	5%	6%	7%	8%	9%	10%	11%	12%	13%	14%	15%
1	1.000	1.000	1.000	1.000	1.000	1.000	1.000	1.000	1.000	1.000	1.000	1.000	1.000	1.000	1.000
2	2.010	2.020	2.030	2.040	2.050	2.060	2.070	2.080	2.090	2.100	2.110	2.120	2.130	2.140	2.150
3	3.030	3.060	3.091	3.122	3.153	3.184	3.215	3.246	3.278	3.310	3.342	3.374	3.407	3.440	3.473
4	4.060	4.122	4.184	4.246	4.310	4.375	4.440	4.506	4.573	4.641	4.710	4.779	4.850	4.921	4.993
5	5.101	5.204	5.309	5.416	5.526	5.637	5.751	5.867	5.985	6.105	6.228	6.353	6.480	6.610	6.742
6	6.152	6.308	6.468	6.633	6.802	6.975	7.153	7.336	7.523	7.716	7.913	8.115	8.323	8.536	8.754
7	7.214	7.434	7.662	7.898	8.142	8.394	8.654	8.923	9.200	9.487	9.783	10.089	10.405	10.730	11.067
8	8.286	8.583	8.892	9.214	9.549	9.897	10.260	10.637	11.028	11.436	11.859	12.300	12.757	13.233	13.727
9	9.369	9.755	10.159	10.583	11.027	11.491	11.978	12.488	13.021	13.579	14.164	14.776	15.416	16.085	16.786
10	10.462	10.950	11.464	12.006	12.578	13.181	13.816	14.487	15.193	15.937	16.722	17.549	18.420	19.337	20.304
11	11.567	12.169	12.808	13.486	14.207	14.972	15.784	16.645	17.560	18.531	19.561	20.655	21.814	23.045	24.349
12	12.683	13.412	14.192	15.026	15.917	16.870	17.888	18.977	20.141	21.384	22.713	24.133	25.650	27.271	29.002
13	13.809	14.680	15.618	16.627	17.713	18.882	20.141	21.495	22.953	24.523	26.212	28.029	29.985	32.089	34.352
14	14.947	15.974	17.086	18.292	19.599	21.015	22.550	24.215	26.019	27.975	30.095	32.393	34.883	37.581	40.505
15	16.097	17.293	18.599	20.024	21.579	23.276	25.129	27.152	29.361	31.772	34.405	37.280	40.417	43.842	47.580
16	17.258	18.639	20.157	21.825	23.657	25.673	27.888	30.324	33.003	35.950	39.190	42.753	46.672	50.980	55.717
17	18.430	20.012	21.762	23.698	25.840	28.213	30.840	33.750	36.974	40.545	44.501	48.884	53.739	59.118	65.075
18	19.615	21.412	23.414	25.645	28.132	30.906	33.999	37.450	41.301	45.599	50.396	55.750	61.725	68.394	75.836
19	20.811	22.841	25.117	27.671	30.539	33.760	37.379	41.446	46.018	51.159	56.939	63.440	70.749	78.969	88.212
20	22.019	24.297	26.870	29.778	33.066	36.786	40.995	45.762	51.160	57.275	64.203	72.052	80.947	91.025	102.444

List of Supplemental
Case Studies

The following case studies are available from Ivey Publishing and include teaching notes for instructors (sample copies and teaching notes are available free of charge to academics). The cases correspond to the material covered in the relevant chapters of this book. For more information, see www.ivey.ca/cases/.

Chapter 2

National Fabricators (case number 9A95B022)

Chapter 3

Financial Performance of Dell Computer (9B00N017)

Chapter 4

SRI Office Products (9A98N014)
Alfred Brooks Menswear Limited (9A89B055)

Chapter 5

Chef's Toolkit Inc. (9A94B026)
Palmer Limited (9B01N020)

Cow's London (9A95B027)
Sophisticated Petites (9A90B042)
London Ski Club (9A99N041)
Peak Roofing Company (9B00N026)

Chapter 6

Border Hotels Corp. (9B01B034)
The T. Eaton Company Limited's Initial Public Offering (9A98N024)

Chapter 7

Telus: The Cost of Capital (9B01N019)

Chapter 8

Rocky Mountain High Ski Resort (RMH) (9A94B021)
Unihost Corporation (9A99N008)

Chapter 9

Pepsico Changchun Joint Ventures: Capital Expenditure Analysis (9B00N016)
Laurentian Bakeries (9A95B029)
Valuing Coca-Cola Stock (9-97N017)

Chapter 10

Scott's Hospitality Inc.—EVA (9A96B034)
Rushway Brothers Lumber and Building Supplies Ltd. (9A92B020)
Canadian Occidental Petroleum Ltd.—The Wascana Energy Inc. Decision (9A97N014)
The Empire Company Limited—The Oshawa Group Limited Proposal (9B00N028)

Index